WEAVING
IS
CREATIVE

Frontispiece:

A BANNER OF TECHNIQUES. Each section has been woven with several techniques and variations, and all techniques shown are covered in the text (see contents). Read each strip from the top down. Left to right:

(1.) Scalloped edge, weft fringes, Peruvian oval tab and tassels. (2.) Wrapped warps, slits. (3.) Joinings: Five-strand, tied weft loops, embroidery stitches, Guatemalan buttonhole, couching; Collected Edge at bottom. (4.) Guatemalan-style tapestry band; knotted openwork end finish. (5.) Peruvian Undulating Edge Braid; Egvedt skirt method finishes warp ends. (6.) Loop and cut pile weaves.

WEAVING
IS
CREATIVE

THE WEAVER-CONTROLLED WEAVES

Jean Wilson

VNR VAN NOSTRAND REINHOLD COMPANY
NEW YORK   CINCINNATI   TORONTO   LONDON   MELBOURNE

TO THE SEATTLE WEAVERS' GUILD—

AND ALL WEAVERS, PAST, PRESENT, AND FUTURE

Books by Jean Wilson

Weaving is Creative
Weaving is Fun
Weaving is for Anyone

ALL RIGHTS RESERVED

Van Nostrand Reinhold Company Regional Offices:
New York Cincinnati Chicago Millbrae Dallas

Van Nostrand Reinhold Company International Offices:
London Toronto Melbourne

Copyright © 1972 by Litton Educational Publishing, Inc.
Library of Congress Catalog Card Number 76-163320

Designed by Visuality
Printed by Halliday Lithograph Corporation
Color printed by Toppan Printing Co. (America), Inc.
Bound by Haddon Bindery, Inc.

Published by Van Nostrand Reinhold Company
450 West 33rd Street, New York, N.Y. 10001
Published simultaneously in Canada by
Van Nostrand Reinhold Limited

16 15 14 13 12 11 10 9 8 7 6 5 4 3 2

Contents

Roman numerals designating chapters were prepared by the author for this book.
Each one is woven in a different technique, or a different combination of techniques.

	NUMERAL	GROUND
I	Greek Soumak	Plain weave
II	Oriental Soumak	Oriental Soumak
III	Plain-weave tapestry, dovetail joining	
IV	Single Soumak	Single Soumak
V	Plain-weave tapestry, stepped-up slant	
VI	Pile weave, cut and loops	Plain weave
VII	Oriental Soumak	Plain weave
VIII	V, Single Soumak, III, wrapped	Oriental Soumak
IX	I, plain weave, slit	
	X, plain weave, wrapped outline	Plain weave

Acknowledgments

• Special thanks to the Seattle Weavers' Guild for permitting use of some of the material prepared for the Guild study of weaver-controlled weaves.

• My sincere thanks to Doris Brockway, Associate Professor, School of Home Economics, University of Washington, Seattle, for her encouragement in the early planning stages, and her belief in the need for this book.

• The following friends gave specialized interest, encouragement, and help: Virginia Harvey, Bill Holm, Leslie McCune Hart, Jacqueline Enthoven—to name only a few. Every one named in a photograph credit line contributed, and this is a warm thank-you to each of you.

• Photographs are most important to a craft book—so particular thanks to Kent Kammerer, whose interest and skillful photography contributed to this book and others, and

• To William Eng, whose fine photographs again add a great deal to my text.

An admiring and very sincere thank-you to Myron S. Hall 3rd, of VISUALITY, designer of this book, for the expert way he arranged an incredible amount of material, and found proper places for everything.

And an all-encompassing, heart-felt, and warm thank you to Margaret Holton, who has expertly and sensitively edited each of my three books. Working with her has added so much to the enjoyment of putting these books together.

As always—loving thanks to my family, for patience; and to my very dear daughter-in-law, Sheri Wilson, who helped with the typing chore.

Jean Wilson

Foreword

The idea for this book grew out of a year-long study course for the Study Groups of the Seattle Weavers' Guild, planned and implemented by Virginia Harvey and the author, several years ago. We had each been interested in doing a book about the weaver-controlled techniques, and considered writing it together. Meanwhile, Virginia became intrigued with the technique of knotting. At the publisher's suggestion, she wrote *Macramé: the Art of Creative Knotting*, followed by *Color in Macramé*, and I wrote *Weaving is for Anyone*, followed by *Weaving is Fun* and the present book, *Weaving is Creative*. Since we had expected to do a book together, but then wrote separate books for the same publisher, at the same time, we consulted each other and compared notes so frequently that Virginia referred to us jokingly as "co-authors of separate books." She has continued to knot and write about knotting, and I turned to the task of bringing all the weaver-controlled weaves into one volume. As Preparator of the Costume and Textile Study Collection, School of Home Economics, University of Washington, Virginia's help in securing examples from the Collection, a rich mine of source material, has been invaluable.

Jean Wilson

Although circumstances prevented our collaboration, my intense interest in the subject matter of this book has never diminished and my conviction has increased that it is a much-needed reference for the textile craftsman. We owe a great debt of gratitude to Jean Wilson for undertaking the arduous task of preparing this handsome, useful reference work.

As weavers and authors, the friendship between us has been a sharing of knowledge, seeking advice, discussion and comparison of our work, consolation in our reverses, and joy in our successes. When Jean made her decision to write this book, I was very pleased. It has been exciting to see it grow and to help her when I could. Although I can take no credit for the completed work, I wish to extend special congratulations and an expression of pride in her accomplishment of a goal that we have shared.

Virginia I. Harvey

What, Why, and How

Written as an interpretation of weaves controlled by the weaver, this unique reference work serves as a guide to techniques you can explore to your own satisfaction. We want to help you find out about the fabrication of interesting, exciting, useful textiles that will be your own personal creative expression of the craft.

While we would have liked to bring you the whole world of techniques, we had to settle for a bit less. Therefore we chose to bring you a maximum of new and how-to material, instead of explanations and directions on looms. We had to assume that your loom is there and ready to go, and we have provided the necessary help to guide you on what you are going to weave. Where it is important to the method, we have suggested the type of loom, the number of warps per inch, the kinds of yarn, and any special tools or whatever else is needed to get the proper result. For those who want more information, many of the books suggested in the bibliography have excellent advice on how to select and warp a loom.

We have examined and analyzed hundreds of textiles. Photographs and descriptions have been studied. New, old, and very ancient pieces have been scrutinized. As a result of our research, and our own experience, a representative number of different ways to treat a weaving are analyzed here for you and shown in photographs. Additional ways are indicated in small sketches. Weighing techniques against available space, we usually decided in favor of those we thought would be new to many of you. Even so, all these only begin to show what can be done. To originate and to adapt—this is part of the weaving craft.

We expect this book to be a handy reference for craftsmen who do not need every detail spelled out, but will go ahead on their own. Consider it a compilation, a reminder of a great many techniques, and a working reference for some of those lesser known and those with an original approach. At the end of each chapter there are pages in notebook style with informal freehand sketches to give you a clue to follow—an idea to enlarge in your own way.

You will find the reference books listed in our bibliography useful. Specific titles are recommended throughout the text as they apply to the subject under discussion.

WHAT AND WHY

"Controlled by the weaver" does not mean decorative effects only. Another weaver-controlled area is shaping your weaving on the loom, from just an edge to an entire piece. Shaping employs the tapestry technique of weaving on a slant. Examples are wedge-shaped mats for a round table; shaped necklines, side seams, or shoulders; Kelim or slit-weave for a neck opening in a poncho or slip-over shirt; slit-weave buttonholes or small eyelets for lacings; slit-weave for pockets, with the pocket sewn on the back, and an inconspicuous slit as pocket-opening in the front. An ingenious shaped shoulder woven into short *quechquemitls* by the Otomi people of Hidalgo, Mexico, is shown in figure 8-10.

What's in a Name?

Sorting out, properly placing, noting similarities and differences in these many techniques is a mind- and hand-boggling effort! Problems of definition occur in them all. So many have been in the world for so long, produced by so many craftsmen, interpreted and adapted by so many weavers and writers and historians and archeologists, some of whom have re-classified, re-named, drawn, and re-constructed, that it is truly a task to put certain of them in a category, and make it stick. It would be presumptuous on our part to claim we can put together a definitive study. After years of search, research, study, and doing— using the best references we can find and agree with, weaving everything we write about and use for illustrations—we present this as our version. While we agree with textile authorities Irene Emery and Harriet Tidball that the ideal situation is to reduce each technique to a common denominator of structure, this, of course, can be extremely confusing, because some of the most familiar methods are known and used under a variety of names.

Many of the knots, for instance, are really wrapped weaves; some of the tapestry weaves should properly be grouped with laid-in; "rug" weaves fall into any number of structural weave lists, knots, plain, wrapped, and so on. Just as surely as your own name means YOU, so do weaving names mean specific articles or techniques: a Kelim rug equals plain-weave tapestry with slits; a Navaho rug equals plain-weave tapestry with interlooping and a special method of weaving the selvedge; Demadesh is a Peruvian way of weaving small slits; a belt weave can mean woven on a belt or back-strap loom, or a belt or sash woven in a number of different ways, such as tablet or card-weave, plaiting. You get the point. We have grouped, defined, suggested, and adapted. You go on from here, and more power to you and your talented hands!

Classification

The classification of fabric structures becomes very involved when you group them into simple and compound weaves.
Simple: One set of warp and weft elements.
Compound: More than one set of warp and weft.

Further, a weave structure is compounded by adding elements in various ways, creating fabric structures with supplementary warps and/or wefts. The ground or foundation weave, plus extra-weft patterning, such as supplementary pile, floats, backing, in turn all create new classifications.

For a scholarly definitive text on classification of fabric structures refer to *The Primary Structures of Fabrics* by Irene Emery. The "inter" words are discussed at length, among them, "Interworking of Elements," which is weaving, "Interworked Structures," "Interlacing" (the simplest interworking, with one element over or under other elements). Interlooping, interlocking, interconnected —meat for you analysts who want to know just what and how you are weaving. One favorite word, which seems to say it all for these weaver-controlled weaves (and we considered this for a title), is:

Intertextures. "The art or act of weaving one thing into another. The condition of being woven in with something else. Also, that which is so woven."

How ideally helpful it would be to have an all-encompassing chart to relate embroidery, canvas needlework, woven techniques, including tapestry, rug, and other methods, with their variety of names. There are only a certain number of ways to cover a surface of warp or cloth. Through the centuries, different names have been given to the same technique, with authors .and craftsmen furnishing a new identity—just as cooks do with recipes. One cook's hash is another cook's stew—one weaver's stemstitch is another weaver's soumak.

There are two different ways to approach creative weaving

• Manipulating warps and wefts, trying all kinds of effects—open weaves, knots, twists, loops, fringes—whatever occurs. Happenings.
or
• Gaining a knowledge of techniques so the designing can come first. This means that you *know* a way of creating the effect you want. Happenings are fun, and contribute to creativity in textiles, but to be a real textile-maker, you ·must know how to *construct* a textile.

Just as "journeys of a thousand miles start with a single step" so weaving starts with an idea and a method—a length of yarn travelling over warp yarns one step at a time. From there on, it is up to you.

Design

Design inspiration is everywhere: In a book of Persian miniatures, pages from the Book of Kells, books on art from past centuries, old prints, *Godey's Lady's Book*—when fashions really were contrived and any one costume might have several kinds of materials, embroideries, braids, trims, and furbelows; paintings, the old masters with their carefully detailed depiction of laces and jewelry, and backgrounds of detailed rugs and tapestries. All these beautiful things made by our forebears provide a wealth of material for study. Part of the interest in weaving is looking for methods, applications, tools, and materials used in years past; we can borrow, adapt, and re-invent, enriching our own efforts. Time and again, while looking through a book of costumes, a bounding pulse signals an idea. A statue with a carefully carved girdle may suggest a woven design for a skirt or belt. An artist's sketch of texture in the cloak of an ancient dignitary may suggest a loop technique. Endless inspiration is in the world around us— nature's colors, forms, and textures.

As this book is written, the vogue for fringes, fancy trims, belts, shawls, ponchos—the costume look and dress-as-you-like—is part of the current scene. In this era of individuality, handcrafted accessories and clothing are worn with imagination and flair. The hours of loving care spent in creating handsome pieces will assure their place in the fashion world for some time to come, regardless of passing fads. We are in the midst of a textile enrichment period comparable to the elegant apparel of older times—Coptic tunics with tapestry medallions and borders, elaborate brocaded waistcoats, paisley shawls. Still being made are Mexican and Guatemalan embroidered and woven clothing. East Indian saris, Kente cloth of Africa, New Zealand *Taaniko* twining, Oriental and European national costumes and the costumes of our own American Indians.

As you study weaving techniques of different cultures and ages you wonder how They did it, and then you realize that all methods are alike or similar. Only the local name, colors, material used, pattern, and tools are different. The detective work is intriguing. There are limited ways to lay in a pattern, lift a loop, insert a knot, but the variations in tools, yarns, colors, designs, sett are endless. When a different name is given to each method and style, the number of variations becomes astronomical. Following a simple loop technique from Spain, to Greece, to Mexico, to Scandinavia, and back to Coptic weaves of ancient Egypt, you find that the loops are put in about the same way. They may be lifted in different ways—over a gauge, picked up with a hook or thorn, pulled up around a finger tip, and so on. But the basic method remains the same. A comparison chart is the device I use to list them in their logical places. Nearly all world-wide techniques, such as tapestry, pile weaves, laid-in, can be organized in this form to show the interrelationships within a technique. Because this has been so helpful to me, I have included two charts for you. (See chapter 3, "Brocade," and chapter 5, "Tapestry".)

HOW

Relax! Learn how to do a technique, then do it—correctly—using your own most comfortable way of working. Sometimes being told exactly what hand to use where creates tension, so we have tried not to be overly specific in our directions. After watching youngsters weave on small frame looms—upside down, sloping and slaunchwise, top and bottom,—I am convinced that a weaving can be done somehow, and right, no matter how unorthodox the position. Use fingers or tools, right hand or left. With experience, all weavers perforce become ambidextrous.

If you just can't weave a plain-weave tapestry from the back, do your weaving from the right side. Don't let the method or prescribed position be a barrier that keeps you from the joys of weaving.

THIS CRAFT OF WEAVING

Weaving has been a major interest and occupation in my life for a long time (about 30 years). It has led me into all kinds of fascinating by-ways of design, color, fibers, history, costumes, looms of all kinds, spinning, vegetable dyeing, creative techniques, stitchery, knotting, and related crafts. Ultimately, it led to writing about the craft.

Weaving, which began as a purely functional method of putting small units of material together (branches, grasses) to make a shelter or garments for weather protection, must be done so it works. Household linens and clothing textiles must be constructed so they can be cut, sewn, pressed, washed and washed, and wear well. A drapery material must hang straight, be opaque or sheer according to need, and so on. Today, when sculptors are weaving, weavers are stitching, potters and jewelers are doing macramé, and even painters are weaving tapestries, weaving is struggling to become an art form instead of merely functional.

All criteria for good design apply to weaving: Color, texture, proportion, and suitability for the purpose. A textile may be beautiful to look at, but if the weaver intended it for suiting material, and it is harsh to the touch, the weave so loose the skirt will become rump-sprung, too heavy for appropriate hems, the design problem has not been solved. Purely decorative weavings can be free-wheeling, exciting, far-out, made of unlikely materials, and that is within *their* purpose. Learn how to make the techniques work for you.

Weaving has been set a little apart from some of the other crafts and arts, probably because it has been a domestic, functional craft, long considered only as necessary work, done by the women as part of their household tasks. After the establishment of factory weaving, periodically interest in hand weaving simmered down, the attitude being—why should I do all that work when I can buy the textiles I want—and very good ones, too? Recently, however, a great surge of our need to be creative has occurred and the craft has had a vigorous revival. At this writing, work with textiles is blooming. Exciting and never-before uses of weaving and knotting are being developed. After the first exuberance, the 3-D experiments, some of them truly creative works, will no doubt be regarded as art forms. Meanwhile, weaving is fun, rewarding, and not necessarily art—it still does have a functional purpose.

2-1

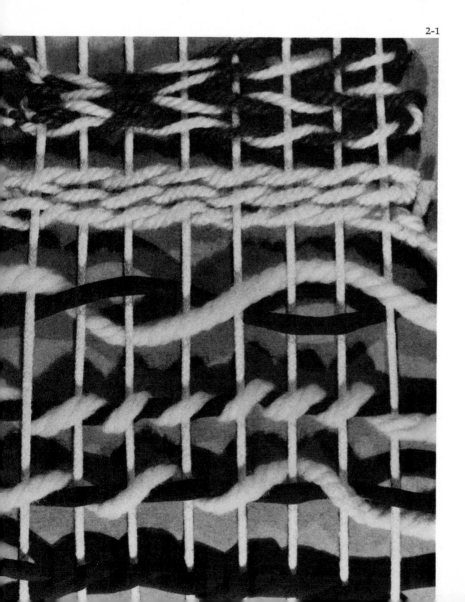

Twining and Chaining

Twining and Chaining are self-descriptive names for the two techniques covered in this chapter. To twine is to twist threads together. To chain is to form series of loops.

Warp-twining: Warp elements spiral about each other.

Weft-twining: Pairs of weft spiral about the warps to right or left, crossing between warps.

Chaining: Weft yarn encloses the warps in chained loops, like a crocheted chain. Loops are on top surface. Chaining can be worked from right or left.

Figure 2-1 shows simple twining variations expanded to show path of the yarn. From bottom up:

• Half turns. One color.
• Half turns. Two colors.
• Full turns. Two colors. Full twist of wefts, between warps.
• Paired, or pairing. Half turns, but over and under two warps.
• Compact. Rows beaten very close together. Half turns.
• Three rows, with different edge treatments. At right, knotted with cut ends. Twisted twice before continuing in the next row. Left, twisted and knotted. Four ends (two rows) braided and knotted.
• Countered twining. Four rows. Resembles knitting, especially when rows are set closer than this. Two colors to show yarn path. (Also see D2-1.)

Figure 2-2 shows chaining techniques. Bottom row is expanded to show progress of the yarn, left to right. Top three rows are in two colors worked right, left, and right. (Also see D2-3.)

2-2

2-1, 2. Large-scale examples of twining *left* and chaining *right*. (Photograph by Kent Kammerer.)

2-3. Twining in 3-D. Hot pink and orange yarns twined and looped into a structure standing on flat feet. Weaver, Hella Skowronski. (Photograph by Paul Gilmore.)

2-4. Warp twining. Belt twined in mercerized cotton. American. Given by Mrs. Mary Atwater, Courtesy of Costume and Textile Study Collection, School of Home Economics, University of Washington, Seattle. (Photography by Audio-Visual Services, University of Washington.)

2-3   2-4

HISTORY

Educated guesses from finds and digs place the use of twining as far back as several thousand years B.C. Incredible as it seems, bits and pieces and parts of costumes have been found in a state of preservation allowing study and analysis. Almost everywhere clues have turned up that indicate early knowledge and use of twining. The Bronze Age craftsmen in Jutland, other northern Europeans, and early craftsmen elsewhere appear to have employed this technique in some way. Major areas where this technique is known to have been used extensively are Peru, North America (Indians), New Zealand (the Maori people), northeast India (Naga tribesmen), Denmark. The first twining was probably related to basket weaving, and other uses of basket-type materials— twigs, willow whips, stiff grasses—followed. It is such a logical way to fasten materials and fashion them into larger units—the strands stay put, it can be open or quite solid, long or short strands will work. No wonder early man discovered this means of putting strands together.

Twining was originally done on a free-hanging warp— that is, a warp not in tension because one end hangs loose. Sometimes the warp was weighted, leaving the ends free for manipulation, but providing some tension. Weft twining can be done on a loom with warp fastened to both beams, but some types, like *Taaniko*, are much easier to do with the free warp; warp twining must be done with the free end. Twining in the classic manner, on free or weighted warp, is done from the top down. The twined rows are pushed up. On a conventional loom, weft twining is made from the bottom up, as in weaving.

WEFT TWINING

Weft twining, which employs two weft elements twisting over warps, was no doubt one of the earliest methods used, probably with fence posts as the warp and pliable twigs as the wefts. Fish traps, baskets, mats, capes, and skirts, made of fibers both spun and unspun, were all constructed in this way. Although this structure is sometimes identified more with basketry than with loom-woven techniques, it has the two elements of weaving—warps with wefts passing over and around them. When employed for weaving a textile, it is sometimes difficult to tell a twined fabric from a heddle-woven fabric. Shuttles and heddles are of no use in this technique. No shed is needed. Pairs of weft twist between and enclose the flat warp.

What the weft does

Pairs of weft change position each time they cross between each warp and are taken one on top and one underneath. If you use two different colors to twine across a warp you will see exactly what happens: Each weft, in turn, is on top, then twisted or crossed (a half-turn) over the other weft to become the lower one—each warp is therefore encircled by the two wefts. This is twining in its simplest form, but it can become quite complicated.

Kinds of weft twining

So far, twining is not being done by mechanical means. It is still a completely hand-controlled technique, and, because it is slow, handweavers tend to limit its use to edge finishes, small decorative bands, or design units employing very heavy yarns that weave up quickly. Twining can make a very solid and compact textile, or one that is lacy and quite open. It can have uncovered warp areas with warps crossed or straight (fitching, in basketry), have a loose tension in both directions to be flexible or elastic, as with knitting. Since it is entirely controlled by you, it can be very easily adapted to the exact density or firmness you need. Twined inserts in clothing can be solid or with tension adjusted for a bit of shaping, or "give." This technique works for you—you are the prime mover. (See the Seattle Weavers' Guild twining samplers, figures 2-24, 25, 26.)

Changes in texture and color are possible in a number of ways: By counter-twining, where each row is twined in a different direction; by putting open rows next to compact rows, or a combination of twining and other techniques such as plain weave, Soumak, or rug knots. The number and yarn size of warps and/or wefts can be changed in any area. In any one row, the wefts can twine, then be woven in for a while, then twined again. More than two weft elements provide a still further variation in color and texture. Twining securely holds feathers, beads, or shells for surface interest. Patterned weft-twining can be tapestry-like, as in Chilkat blankets; with geometric patterns, as in Maori *Taaniko;* ornamented with tags of fur or wool. Stripes can be made by changing weft colors in the rows. Rows of twining can be pushed into curves or diagonal lines.

Other uses

On some of the most ancient finds, a row or two of weft twining is seen at the beginning of other weaves. Twining is commonly used today to put a warp on a frame "in neutral"—all on one level. A row or two is used to begin a tapestry, as part or all of the heading. It makes a good heading for an edge finish like fringe, especially on a rug.

MORE ABOUT WEFT TWINING

There is infinite variety in the methods and variations of twining within each type of turn, direction of twining, the sett and sizes of yarn, color changes, and beating. To help you find references for further study, following are some descriptive names together with brief explanations of a few of the many ways to do weft twining. We found two quite different sets of names for classifying weft twining variations, and there may be more. Our names are those used in the Shuttle Craft Guild Monograph *Weft Twining*. The Seattle Weavers' Guild samplers pictured and described later follow the classification in Verla Birrell's *The Textile Arts*.

Half turns: Each weft is taken over and under the warp, alternately, so they twine over each other.

Full turns: The same weft consistently goes over, the other weft always under the warp. In two colors, with the warps close together, the result is a solid line of one color.

Paired warps: The twist is the half turn, but over and under a pair of warps at one time. Also try variations. Alternate pairing—each row is twined on alternate pairs of warp. Alternate warp pairs with single warps for still another effect, with each row offset. Or use groups of pairs, then a few singles, and so on ad infinitum.

Compact twining: Warp is set fairly close, and rows of twining, with half turns, are beaten firmly so a flexible but thick fabric is made. When full turns are made, the textile is even more firm.

Countered twining: Rows are twined right to left, then left to right. The twist between warps is in the opposite direction each row, so the "stitches" slant in opposite directions and the look is that of knitting or countered Oriental Soumak.

TWO SPECIAL KINDS OF WEFT TWINING: *TAANIKO* AND *CHILKAT*

Maori mantles—*Taaniko* weaving, or twining

The twined mantles made by the Maori people of New Zealand are a fascinating study in design and craftsmanship. The *Maori Mantle* by H. Ling Roth, published in 1923, presents an exhaustive study of the subject, with photographs, drawings of construction details, and an anthropologist's careful measuring and analyses. He compares these mantles with the Northwest Indian Chilkat blankets, although there are many differences in materials used and methods of construction as well as design. Captain Cook characterized the mantles he saw in New Zealand as "thrumb'd matts." Since weavers, for years, have used the term "thrums" to mean the leftover ends of warp, Roth's use of the word "tags" seems more appropriate for the bits of wool or fur put into the mantles. The construction was called "twining" because of the weft twist; it was also called "weaving." We call twining a "weaving technique."

Design

The Maori, somewhat scornful of plain rectangular blanket-type mantles, worked out a number of methods of shaping. Elliptical inserts and vertical

2-6

2-5

2-5, 6. *Taaniko* weaving from New Zealand. A narrow belt and a wide band twined in typical patterning. From the Harriet Tidball Collection.

wedges were worked in. Shaping was usually done across the shoulder area to round it to the shape of the body. Sometimes an elliptical section was put in lower down, for "sitting-room." Here the skill of the weaver was apparent, since a slightly longer warp was used to accommodate the take-up. "Kilts"— short skirts—consisted mostly of fringe hanging from an elaborately patterned *Taaniko* band, much like a short cape.

Ornamentation

Tags—slightly twisted bits of unscoured wool were fastened into the twining to ornament the surface. Strips of dog hair, skin, rolls made of leaves, pompons, and tassels of worsted yarn, as well as worsted pieces were inserted into the twining rows to make each garment unique. Feather-work, hair tassels, and very fine, geometrically-patterned taaniko-twining borders and bands were employed for decoration.

Basic materials used

The New Zealand flax plant (*Phormium tenax*)—a tall-growing, pointed-leaf plant—was the source of the twining materials. In this plant bast fibers are produced in the leaves, unlike the linen fibers which come from the stem of the flax plant. *The Art of Taaniko Weaving* by Sidney M. Mead, a recent book on *Taaniko* methods, materials, and design, has excellent photographs that show the process of obtaining the fibers. This beautifully illustrated book was written by a New Zealand Maori, an anthropologist and authority on Polynesian art forms.

About the word *Taaniko*: Formerly this word was spelled *taniko*, sometimes *tāniko*. The University of Aukland system uses the double vowel to indicate the length of the sound, in order to assist in the correct pronunciation of Maori words.

How to do it

Throughout years of change and growing sophistication of patterning and styling, the basic method of *Taaniko* weaving remains the same. Mr. Mead's instructions, his illustrations for making a sampler and using the patterns, are unusually clear. We recommend his book if you wish to pursue the study of this rich and beautiful method of twining; here we must confine ourselves to directions for the basic system, and explanation of how it differs from other methods of twining.

The major difference between this and other twining methods is that all the wefts of different colors used to make the patterns are carried along together. Only one is worked on the surface at a time. Wefts are put back and brought up to the surface again as needed to make color changes. This results in a very solid textile, for of course the more wefts you have, the heavier your fabric will be. The possibilities of design are free, too, and you are not necessarily restricted to the classic Maori triangles, diamonds, and squares. (See figures D2-4, 5, 6.)

For sampling, we suggest you put a warp on a frame or regular loom, so you can concentrate on manipulating the wefts. Refer to D2-5 in the notebook pages at the end of this chapter.

CHILKAT BLANKETS

The Chilkat People

Northwest Coast Indians of southeastern Alaska, the Chilkats are a division of the Tlingit group. The center of Northwest Indian design development rests with the Haida Indians of the Queen Charlotte Islands of totem-pole fame; of these, the Chilkat weavers were the most proficient, and the blanket-style bears their name. Dance shirts, leggings, and aprons were also woven with the same symbolic patterning. Similar items were woven by most of the Alaskan and British Columbian tribes.

2-7. Chilkat dance shirt. Note fur trim. From the Rasmussen Collection, Portland Art Museum, Portland, Oregon.

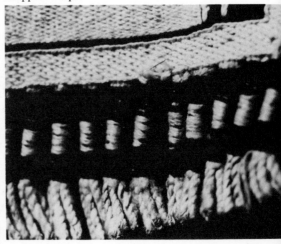

2-8. Bottom border of dance shirt with fringe of wrapped warps.

Designs

Sharp black outlining of design units, deep fringe following the pointed blanket shape, prescribed proportions, symbolic patterns, and color plans all contribute to make the Chilkat blankets unique and instantly recognizable. Men painted the schematic design on pattern boards—women were the weavers. Space is filled with a subtle balance of lines and areas. Creatures of nature inspire the highly stylized design elements.

The partially-woven Chilkat blanket we show in figures 2-10 to 2-14 is an important acquisition by the Portland Art Museum. Bill Holm photographed a

2-9. Pattern board for Chilkat blanket. From the Rasmussen Collection, Portland Art Museum, Portland, Oregon.

2-10. Chilkat blanket. *At left*, the reverse side is shown partly folded over the front side *at right*. Note the joining of black and yellow along the border on the reverse side. This is like an interloop joining in tapestry weave. Colors are always black, white, yellow, and blue-green.

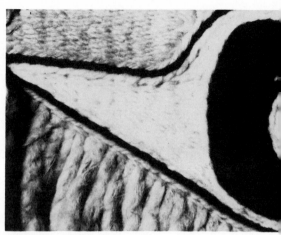

2-11. Detail of partly-woven Chilkat blanket showing the heavy, close-set warps and the three-strand twining that outlines the design units. The wefts are tied into loose hanks.

2-12. Close-up of the eye in upper left corner of figure 2-11. The "scale figure"—a penny—can be partly seen in the lower right-hand corner.

2-13   2-14

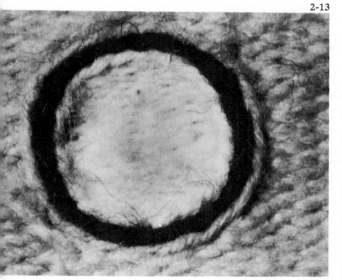

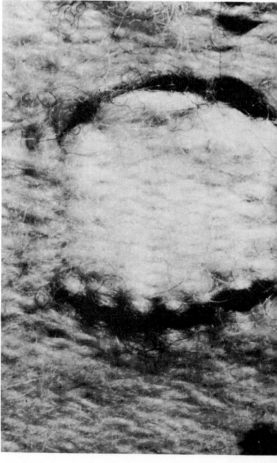

2-13, 14. Detail of Chilkat blanket. Top and reverse sides, showing the construction of the round units. Note how the three-strand twining makes a smooth line on the surface. The color-change, white and yellow, is made by interlooping, approximating a circle.

series of details showing how these beautiful textiles are constructed. We regret that space permits us to reproduce only a few, and in black and white instead of color, particularly since this is an unfinished piece with the colors still bright. In old used and treasured blankets mellowed by time, the colors are usually quite pale. The color plan is always black, white, yellow, and blue-green.

At first glance, the blankets look like tapestry. They are twined, with rows packed in tightly so the textile is very solid and heavy. The weaving sequence is weft twined over alternate pairs, back and forth within each pattern unit. Twined rows are interlooped at the color change points in the manner of tapestry. Sections are joined with an extra cord in what Bill Holm calls a "drawstring joint," worked from edge to edge. This seam is then covered with three-strand twining, giving the smooth unbroken line that conceals the join. These designer-weavers showed an extremely high degree of sophistication in areas of design and craftsmanship.

Use of cedar bark

Twined cedar-bark capes (figure 2-15) fashioned from bundles of soft, shredded inner bark from cedar trees, twined with string, were useful for warmth and protection from rain. The loom used was a simple cross-bar holding the warp of cedar bundles free at the bottom. The twining rows stopped near the bottom edge, leaving a warp-fringe finish. Some were circular, some oblong. Mats were also made in the same way.

For more about Northwest Indian designs, we refer you to Monograph No. 1, *Northwest Coast Indian Art, an analysis of form,* by Bill Holm, lecturer and curator of Northwest Coast Indian Art at the Thomas Burke Memorial Washington State Museum, on the campus of the University of Washington, Seattle.

2-15. Twined cedar bark cape, Northwest Coast Nootka Indians. (The necklace is made of shells and beads.) From the Rasmussem Collection, Portland Art Museum, Portland, Oregon.

2-16. Tumpline (forehead band). A Puget Sound Salish Indian patterned tumpline. Twined with both commercial and handspun wool, red, black, and white. The warp is native hemp, and the cords narrow down to a hemp braid. These tumplines were used to hold backloads, with the wide wool part of the band across the forehead.

2-17. A Chippewa Indian twined bag. Red, black, and brown wool on vegetable-fiber warp. Note the good-looking and serviceable edge-finish at the top. Warps are wound, with open space between, then a heavy rim, buttonholed around a core, is worked along the top.

2-18

2-19

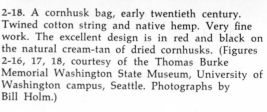

2-18. A cornhusk bag, early twentieth century. Twined cotton string and native hemp. Very fine work. The excellent design is in red and black on the natural cream-tan of dried cornhusks. (Figures 2-16, 17, 18, courtesy of the Thomas Burke Memorial Washington State Museum, University of Washington campus, Seattle. Photographs by Bill Holm.)

2-19. From Nagaland in northeast India, a Naga hill-tribe jacket.

TWINING FROM INDIA

From northeast India on the other side of the world we show a Naga hill-tribe jacket (figure 2-19) and a textile from the Angami tribe (figure 2-20). The jacket, with very tightly woven ground, has an insignia on the back. This motif is a combination of twined rows and diamond-woven laid-in pattern. Note the reinforcement at the neck—a plait stitch in coarse wool.

The fine cotton textile has so many techniques going for it that it is almost a little sampler. Rows of twining at the hem put it in this chapter, but it also has: Warp stripes beginning at the selvedge on the two outside strips only; four twelve-inch strips are sewn together, so there is joining; some seams are firmly overcast with selvedges up tight, making a ridge, and some parts have a more open joining. Above the twined border is a woven weft pattern. The warp ends are twisted into cords, then grouped into tassels, with a twist in the group before wrapping with fine thread. Where the twined rows end, at the edge of each strip, the ends have been twisted and wrapped into a tassel that falls just above the other fringe, at the seam. And if all of this is not enough—in the body of the robe is a group of eight exquisitely designed and laid-in motifs. These are shown in chapter 3, "Laid-in," figures 3-28A,B,C,D,E,F,G,H.

Traditional blankets (*chadar*) with borders of twining that show tribal affiliation are woven on backstrap looms by the Naga weavers.

2-20. Naga textile from India's Angami tribe. Both textiles courtesy of the Costume and Textile Study Collection, School of Home Economics, University of Washington. (Photographs by William Eng.)

2-21. Two twined bags, both well made. *Right:* The weft ends at the bottom are knotted to close the edge and left in a fringe. The rows of open warp separated and wrapped in an attractive pattern band are a nice contrast to the solid twining. Woven by Diana Leonhardt, Renton Senior High School student. *Left:* Well spaced stripes, with some open warp, Leno. The bottom is closed on the inside with knotted warp ends. A spiral macrame' button is made of the same yarn. Woven by Mrs. Dorothy Stickney, teacher, Renton Senior High School, Renton, Washington. Both bags have strong handles, thoughtfully designed along with the bag. (Photograph by William Eng.)

2-22. Open weave at the top of a basket. Combines twining and wrapped techniques. Flat strips of bamboo are wrapped over pairs of warp, in a diamond pattern. Twining is in simple, paired, and half turns. (Photograph by Kent Kammerer.)

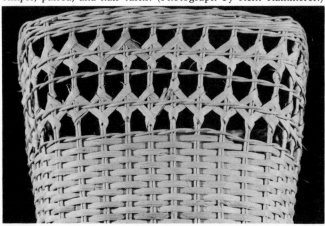

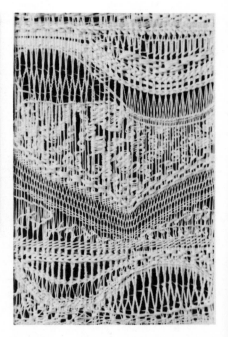

2-23. Adult student example of twining and chaining, showing how it can be curved, slanted, and pushed about. The warp is covered or left open, wrapped, twisted, crossed with an occasional woven row. Teacher, Larry Metcalf, Chairman Art Department, Seattle Pacific College. (Photograph by Larry Metcalf.)

HOW TO DO IT

General ideas on handling any type of twining

Yarns to use

Linen, macramé cords, firm wools, jute work well. Generally, a smooth yarn with some crispness makes the best-looking twined fabric. Many of the synthetic fibers are satisfactory. Hard-spun wools work well, but softer ones, like knitting worsted, pack in and the effect of the technique is lost. Voice of experience: Use a warp that is smooth, not hairy, otherwise the little loose fibers will get looser and come up through, spoiling the neat lines of the twining.

Working from left to right, the twist is made with the right thumb and fingers, the warp is brought up in position with the left fingers. Both hands work at the same time; steps follow along easily.

Start

Double the weft. Put half under the first warp, half over. Pull, so bend is at the warp, and start twining. The first twist will hold it there.

Another way to start

Tie the cut ends of wefts together. Put half under and half over the first warp. The knot and ends can be made into a decorative selvedge finish, ornate or small, made into a tassel, frayed out in a pouf.

Selvedges

Wind one yarn around the outside warp once or twice as needed, to make a smooth edge and fill any space. If more than one color is used, make sure the yarns are turned smoothly, and that the proper color is on top to begin the next row in the color sequence.

Ends at the selvedge: A twined textile offers some interesting ways to make a selvedge important in the over-all design. One method is to twine each row and leave cut ends at each edge. These can then be twisted, knotted, wrapped, braided, made into tassels or any of the fringe techniques. When rows are twined with continuous wefts, turned, and continued in the subsequent rows, you have the option of decorative treatment here, too. See figure 2-1 for possibilities. The wefts can be twisted once or several times before turning in. They can be chained, crocheted, knotted, or wrapped. See the rug with chaining selvedge treatments, shown in figure 2-32.

Checking for the proper sequence

At the beginning, remember to have wefts alternate over and under on the first warp. To help remember the sequence: Each single weft goes over and under each time. The second weft also goes over and under, alternating with the first weft. The twist comes between the warps.

Warp ends

The ends of a twined fabric are quite bulky, so the edge finish is seldom a hem. See chapter 7, on edges, and chapter 9, on fringes, for suggestions on what to do with warp ends. If a plain, unadorned edge is desired simply turn each warp back into the edge, through several rows, using a needle or crochet hook. Trim the ends close. Where it is necessary to have a very secure edge a row of machine or hand stitching with matching thread may not be noticeable.

Joining in a new length of weft

Add the new length to the old weft and twine the two for an inch or a few turns. Do not join several wefts at the same spot. Space them out to avoid a lump.

To widen the fabric: Twist two or more times between the warps. This pushes them apart; the spread will make the fabric wider.

Samplers of twining methods and patterns

For the Seattle Weavers' Guild study program on twining techniques, member Alice Leffler made these samplers. We suggest them as a very worthwhile exercise to study and learn the ways of twining. Brown, white, and yellow-green cotton rug yarn was used, making good-looking as well as useful little samplers.

Twining Sampler 1

From the top down:

• One color twining, counterclockwise, over and under pairs of warps, with two wefts. Half turns between warps.
• Chevron. Two colors of weft. Countered twining, with one row right to left, next row left to right. On split warp—note the little open triangles that occur when a different set of warps are used than the rows above and below. Useful in designing.
• Chevron (countered). One color.
• Three-thread twining. Note that the three colors are started between successive warp pairs.
• Chain stitch on closed shed. Note how it resembles the countered twining.
• Decorated chain stitch. Loops can be added as the chaining proceeds, or with a needle afterward.
• Maori *Taaniko* (Taniko) twining on single warps. Two, then three colors.

Twining Sampler 2

From the top down:

• Counter clockwise, five rows. One color.
• Chevron, six rows. One color.
• Vertical stripes. Two colors.
• Zigzag stripe, two colors.
• Soumak. Two rows with one row of reverse Soumak between. The center row of Soumak is unusually open.
• Soumak, over four and back two warps. All in the same direction.
• Chilkat twining. Each row is on a split warp. Used in the tapestry-like Chilkat blankets of the Northwest Indians.

Twining sampler 3

From the top down:

• Checkerboard. Two colors. Over pairs of warp.
• Checkerboard. Double the size of the "checks" by twisting the weft twice to bring the same color up again.
• Diagonal. Make chevron by turning after four rows, working in the opposite direction. Two colors. Turn is made on the chevron.
• Diagonal with the turn made on the point. Note the subtle difference by comparing with the one above.
• Surface twining (the imbrication technique used on Alaskan and Pacific Northwest Indian baskets). The pattern appears only on the face of the twining.

2-24. Seattle Weavers' Guild Twining Sampler 1.

2-25. Seattle Weavers' Guild Twining Sampler 2.

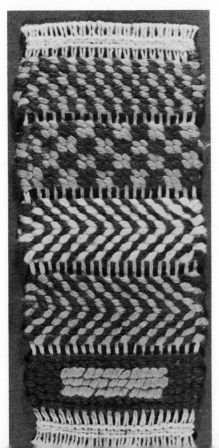

2-26. Seattle Weavers' Guild Twining Sampler 3.

OBSERVATIONS ON TWINING

• In your first twining sampler, use three colors—one in the warp, and each weft a different color to check yourself on the correct placement of each. It is easy to become confused, and you may be twining with a warp before you know it!

• To avoid getting tangled before you have the system worked out, learn with short and narrow warp, fairly short wefts.

• We urge you, as always, to do a lot of sampling. Don't plunge right in making a finished Thing. Time enough for that after your fingers learn.

• Twining can be done on either a free-end warp or a conventional warp in tension.

• On a free-end warp, work from the top down. On a warp in tension work from the bottom up as in regular weaving.

• Twining is usually done on pairs of warp except for the *Taaniko* where close-set single warps are used.

• For an open-work design with warp threads showing, alternate rows of weft, work on alternate pairs of warp, making triangular open spaces. This is called split warps.

• Tension and placement of the twining row on a free warp is readily adjusted by pulling warps down with one hand, while pushing the weft row upward, close to the previous row.

• Working on a free-end warp, the warps can be moved from their usual vertical position, and can be twined (warp twining), twisted, or slanted.

All yarns have an "S" or a "Z" twist. If you work with the twist of the yarns the result is a smoother, cordlike product. Working against the twist so that the yarns are slightly unspun, the result is softer and a bit fuzzy.

• Rows of twining can be modelled, making wavering lines, angles, curves. The warp is passive; the twisted wefts can be pushed up and down. They must be tight enough, however, so they won't move out of place too easily, resulting in a sloppy fabric.

• Advantages in working on a warp in tension: Your textile will be more uniform—twists and rows more evenly spaced. If you twine on an open shed, change shed and weave some plain weave. Then the fabric will be a firm one with plain weave backing the twined rows.

WARP TWINING

Warp twining is also known as card weaving, tablet weaving, or card-heddle weaving. It has been traced back to ancient Egypt and is sometimes called Egyptian card weaving. In warp twining, the warp yarns are fully twisted around each other. It is a finger-weave process like weft twining. Elaborate patterns and a great variety of color-play are possible. The two faces of the fabric can be different colors. Solid color areas can alternate with pattern. Unlike the crossing of warps in gauze weave, the twining of warps produces a compact, corded fabric. Variations can be made by spiralling to right or to left, by using more than one yarn, by using a heavy yarn, or by using more than one color.

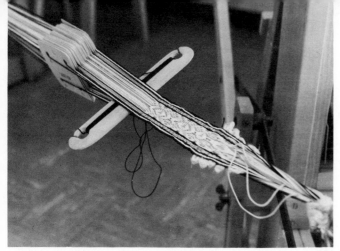

2-27. Card, or tablet weaving. The shuttle is a Norwegian belt shuttle, tapered at one edge. It holds the weft, and is the beater.

2-28. Examples of card-woven bands. The warp-face fabric is extremely strong, since the warps are twisted to create the pattern, and the weft is beaten in— almost out of sight—making the belting very firm. Both the above, courtesy of Russell E. Groff, of Robin and Russ Handweavers, McMinnville, Oregon.

Card or tablet weaving

This is a method used to speed up warp twining. Card weaving is a big subject, involving how to make and use a system of cards, and the many weaving variations possible. With limited space, we cannot do much more than introduce you to the subject.

Cards are perforated with from two to eight holes, through which warps are threaded, creating a free-wheeling shedding device that allows the warps to be twisted in any desired combination. The technique is a natural for belts because of the firm result, and the easy handling of a narrow set of warps. Figures 2-27 and 2-28 are from an excellent small book on card weaving, with methods and designs well illustrated. It is published by Robin and Russ, McMinnville, Oregon. This family of weavers, teachers, and suppliers of all weaving needs developed a first-rate series of card-woven bands for busy-work on camping trips, and found enough interest and challenge in card weaving to make a helpful book.

References

There is a world of twining information available for those who want to pursue the subject more deeply. Our most-used and helpful references are Irene Emery for terminology and construction, the Shuttlecraft Guild Monograph on weft twining, and the following more specialized works: Raoul d'Harcourt tells how Peruvian craftsmen combined plaiting with twining. Peter Collingwood explains how to use warp twining in rug weaving. Verla Birrell details various methods of warp twining, including some she worked out using tubular beads and two-holed cards. Detailed studies of *Taaniko* and Maori twining methods are in the works of H. Ling Roth and Sidney Mead. We think you would enjoy further study of this very old and interesting method of covering a warp.

CHAINING—WHAT IS IT?

Chaining is not the same as twining, but there are similarities and it seems logical to group it with the twining. Essentially, it is just the same as a single crochet chain stitch, only it is worked on a closed warp, with a single weft which encloses each warp. A complete loop is made on the surface. Rows of chaining have the appearance of rows of counter-twining, except that the twining is usually flatter, more tightly pulled in; the chain loops are raised and looser. (See figure 2-2.)

2-29. Seated Figure. This, too, is chaining—mostly. Bonnie Meltzer creates people, creatures, and masks in crochet and weaving techniques. Here she employs chaining and wrapping over a core of sticks or cords.

Observations on chaining

• Because the chain is made on the surface of the textile most of the yarn shows. It can be loose or tight, raised or slightly pulled in.
• It is a very decorative accent for shadow lines in rows or isolated spots.
• It combines well with twining, and a textile with alternate chaining and twining rows will have an interesting ribbed look.
• Color-change is easy—just carry more than one weft along and lift up whichever color you wish (see "How to do it").
• Use for spot motifs and raised texture in a flat weave.
• Rows of plain weave and chained rows are attractive.
• Reversed rows look like knit or herringbone weave, with stitches slanting in opposite directions. Combinations of reverse rows and those in the same direction are an interesting design element to play with.
• One accommodating thing about chaining—if you don't lock the end loop, you can just tug and it will unchain. Handy, if you don't like the look of the row you just put in. But *do* lock the end chain if you want your fabric to stay!

How to do it

The beauty of several rows of chaining is in the even tension of the chain. You will get the feel of it after a row or two, then the yarn will flow smoothly, the tension will be uniform, and your warps will be covered quite rapidly.

How much weft for a chain row? To avoid running out of continuous weft, try to have plenty. You can work from a spool or large ball of yarn, because the free end is not actively involved—it just provides more and more weft. When you reach the end of your chain, you can cut the weft to bring it through and fasten the last loop. Or, if you are returning with chaining, simply place the yarn under the warp with the free end at the other side. Another way is to do a sample row and measure the amount used. It will vary with size of yarn, size of warp, how tight a chain you make. With a heavy yarn, over pairs of carpet warp, we used almost seven times the width for one quite loose chain row.

Start the chain row: Tie the chaining weft to the outside warp, or tie a loop in the end of the chaining weft. Lay it on top of the first-warp, bring the first loop up through it. Lay the chaining weft under the warp, with one end free.

Begin the chain: With fingers or crochet hook, pull up a loop, lay over next warp, reach down and pull weft up through, and so on. Each warp is encircled. The left side of the loop controls the size of the chain stitch. A crochet hook may be more convenient to use than fingers; it depends upon the size of the yarns, warp spacing, and the size and skill of your fingers. When using fingers, you are more sensitive to the tension and can regulate the size of the loop. Do it the best way for you, your project, and the material.

At the end of the chain row, pull free end of weft up through the last loop to lock it; tighten, tuck end in around last warp, weave back into a few warps. If you are making more than one row, going in both directions, turn chain weft around the last warp and chain the other way.

For a relaxed and neater selvedge, make one chain loop "in the air" before beginning the first loop on the new row. If you want the successive rows of chain to be made all in one direction, weave a row of tabby with the chaining weft to get it back to the other side.

Add color and texture

A band of chained loops can alternate colors each loop, or in groups of color-change. A third and fourth weft can be carried along for more color and texture effects.

Bring a chaining weft or two from the back, up to the top, then chain several times before continuing a regular chain row, or weave the chain weft in. With this little trick you can make bumps and mounds for a spot of high relief. The small pillow shown in figure 6-25 is covered with these. (Also see figure 9-22B.)
• Loops, cut ends, feathers, beads, all can be incorporated into your chain rows.
• Try a sampling of all the ways to use and design with the chain.

A versatile technique

Chaining has a very useful place, too, just as twining has, at the beginning of weaving or to make a line or two at an edge that will be fringed or hemmed. Some very old weavings have chained borders at the edge. Try it as a spacer of warps to be braided or fringed, as a holder of warps at the top of a primitive vertical loom. On a frame loom, where the warp is taken round and round the frame, a row or two of chaining (or twining) at top and bottom will level the warp and make it flat to weave upon.

When chain loops are flat and snug, chaining is firm enough for a rug. Use a good strong linen warp and wool weft. Weave several rows of tabby between the chain rows for a solid fabric, so your rug will stay put. A rug can be made with alternating rows of Soumak, plain weave, and chaining. Most of the weft is on the surface, effectually displaying your beautiful rug wool. Chain rows can be beaten in to completely cover the tabby weave, therefore tabby weft can be a different yarn, instead of your special rug wool. Just be sure it is a strong yarn of durable quality; it will in no way detract from the appearance of the rug. Best if it is the same color.

2-30. To separate two design areas in a double-weave hanging, the open warp is left unwoven, divided by a single row of chaining with beads slipped over the loops. A pleasant, simple repetition. The complete hanging is shown in figure 3-24. Weaver, Bernice O'Neil. (Photograph by Kent Kammerer.)

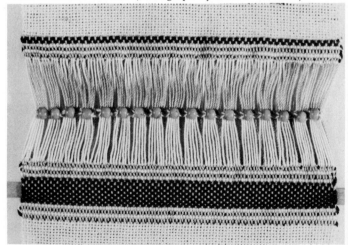

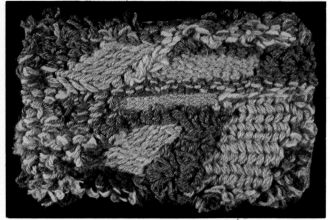

Three thumbnail-sketch Irish tapestries by the author.
(Photographs by Kent Kammerer.)

C-1, *top.* Bainen Sky. Plain weave tapestry and Greek Soumak.

C-2, *left.* St. Brigid's Cross. Background of plain weave
and slits.

C-3, *right.* Hedgerows and Fields. Soumak, pile loops, and
cut pile.

2-31. Make a chain-pile surface by chaining wefts together, or chain weft outside of the shed, then tuck it back; repeat for a row of chained loops. The longer points are caught down with a ground weft. Also see the little pillow covered with these, figure 6-25.

2-32. Example of chaining techniques used to make rugs. Combined with flat weave, chained at the edge for different finishes and textures. (Photograph by Kent Kammerer.)

Chaining sampler

Chain rows make a rug. The squares are made of three rows of chaining worked back and forth over three pairs of warp. The slit that occurs is minimized by lines of chain and tabby that go from side to side. (Figure 2-31.)

Rug of flat weave and chained rows—
A sampler of ideas for making a decorative selvedge

To add interest as well as weight to a flat-weave rug, chained rows separate rows of herringbone, plain, and other weaves. Very large rug wool is used in the chained rows, so they are big scale, and quite thick. Wools and chenille make the flat part. These edge finishes solve the problem of what to do with an enormous weft end. Chaining is continued out from the selvedge on two bands, brought together and knotted. The ends are left as a tassel. In other rows one or two extra chain loops are made outside the selvedge, the ends darned back in; rows are unevenly spaced, with chain returning into the next row after one or two extra loops are made at the turning. Some of these turns are very small, giving just a rounded look—another is extended out a bit more, making a flat open scallop. Many possibilities here for interesting edges. The reverse twill bands echo the pattern made by the slanting rows of chain loops. (Figure 2-32.)

Our notebook sketches and directions for quick reference follow.

Notebook

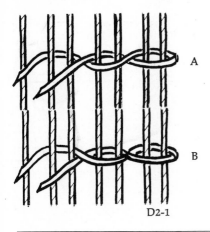

D2-1

Weft twining (D2-1)

A. Simple weft twining, with half turns.
B. Twined with the opposite twist. Alternating rows of A and B produces countered twining.

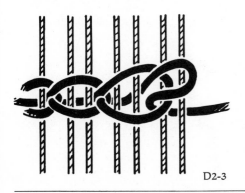

D2-2

Division of space (D2-2)

Typical plan of division of space in Chilkat blanket design. Each one is different, but all follow a general scheme and proportion.

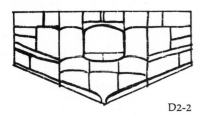

D2-3

Chaining (D2-3)

Work from left to right.

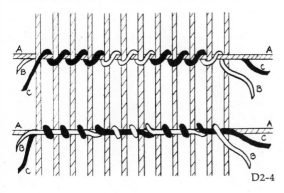

D2-4

Taaniko twining (D2-4)

The top row is the face. The bottom row is the reverse side. Note that weft A is stretched the width, and the two colors, B and C, are worked over A.

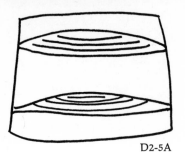

D2-5A

Details of Maori methods according to H. Ling Roth (D2-5, 6)

"Sitting room" and shoulder shaping is done by adding extra short rows and modeling them into curves.
A. Horizontally, in a mantle.

B. Vertically.

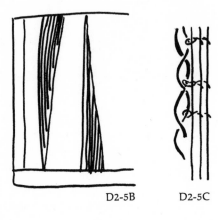

D2-5B   D2-5C

C. Twined selvedge.

D. Method of attaching feathers, for decoration and for entire feather mantles.
E. Tags or ends of wool inserted into the twining rows.

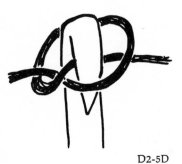

D2-5D

D2-5E

Typical Maori designs (D2-6)

D2-6

Brocade Weaves
and
Pick-up Weaves

There are two types of patterning with supplementary wefts:

1) *Brocade.* This is where the pattern weft is woven in the design area as the weaving proceeds. Added weft is limited to the unit of pattern.

2) *Pick-up.* In this method the pattern warp is picked up from the shed. The background, usually tabby, is woven first. Below is a brief comparison of these two pattern weaves.

Pick-up	*Brocade*
Definite right and wrong side.	Definite right and wrong side.
Pattern weft is put in during the weaving, in areas of pattern only.	Pattern weft is carried along from selvedge to selvedge and picked up where the pattern requires.

Definitions from Harriet Tidball:
Method—Brocading.
Pattern yarn—Brocading weft.
Fabric—Brocade.

These weaves include other names and types: laid-in, inlay, overlay, underlay; *Brocades*, overlay-underlay, wrapped, bouquet, spots, combinations; *Pick-up*, combinations, underlay, overlay, variables. On page 55 there is a comprehensive chart prepared by the author defining common names of techniques, distinctive effect, method, yarns, with comments on each technique.

Listed below are terms with brief descriptions accompanied by photographs. We have titled it "What's in a Name?" For the least confusion of terms, since there are so many overlapping ones for similar techniques, we use "laid-in" as a general term meaning a supplementary weft laid into a shed. For special ways of placing the weft we use the particular term accepted for that method. Laid-in weaves are sometimes called "embroidery weaves," a term that is descriptive but rather misleading, especially as the description of a laid-in weave may include a comparison to the embroidery stitch it resembles. However, although they can be copied with a needle, true brocade weaves are done with a pattern weft on the warp during the weaving. In some ancient textiles—particularly those of Mexico and Guatemala—it is often difficult to tell whether you are looking at a weaving or embroidery. If you want to authenticate such textiles, here are two clues—embroideries have knots where the thread is started and, under a microscope, show warp and weft threads split or skipped.

WHAT'S IN A NAME?

Brocade: Name of a textile patterned with supplementary wefts. Usually has a richly covered ground. In use, brocade has come to mean many types of inlay. The term has been broadened to include both the methods of putting in pattern and the luxurious fabric.

Brocade weaves, brocaded, to brocade all indicate the structure, definitely and distinctly handwoven. As yet, no mechanical means has been devised to do exactly what the weaver's eye and hands can do, although some methods achieve a resemblance.

3-1. Silk Brocade from Japan. Fine and intricate.
Collection of the author. (Photograph by Kent Kammerer.)

3-2. Detail of the Naga jacket from India shown in chapter 6, figure 6-17. Diamond pattern is laid in on one of the white stripes. A laid-in and woven band crosses the background stripes above it. The ends of pattern wefts are simply cut at each row. A row of small loops divides the plain stripes above from the stripes with overlaid pattern below. Done in black and white, with fine yellow lines in the black stripes. Courtesy of the Costume and Study Collection, School of Home Economics, University of Washington. (Photograph by William Eng.)

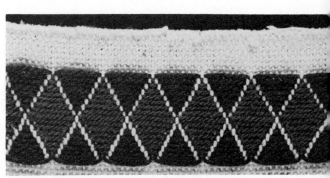

3-3. Reconstruction of a typical Angami (India) design. Woven in coarse wool, it becomes an overlay and the points are not as elongated as they are in the very fine weave of the Angami bag shown in figure 3-9. Woven by Ann Johansen. (Photograph by Kent Kammerer.)

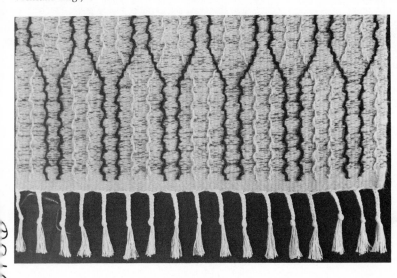

3-4. Rug from Euobea, Greece. On a warp of tightly-twisted seine twine, only about four to the inch. Weft of background is heavy white wool, double, with a smaller, quite harsh dark gray goat or cow-hair yarn. Pattern yarn is 2-ply tight twist, harsh. Black and white alternate in lines of overlay that cross and recross for the whole length of the rug. The line is wavering, because of the method, which is somewhat like a vertical Soumak technique and Swedish finger-weave. Very effective—looks much more complicated than it is. Collection of Irma Robinson, Seattle.

Laid-in, Inlay, Onlay are synonomous terms.

Overlay: When most of the supplementary weft floats are on the top or face of the fabric. (Figure 3-3.)

Underlay: When most of the supplementary weft floats are on the back of the fabric.

Overlay-underlay: Long floats on top and underside.

All three have floats over more than one warp, tied down at intervals with one or more warps. (Figures 3-4, 5.)

3-5. Appropriately enough, a Greek key border is used on a flat wool rug from Greece. Red and black random stripes are done in close-packed weave, like a plain-weave tapestry. Overlay-underlay. Collection of the author. (Photograph by Kent Kammerer.)

3-6. Oaxaca, Mexico, *servilleta* (tortilla mat). Red pick-up weave on white cotton. The pattern weft is woven from side to side, and makes a third value and contrast for the all-red birds and animals. Collection of the author. From La Tienda, Seattle. (Photograph by Kent Kammerer.)

Pick-up: A weaving sword, pick-up stick, lance , or fingers are used to pick up and isolate the pattern warps. The pattern weft is put in the shed. (Figure 3-6.)

Pick-up weave can be done by some mechanical means on Jacquard (card) and draw-looms. The handweaver can add doups or string heddles, operated by hand, which speed up the making of pattern sheds.

THESE ARE ALSO BROCADE WEAVES

Laid-in on every shed, on every-other shed, on opposites, on a pattern weave: The terms are self-descriptive and techniques are shown in our sampling illustrations. (Figures 3-7—3-21.)

Boutonné : A French-Canadian technique done with a single line of weft inlay, ending in a loop. Used in borders or isolated pattern areas. Harriet Tidball included it with the brocade weaves. In this text, however, it will be found with the loop techniques in Chapter 6, figures 6-26 and 6-43.

3-7. Band of Greek Key pattern laid in across a plain-weave pillow cover. The pattern weft is chenille. The turns in each row are made underneath. Weaver, Lila Winn. (Photograph by Harold Tacker.)

3-9. Angami tribe shoulder bag, Naga, India. Laid-in, black and white with a few orange wefts. Construction of the bag is much like the one from Burma (figure 3-37), the shoulder strap folded, attached to the sides, and with a warp fringe.

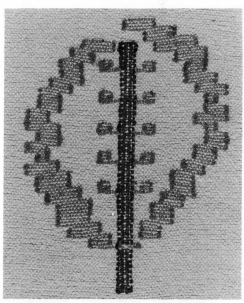

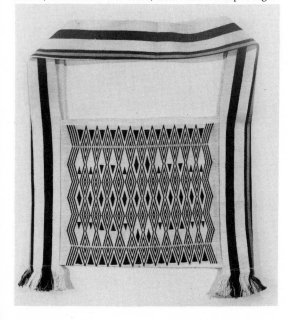

3-8. Knowingly balanced curves, stepping up in simple laid-in on every shed. The turns are made on the top, creating a little punctuation mark that adds greatly to the design. Woven by Hella Skowronski. (Photograph by Kent Kammerer.)

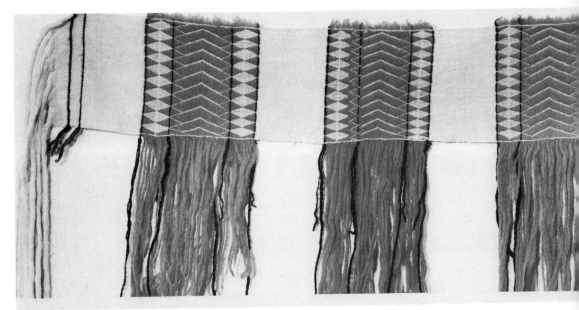

3-10. Angami tribe warrior sash. Red and black wool on white cotton. Laid-in. Wefts continue along one side, hanging in a long cut fringe. The warp ends twist into an even deeper fringe at the ends.

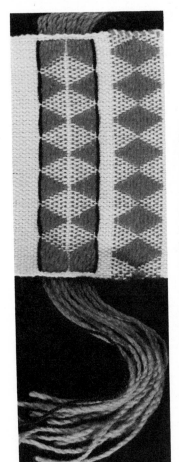

3-11. A reconstruction of the warrior sash in coarse wool and cotton. The diamonds are a bit broader, because of the large yarn. Woven by Ann Johansen. (Photograph by Kent Kammerer.)

The Angami tribe weavings from Naga, India, are shown courtesy of the Costume and Textile Study Collection, School of Home Economics, University of Washington. (Photographs by William Eng.)

3-12. Laid-in on a pattern weave. Soft, fine brown wool scarf, with yellow-green wool initial laid-in on the treadled pattern sheds. Woven by the author. (Photograph by Kent Kammerer.)

3-13A. French laid-in. White on brown linen. Pattern weft on every shed with a single line of weft used to connect the pattern areas.

3-13B. On a Monk's Belt threading, the pattern weft is laid-in on treadling that brings out little flower forms. Fine green mercerized cotton is employed for the leaves and stems; nubby yellow cotton bouclé for the blooms; all on a very fine white cotton.

Italian, Calabrian, Reverse Calabrian: All these are laid-in, each one done in a particular method of turning, shed, and type of pattern.

In the sampling illustrations—

Russian or Guatemalan brocading: Tabby and pattern alternate. Characteristic ethnic patterns.

Ryss weave: Looks like a simple laid-in, with turns made on the back. Woven "wrong" side up, following a system of treadling.

French laid-in: Over two and under two warps, alternating with tabby weave. Units of design are isolated, with a single line of weft connecting them.

Spots: There are as many ways to lay in spots as there are weavers doing it. A spot of many rows will distort the ground weft, but you may want to exploit this as an element of design. Spots can be laid in with any arrangement of turns, number of warps, rows, or colors. If they are arranged carefully, the distortion can be minimized or offset.

Dots and dashes: Single bits of pattern weft can be laid in at random or in a planned pattern. Any length, size, color, texture. Ends can be left on the surface for almost a pile effect, or left at the back for a smooth line on the face.

3-14. Swivel weave from Mexico. White-on-white cotton. This is swivel weave done as described by Verla Birrell, with the typical small animal, bird, and people figures on a sheer ground. From the Arthur Loveless collection, gift of the Seattle Weavers' Guild to the Costume and Textile Study Collection, School of Home Economics, University of Washington. (Photograph by William Eng.)

3-15. Swedish finger-weaving. Six strands of very fine linen are used for the pattern weft, which wraps around and up the warp. (Photograph by Kent Kammerer.)

Swivel weave: Small areas of pattern woven back and forth like a laid-in. However, this term is also applicable to a mechanically woven textile. "Swivel" is a catchy, apt term for what happens in a certain method of laid-in, but there are differences of opinion, so we give two versions. Harriet Tidball said swivel weave is a mechanically produced brocade weave that requires a special type of Jacquard loom with small shuttles, known as swivels. These work the pattern wefts back and forth in limited areas. Verla Birrell, on the other hand, relates swivel weave to Guatemalan and other inlaid weaves, and has directions and photographs under that name.

Finger-weaving, relating to the brocade weaves: Lila O'Neale wrote that it is brocading of the freehand variety, also called "picked-in." Her description, however, is that of a pick-up weave, using a weaving sword to pick up the pattern warps, making a shed.

Swedish finger-weaving: Related to wrapped weave, something like a vertical Soumak. (See Greek rug, figure 3-4.) It is a system of counted warps and exact shedding, an onlay, with the pattern raised over a plain weave ground. (Figure 3-15.)

HV: Abbreviated term for *Halvobeland*—half tapestry—a Swedish method of weaving pattern against a ground that is almost sheer. A simple laid-in. (Figures 3-16, 17, 18 show three examples from Sweden.) This is the simplest of inlay

3-16. H V technique. A beautifully balanced composition of rectangles, one extra weft of gray-green, blue-gray, white or natural dark linen color is introduced in some of the blocks to make a slight change in color. H V—with more pattern than background.

3-17. H V. Background and pattern are almost equal. Done in natural linen, and gold tones of fine wool and linen.

3-18. Detail of H V. The sheer area outlines a circle and segments. Courtesy Irma Robinson. (Photographs by Kent Kammerer.)

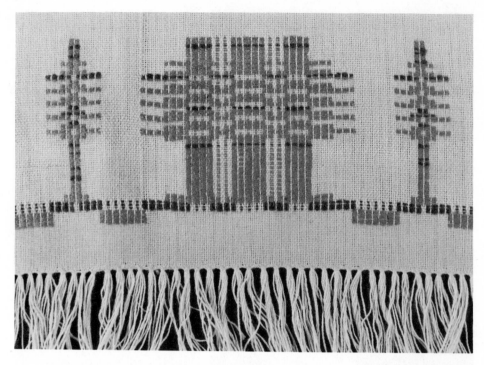

3-19. Half-Dukagang border woven at the edge of a fine linen towel. Pattern is two shades of green. The Scandinavian term—translated "path of cloth"—is an apt one, a distinguishing feature being the straight line of background color showing between the paths of pattern. Full Dukagang is woven in the same way, except that it covers all of the background, with no plain areas between the patterns.

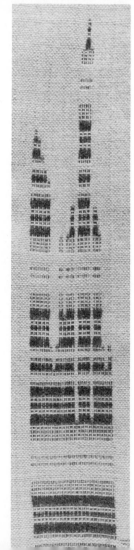

3-20. Half-Dukagang. A city-scape, or cathedral spires, woven in extremely fine wool.

3-21. Krabba and Half-Krabba. Small rug, rose-red and navy blue, woven on a two-strand natural linen warp. Fine stranded-wool weft. Laid-in (overlay-underlay). One row of knots and straight fringe finish the ends. The technique is Half-Krabba for the lines on diagonals; Krabba for the blocks and rectangles, stepped up.

methods, with the pattern yarn put in every shed, and returned on the surface. The background is almost sheer, of very fine linen. The pattern wefts are usually of very fine wool, often two colors in one shuttle. Frequently the pattern covers most of the surface, with narrow lines dividing the geometric designs.

Dukagang (cloth path) either Whole or Half: Usually associated with Scandinavian weavers, since they use it a great deal, but it is found in weavings from many cultures. History records use of this technique as far back as the early Egyptian weavers. Also called pick-up, because the warp threads are picked up to make the pattern shed.

Whole (full) Dukagang: The pattern covers all of the textile.

Half Dukagang: Patterning is scattered, and part of the ground weave is left unpatterned. (Figures 3-19, 20.)

Krabba: A Finnish weave, a pick-up, this involves pattern wefts and warps in a specific way. Blocks and rectangles are stepped up.

Half-Krabba: Related to Krabba, but has its own ways. It is always woven on a diagonal pattern involving a specified number of warps and wefts. (Figure 3-21.)

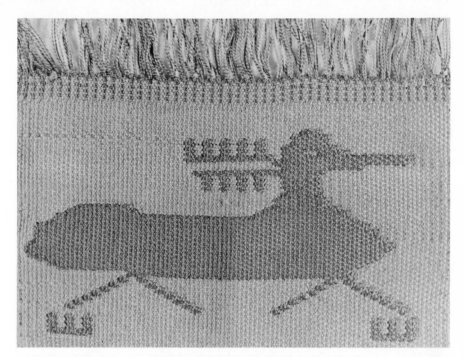

3-22, 23. Both sides of a pick-up weave. The two warp colors are reversed in pattern and background. Gertrude Mortensen, the weaver, laughs at this bird because he turned out to be rather more elongated and compressed than her diagram on graph paper. We think he has a lot of dignity and poise, though! A distortion of your design can easily happen in the laid-in and pick-up techniques, if the weaving closes up more than you thought it would, and you had allowed too few rows to build up some areas. This is something to watch out for and correct early in the weaving. It also points up the value of sampling with different yarn sizes and setts. (Weavings pictured in figures 3-19—23 are all by Gertrude Mortensen. Photographs by Kent Kammerer.)

PICK-UP WEAVES

Methods and types of pick-up weaves are many and varied. Directions are lengthy. We regret having to limit our text to names, together with some general notes, in order to bring these weaves to your attention. We urge further research and study.

Methods

Briefly, pattern weft is put into a shed made by a pick-up stick. Selected warps that define the pattern are picked up by the stick. Rows of tabby are woven between the pattern rows to make the background fabric. Many variations are known and used: underlay, overlay, overlay-underlay, combined with brocade weaves. On a closed shed, or on an open shed. Tabby and pattern. Pattern with no tabby, where two or more pattern wefts interwork to make a ground weave. Surface effects differ with floats over the warp in isolated pattern areas, floats over the whole surface, floats tied down with certain warps to make a warp outline.

Double cloth pick-up weaves: Two sets of warp are employed, usually in contrasting colors. The pattern is picked up and the design is identical on the reverse side, in the second color. The picked-up warp is bound to the opposite color warp in the weaving. Weaving is done with two shuttles, one of each color, with both warps the same weight yarn. The Peruvian, Scandinavian, Mexican, and Guatemalan weavers were, and are, masters of this technique. Look for *Finn-weave* and *Mexican style.*

3-24   3-25

3-24, 25. Two long hangings in double-weave pick-up. Sections of these appear in other chapters because so many interesting techniques are incorporated. Each panel has a complete reverse of design and color. The right side of one seems to be black on white; the other, white on dark. Note how suitable the top and bottom treatments are, especially on the black one, and how much the varied division bands contribute to the white one, making each design a separate section. Weaver, Bernice O'Neil. (Photograph by Kent Kammerer.)

Patterns

Pick-up weaves require careful planning of the pattern and counting of warps. Pick-up is not spontaneous or casual, as the brocade weaves can be. Patterns must be carefully planned out on graph paper with one square equal to a fixed number of warps and wefts. Patterns are clean-cut and precise.

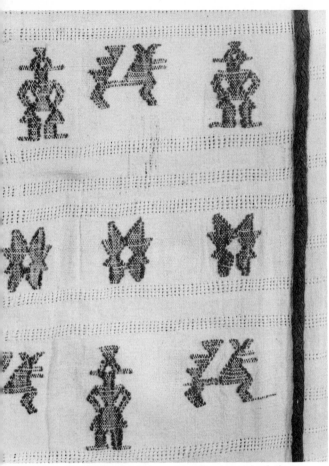

3-26. Detail of the center front panel of the Mexican *huipil* shown in chapter 8, figure 8-7A. Red on white. Three rows of laid-in figures are woven just below the neckline, between rows of Leno woven into the background fabric. Laid-in on every-other shed, the turnings are made on the top side, giving a little textured edge. Note the pattern yarn run out into the fabric in the lower right creature. This characteristic way to dispose of the weft end often occurs in these weavings. From the collection of Mr. and Mrs. Fred Hart, La Tienda, Seattle. (Photographs 3-26, 27 by William Eng.)

3-27. Peyote bag, carried by men in Huichol, Mexico. Another example of many techniques combined to make an article of great interest. Double weave of fine wool, royal blue and golden tan, with a deep pink edge and joining. Note one row of animals upside down! On reverse, all are right side up but we show this side—again pointing out the little touches that make these weavings so endearing. The joining is Blanket Stitch, grouped in two's. *Top edge:* Turned in one-half inch and blanket-stitched like the joining. *Bottom corner decorations:* Double pompons in blue and light yellow, on pink twisted cord. *Shoulder strap:* Three-quarter-inch-wide woven band, same colors as the bag, plus white; sewn on as separate strips, tied together at the shoulder. Warps are divided into three groups, twisted and knotted, leaving a small tassel at the end. Collection of Mr. and Mrs. Fred Hart, La Tienda, Seattle.

3-28A, B, C, D, E, F, G, H. Eight motifs from the Naga, India, textile shown in chapter 2, figure 2-20. White cotton plain weave ground. Black pattern weft. The patterns are woven in from the selvedge, then strips are joined to make a robe. You can see the joining at the left edge of some. The black weft is carried along in the shed, and you can see where it is returned, leaving a black outline at the right edge of the design.
A heavy weft is woven across, top and bottom, and a few times in between, each one into the ground weave for a way. Courtesy of the Costume and Textile Study Collection, School of Home Economics, University of Washington. (Photograph by William Eng.)

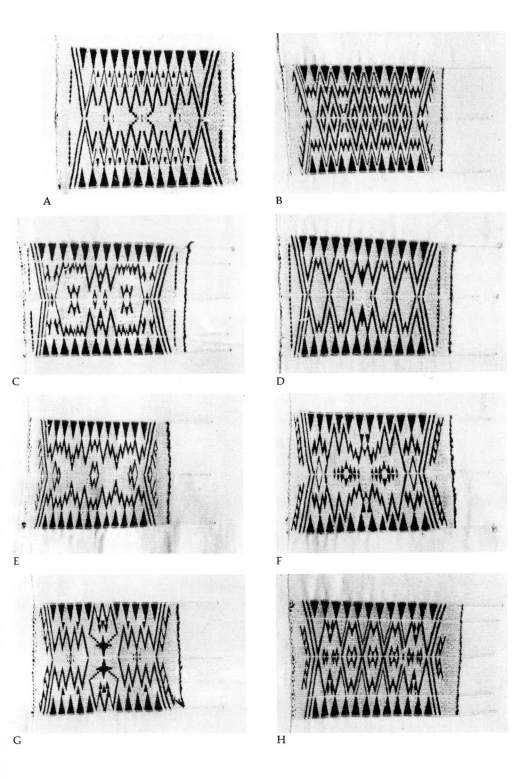

A

B

C

D

E

F

G

H

C-4

C-5

Pick-up sticks

Warps are picked up with smooth, narrow pick-up sticks. On small weavings, the fingers or a knitting needle will suffice. These sticks perform the same work as a heddle. Often more than one pick-up stick is used, and often—especially on primitive back-strap looms—a whole series of sticks will be employed. The first pick-up stick is usually removed after weaving the row and after the second pick-up stick has been inserted to make the next pattern row. Sometimes a shed stick or weaving sword of smooth wood, wider than the pick-up stick and usually knife-edged with rounded point at the ends, is used, turned on edge to make a wide pattern shed. The pattern weft is put through this shed with shuttle or bobbin.

3-29, 30. Inlays on twill, from Bhutan, India. Woven of heavy wool, rich colors. Elizabeth Bayley Willis Collection, courtesy Costume and Textile Study Collection, School of Home Economics, University of Washington. (Photographs by William Eng.)

Opposite:
C-4. Igorot skirt from the Philippines. Warp-face pattern, woven in three pieces. Border of narrow weaving, with fringe laid in. From the collection of Zada Sigman. (Photograph by William Eng.)

C-5. Greek table-runner. Heavy wool tapestry weave on white cotton warp. The edge is finished with a fringe made by tying bundles of the colored wools with groups of the white warp. Courtesy Zada Sigman. (Photograph by William Eng.)

A CHART OF TECHNIQUES

We urge experimental sampling of the weaves listed on the chart that follows. You will discover the relationships, distortions, limitations, and so on, of warp, ground, and pattern wefts. Refer to "General notes" for more on these techniques.

• Learn on samples, then you won't have to re-invent the technique to get the look and weave you are after. (See the laid-in samples shown in figures 33A,B—36A,B.)

• Try the effects of colors and yarn sizes, different combinations, in each different technique.

• Most of the brocade weave designs are easier to do if worked out on graph paper, especially Dukagang, Half-Krabba, etc.

• The inlays cover only the pattern units. The ground weave for the width of the fabric is woven at the same time, with the tabby rows between pattern rows.

• Unless otherwise mentioned, these weaves are done on a four-harness twill threading—1,2,3,4. The ground weave is tabby or plain weave.

• Unless otherwise mentioned, they are woven with the right side up.

• Yarn sizes are suggested where necessary to get the correct relationship of pattern to ground. But do try others, too.

• Numerous refinements, usage, exceptions, variants, original adaptations will be discovered.

See these helpful references, listed in our bibliography: Irene Emery, for analyses of techniques by structure; Harriet Tidball monographs; the Peter Collingwood rug book for detailed methods and techniques worked out in individual ways; Jeanetta L. Jones for a notebook with woven swatches of many of these techniques.

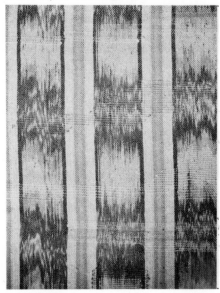

3-31. Painted warp, plain weave, has inlaid lines meandering over and back to give a floating, third dimensional quality. Woven by Margaret Burlew. Courtesy Henry Gallery, University of Washington (Photograph by Audio-Visual Services, University of Washington.)

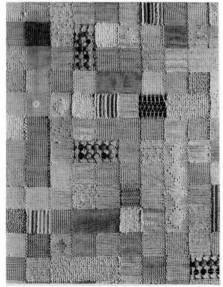

3-32. A "bug" screen for a small window shows an interesting collection of inlay techniques, in light warm tones with amber beads. Stretched on a simple wooden frame, the light filters through, it screens for privacy—and keeps the insects out! Woven by Virginia I. Harvey. (Photograph by William Eng.)

BROCADE, LAID-IN—INLAY—ONLAY—INLAID, AND PICK-UP WEAVES

Common name	Distinctive effect	Method	Best choice of yarns	Comment
Laid-in on every shed Top side turns	Well-defined pattern. Both pattern and ground weft in each shed.	1. Tabby row. 2. Pattern weft in same shed. 3. Turn on top side.	Color and/or size to set pattern off. Fine enough not to distort.	Also called: Simple or Plain Laid-in.
Laid-in on every shed Underside turns	No outline of pattern.	1. Tabby row. 2. Pattern weft in same shed. 3. Turn made underneath.	Same as above.	Same as above.
Random or casual Laid-in	Cut ends of pattern wefts add to surface interest.	Cut ends are laid in at random or to build a pattern. Ends are brought to surface.	Heavier than ground weft. Use doubled.	Effect is like that of cutting a long overshot.
H.V. Swedish Half-Tapestry	Ground weave, sheer. Pattern heavier.	Like Simple Laid-in. Surface turns	Ground weft, fine. Pattern weft, many fine yarns or one heavier than ground.	Usually geometric patterns.
Laid-in on every other shed	Pattern defined, but ground shows between pattern rows.	1. Tabby 1,3. 2. Pattern weft in same shed. 3. Tabby 2,4. 4. Tabby 1,3. 5. Pattern weft in same shed. Turns made on the top side.	Fine ground, heavy pattern weft.	May be woven on a pattern threading. Pattern shows up always on the same warps.
Laid-in on opposites	Pattern weft is in continuous-looking lines. Similar to double running stitch in embroidery.	Pattern shots over and under two warps at a time, or single. 1. Pattern weft. 2. Pattern weft row on opposite shed. 3. Two rows of tabby. 4. Repeat pattern rows.	Tabby, light. Pattern, heavier.	Yarn may be doubled in pattern rows—all one color, or more. Each row can be a different color. Careful beating to minimize distortion.
Laid-in on a pattern threading	Pattern or unit of design threaded in is picked out with a heavier or contrasting pattern weft. In rows, areas, or single units.	Any pattern threading provides a ready-made design for an inlay. Treadle the pattern, and lay in a pattern weft where desired. May be woven with conventional tabby and pattern system, or any variation of turns or method that suits the design plan.	Heavy, textured, contrasting color.	See flower pattern on a Monk's Belt threading. Figure 3-13B.
Outlined Italian Laid-in	Pattern is outlined by surface turns and double rows of pattern weft in the same shed.	Pattern weft is centered in first row of the inlay, with cut ends at each side. Work with first one end, then the other. 1. Tabby row. 2. Pattern weft laid-in, as above. 3. Uneven number of tabby rows. 4. Pattern weft in same shed as first row, first one end laid-in, then the other end. The pattern weft ends cross and change sides as they are moved up to outline the design.	Most effective with a heavy pattern yarn.	
Calabrian Laid-in	Pattern raised above surface. Can look solid. Weave on pattern threading.	Pattern weft is put in just like the Italian, but treadling is different to put more pattern weft on the surface. 1. Tabby row. 2. Three warps down and one warp up. Put pattern weft in. A one-warp tie-down, always in the same shed. 3. Tabby row or rows between the pattern rows.	Very heavy, soft pattern yarn will give a raised, puffy pattern.	Can be woven on other pattern tie-ups, but a one-warp tie-down of pattern weft gives a more solid look.
Reverse Calabrian	Pattern outlines the ground weave where returns are made in the rows.	The same as Calabrian, but reversed, with pattern weft put in on the sheds with three warps up and one down. Rows of tabby between. The turns form the design outline.	Very heavy pattern weft.	
Spots, Dots, Lines	Small areas laid in at random or in a regular design. Some distortion of ground weave.	Weave in over and under two or more warps, step over a warp or two. Beat firmly. Tabby rows will fill in around the spot.	Pattern weft larger than ground weft, but too heavy p.w. will cause emphatic distortion.	A slight distortion is compensated when other spots are put in. A pleasant, curving weft effect occurs.
French Laid-in	Pattern areas connected with one row of pattern yarn.	Pattern weft: over two and under two warps. Ground weft: Tabby. Pattern weft leaves one unit of design and connects to the next one, with one row of weft.	Strong contrast in color with both wefts and warp in about the same size.	

(Continued)

Common name	Distinctive effect	Method	Best choice of yarns	Comment
Dukagang—Whole	Pattern on wide vertical lines. Pattern covers background.	Weave with wrong side up. On any pattern tie-up that allows for a single warp tie-down. Rosepath, twill, Summer and Winter. Pattern rows always on the same shed. Alternate tabby rows between pattern rows.	Pattern, heavier.	Pattern may be picked up.
Dukagang—Half	Pattern is the same as Whole Dukagang, but background is plain weave, and pattern is scattered.	Weave with pattern on shed with three warps up, one down. Pattern will be mostly on the surface with a minimum warp tie-down. Patterns are woven on a plain-weave ground.	Pattern weave heavier or stranded.	
Swedish Finger-weave	Pattern yarn all on surface—spirals up on warps. Patterns can be isolated units of design, or a line of pattern weft can be woven in at the beginning and end to make a border.	Tabby ground weave. Pattern weft is wrapped around raised warps. P.w. is put in with two free ends, as in the Italian laid-ins, but moves up, outlining the design, one end on each side of the pattern. Pattern is woven over an uneven number of warps. Symmetrical designs with center warp always down, and outside warps always raised. Pattern yarn is always taken over the same warps.	Pattern weft is made up of several fine strands for the best effect, but a single, heavy yarn may be used.	
Ryss	Pattern lies on top ground weave.	Weave wrong side up. Turns are made on the wrong side. Alternate tabby rows important, in order, so pattern weft does not slip out of place. 1. Three warps up, treadle 1,2,3. P.w. under group of 3 warps. 2. Tabby, 1,3. 3. Treadle 1,3,4, p.w. in. 4. Tabby, 2-4. To keep the warp lines from being distorted at the turns, be sure the p.w. is brought up through the correct warps each time.	Heavy pattern yarn.	Similar to Guatemalan and Russian brocading.
Guatemalan Brocading Russian Brocading	Pattern is outlined by surface turns. Like the reverse of Ryss.	Weave with right side up, the same procedure as Ryss weave. The turns will emphasize the outlines of the pattern.	Heavy pattern yarn.	
Swivel Brocaded Guatemalan Brocaded	Separate patterns laid-in, often on sheer background. Rows of figures and small geometric patterns, often white on white.	Can be woven from right or wrong side. Alternate rows of tabby and pattern. Also alternate the tabby and pattern sheds.	Pattern weft a little larger than the ground. May be stranded. Figures usually in one color, but may be in many.	See explanation of controversial naming of this technique, page 44.
Krabba	Diagonal lines. Pattern is woven over several warps. Usually combinations of lines going up to left, then to right, forming parentheses and diamond shapes.	Weave pattern rows on a closed shed, followed by a row of tabby. 1. Tabby rows. 2. Closed shed. Put pattern weft down, under group of warps, and up to the surface. 3. Weave tabby, 1,3. 4. Close shed. Pattern weft down under group of warps, but advance, or step over, one warp—take either to right or left. 5. Tabby, 2,4. When angle is reversed, rows of tabby can be woven in between if design requires, or reverse can be woven without a space.	Stranded or heavy pattern weft.	Two to five warps covered in the pattern shots give the best effect. Cartoon helpful.
Half Krabba	Design is made up of small squares woven on a stepped-up diagonal. Usually in diamond pattern.	Weave on closed shed, wrong side up, like Krabba. Tabby rows alternate with pattern rows. Pick up groups of warps, lay in pattern weft. Alternate tabby 1,3 and 2,4. Follow design worked out on graph paper, and pick up pattern where required. Weave over same warps at least twice, with fine tabby between, to make typical squares.	Heavy pattern weft, usually one color. Fine tabby.	Cartoon helpful.

Common name	Distinctive effect	Method	Best choice of yarns	Comment
Clasped Weave	Like an interlooped tapestry joining. Pattern made by joining the double pattern wefts in each shed. The pattern weft, two colors, is woven from selvedge to selvedge.	See text for more about this weave. Two colors are laid into the shed in a special way, looped around each other and returned. The point of joining can be moved back and forth in the shed to control the design and color. Each pattern row is filled with two strands of two colors. Tabby rows between.	Heavy pattern weft. Fine tabby.	

EXAMPLES OF TEN LAID-IN WEAVES, ALL WOVEN ON A PLAIN WEAVE, TWILL THREADING (3-33A—3-36B)

Read pictures from bottom up.

3-33A. Laid-in on every shed: surface turn. Laid-in on every shed, with the turns made on the underside; it is easier and less awkward to weave this type with the "wrong" side up. Random, or casual: cut wefts are laid in with ends left on the surface.

3-33B. The reverse side of 3-33A.

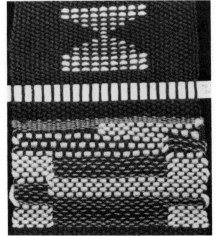

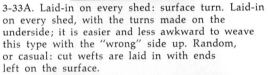

3-34A. Laid-in on every other shed; turns made on the reverse side. H V—half-tapestry: coarse and fine wefts; thin and heavy areas.

3-34B. The reverse side of 3-34A.

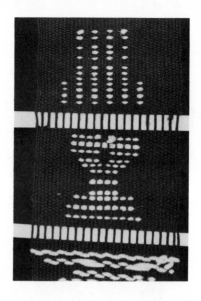

3-35B. Reverse side of 3-35A.

3-35A. On opposites: Two pattern rows, then tabby rows between; pattern yarn and background yarn in different sheds. Outlined Italian: Some pattern rows with double weft; turns made on the surface which outlines pattern. Calabrian: Pattern mostly on surface, covering three warps at a time.

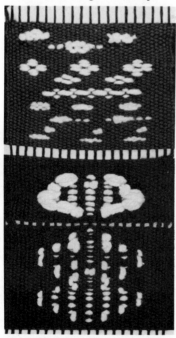

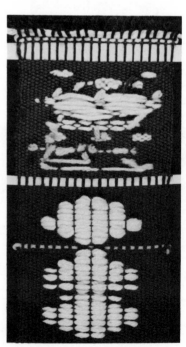

3-36B. Reverse side of 3-36A.

3-36A. Reverse Calabrian: On the surface, only one warp at a time is covered with pattern yarn and three warps are woven between in the ground; the small design is Outline Reverse Calabrian, where the heavy or doubled pattern weft emphasizes the turns. Spots: Pattern weft is laid in, in rows or spots; can be done on any pattern weave, as well as on plain.

JUST ROOM FOR A MENTION

Terms and techniques you may want to look for. They are all challenging and interesting to do, with effects that are a little different from the usual weaves. Well worth trying.

Two Navaho techniques found in very old rugs and blankets

Twisted Weft: Two contrasting weft yarns are woven into the same shed, then twisted in the open shed. If twisting in succeeding rows is done always in one direction, a diagonal pattern will result. If twist is alternated, an arrow pattern appears. This has many possibilities of design, either as a band, or an accent area. Carefully planned and executed, a repeat pattern will be possible. This technique is also seen in Moroccan fabrics.

Another version, used in rag rugs, is to wrap a length of rag in pattern color over the weft rag where required to build your design. A very good way to lift a rag rug into a special design class.

Jaspé is still another name for this twisting method, where indistinct and come-and-go stripes appear. We have our own name for it—union suit or long-john weave, because it is so much like those old fashioned long-handled under-garments made of mixed gray and white wool.

Wedge-weave, or pulled-warp blankets: Either of these names describes very well what this technique is about. Slanting wefts are woven in, beaten with a comb beater. Starting with a triangle built up in the right-hand corner, like a tapestry weave, the wefts then "lean" on this slant all the way across, and an upside down triangle is woven at the other side. To exploit this technique, use several colors so your angled wefts are in stripes. If you continue with bands, the next one starts at the left, and your stripes will make a herringbone weave with the first band. The selvedge will be somewhat distorted. For strength, the succeeding bands should be woven around warps offset from the preceding ones. Peter Collingwood has an extensive discussion and diagrams of this technique.

More unusual techniques

Ingrain weave: Found in Peruvian belt weaving. The warp intermeshes and forms a single fabric. The pattern is reversible, as in a double weave, with colors opposite. Tablet weaving is a form of ingrain weave. Mechanically-woven ingrain carpets are made with two or three sets of warp. (Verla Birrell.)

Finnvav: Double-weave pick-up. A pick-up stick is used for making the pattern shed. (Mary Black, Verla Birrell.)

Wrapped wefts: A Peruvian method—warps were wrapped before weaving, as well as being lifted up and wrapped during the weaving for a still different effect. (Raoul d'Harcourt.)

Cross-cording: Two or more wefts laid into a shed create a slight change of pattern in the ground weave in addition to inlay or other designs. In con-trasting or matching color. (Lila M. O'Neale.)

Counterchange, Countercolor, Tessellation: Repeated reversal of pattern.

Clasped Weave: Pattern weft laid in from both sides, looped around each other and returned; something like the interloop tapestry technique, but the two wefts always fill the whole row, from selvedge to selvedge. The effect is like hatching in tapestry weave, blending colors in a design area by alternate color changes. Useful where you want a color change in a shed. The fillip is that you work with one shuttle and one spool or ball. Two wefts always fill one shed, so choose your yarns accordingly.

The weft in the shuttle comes from the right, and is thrown the full width. The weft from a spool on the floor, at the left, is caught up by the shuttle and brought into the shed, so you are weaving a full-width weft row of double yarn. It's a kind of movable feast of pattern, because, by pulling back and forth with the two looped wefts, you can place their meeting, and the color change, wherever you want, before beating. Peter Collingwood calls this "Meet and separate" and has drawings and directions for weaving.

Shoulder bag from Burma, with laid-in spots and lines

This bag is an excellent example of the admonition to plan your weaving and the method of putting it together, using material suitable and available (figure 3-37.) In Burma, a lightweight cotton bag is much more appropriate than a heavy wool one, such as those made in the colder countries. The construction plan is well worked out, and you may want to follow it. Essentially, the bag is made of three strips of fabric, each about six inches wide. A heavy rib weave, woven of red cotton, has small patterns and bands laid in, in other colors and white. The warp and the shoulder band are black, very fine thread. The black and the red are woven in one continuous length.

The center is one strip, doubled.

The sides are each of one six-inch strip, folded lengthwise. These strips are woven so that the patterned section matches the center piece. Then plain black continues, to make the shoulder band, and then again the pattern area is woven to match the center piece. At each end of this long strip is a black and white stripe in the rib weave, ending in a band of plain black as a heading for warp-end fringe. Warps are grouped, twisted, then knotted at the bottom. Some of the measurements are: 6-inch wide strips; 12 inches of red-patterned area (24 inches doubled); 38½ inches of the plain black, with 12 inches of red-patterned weave at each end. The two narrow side strips are stitched across to close, on

3-37. Red and black cotton shoulder bag from Burma. Laid-in spots and lines. Courtesy, Cleo Francisco. (Photograph by William Eng.)

a line with the top of the center section. The shoulder band is simply pressed along the folded side, and selvedges are left unsewn.

GENERAL NOTES

All these techniques, under any name, are relatives, because they add pattern to a background weave with weaver's choice of method and placement.

Points of difference

• Which shed: Woven with tabby or opposite tabby.
• Yarn: Warp, ground, pattern—all the same, or different. A soft spun or plied yarn is best rather than a slick, crisp one. A design area is more prominent if pattern wefts are larger than warp and ground weft, and soft enough to pack together.
• Sett: Number per inch in the warp and in the weft beating makes a difference in the look. In some cases, a specific sett must be used to be right for the technique. It should be fairly open so there will be room for the added wefts.
• Color: One or many—whatever is required for the effect desired.
• Turns of weft: Where they occur—top or underside—makes a difference in the appearance of the weave.
• Ground weave: Pattern or plain. Plain is usually the most satisfactory to emphasize the laid-in pattern. While a balanced tabby weave is the best choice for background, and is usually used, you can have an all-over loom-controlled ground pattern. This will provide you with a ready-made set of patterns to treadle for your pattern inlays. You can lay in a unit of pattern anywhere you choose.
• Beat: Warp is completely covered, the weft just eased in. A light, even beat is best, so the ground weave does not close up completely. Leave room for the pattern weft.
• The ground wefts go from selvedge to selvedge. The pattern wefts are put in only where required to build the design. A complete web is woven in addition to the pattern.
• If your design is any but a very simple one, draw it on graph paper, or make a small cartoon. You may ink lines for guidance on your warp where they will be covered.
• If you use one of the techniques best done with the underside up, be sure to reverse the design if it must be in a certain direction.
• When the foundation weft is entered first, beaten, then the pattern weft entered, the distortion from the added weft is slightly reduced.
• The pattern yarn can be wound into butterflies, hand hanks, or put on small plastic bobbins used in knitting. Or use a tapestry needle for small areas.
• Fastening the ends: The patterns are superficial—there is a good basic structure underneath, so it is safe enough to leave short tails on the under side. These may be snipped closely either on the top or underside. For better wearing quality, they can be turned and woven in, or darned in, just so they do not distort or spoil a small motif. The clipped ends may be a part of the design if you cut them uniformly, and they add to the effect.
  The Guatemalan weavers have an informal way of disposing of the ends, which adds character to their patterns—and greatly simplifies the problem. They simply run "streamers" out into the shed an inch or so. Sometimes these are run out for several inches, almost meeting the next motif.

USES OF LAID-IN TECHNIQUES

Appropriate for almost any textile, in any weight, for any use—just so the design, placement, yarns, and method are suitable for the purpose. Long over-shots would not be practical for a chair seat, while a plain weave-inlay would be very well chosen.

• Using a needle as a shuttle to put in small design motifs while weaving does not change the technique to embroidery! The technical difference is in *when* it is done. It is weaving, when done on the loom as the ground is woven. It is embroidery, when motifs are added to a woven fabric.

FINALLY

Don't give up on the first sample. These techniques are a bit slow and pains-taking until you learn them. Plan to put in and take out until you know just how a method works. It is worth the time and effort, because then you can weave truly one-of-a-kind creations, and know that they cannot be exactly duplicated by a machine—that human hands are still very much needed.

Our notebook sketches and directions for quick reference follow.

Notebook

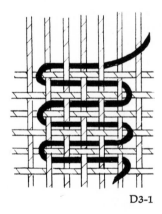

D3-1

Some laid-in methods
(D3-1—4)

Laid-in on every shed. (D3-1.)

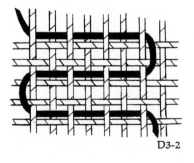

D3-2

Laid-in on every other shed. (D3-2.)

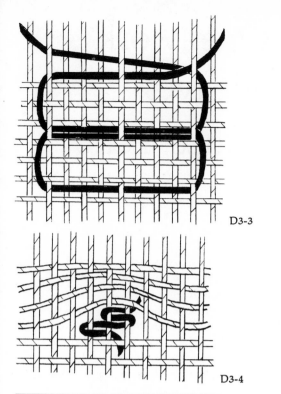

Calabrian. The turns on top outline the pattern. (D3-3.)

D3-3

Laid-in spots. (D3-4.)

D3-4

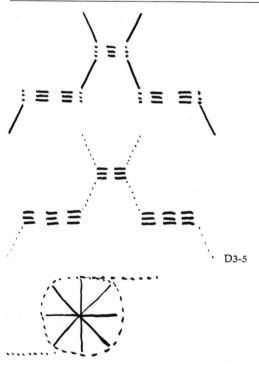

Laid-in patterns seen on Indian saris (D3-5, 6)

Similar to Coptic and Guatemalan ways of inlay with a long overshot overlay. On the top, just the straight floats like a running stitch. The long cross-over on the back shows through the sheer material, giving depth and interest to the simple pattern. (D3-5.)

D3-5

The small patterns are laid in with the design weft ends run out in a few stitches. This is just like the Guatemalan "streamers"—weft ends carried out into the ground weave. (D3-6.)

D3-6

Openwork Weaves: Gauze, Leno

Openwork, Lace, Gauze, Leno, Eyelet—dozens of terms for openwork are used interchangeably, confusingly, and sometimes incorrectly. They mean different things to different weavers. Lace, openwork, lace weaves, lacy or lace-like weaves, bobbin lace, knitted lace, crochet, needle-made lace—while all these are lacy and open, they are quite different in construction and in the meaning of the term. With the help of references, study, trial of openwork weave techniques, and examples by accomplished weavers, we will try to help you sort them out. We are concerned in this book with the woven types of openwork—those which, under any name, incorporate more or less open areas and a pattern of thread made with transposed warps, pattern wefts, and plain weave. From this basic system they take off in every direction, with every variation a weaver can think of. They involve more than two warps in the twist, combinations of gauze weave and plain weave (Leno), interrupted wefts that make slits and eyelets (Kelim), wrapping to make bouquet weaves, deflecting and diverting warps (Peruvian lattice), meandering weft and unwoven warp (Spanish Lace), hooking weft through to make medallions (Danish Medallion). Each one is named, each has its own distinctive style, patterning, and exact working method. All these weaves require only two harnesses, or some means of making a shed, plus a few simple tools.

Although gauze weaves are done commercially, and by mechanical means employing special heddle arrangements, every weave discussed here is truly controlled by the weaver.

SOME DEFINITIONS

In a brave attempt to classify different kinds of open weaves, or at least to sift through them to learn the difference between Gauze and Leno, we found ourselves writing descriptions, definitions, and comparisons. After briefing down a lot of information, here are our findings, with examples, references for further study, photographs, and informal sketches of procedures.

Openwork weaves: This is a proper descriptive word that covers all these weaves, since they are all composed of open and closed spaces.

Transposed, crossed: Transposed is the correct term to use for what happens to the warps in gauze weave—they are twisted, so they change position. "Crossed" or "twisted" are the terms more often used, even though technically not as accurate as "transposed." We use all three.

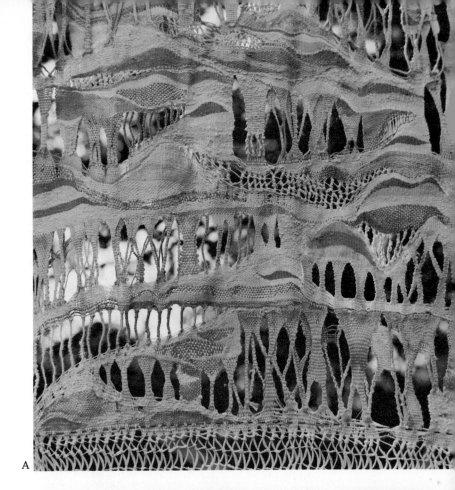

A

B

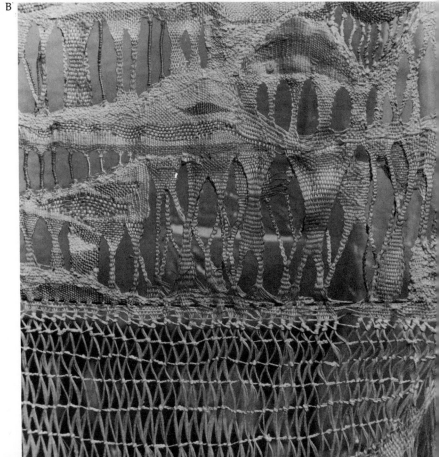

4-1A, B. Details of an airy wall hanging of all natural linens, employing slits, Peruvian lattice, Leno, wrapping of diverted warps, wrapped warps, and modeling of plain weave. The bottom is an elipse of plain weave and a very long, straight fringe. Woven by Linda Borland. (Photograph by Kent Kammerer)

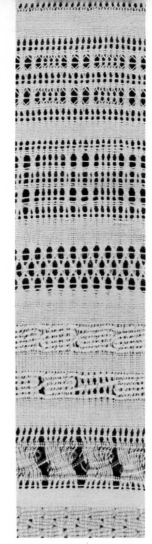
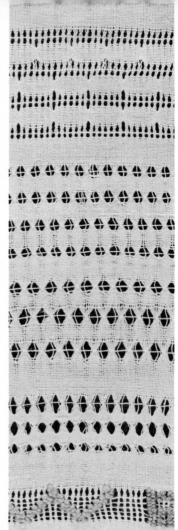

Right:
4-2. A long sampler worked mostly in white mercerized cotton to try out various gauze, Leno and other open weaves. *From top:* The beginning band is a row of one weft over four crossed warps. The next three bands are combinations of gauze weaves, multiples and divisions. The following three bands are variations of Spanish lace, first alone, then combined with Leno. There is a bit of eyelet at the bottom.

Far right:
4-3. *At top* is a row of Danish medallion done with heavy thread. Then comes a band of rows of Leno separated by Danish medallion, forming a pleasant repetition of ovals between the open rows. Several rows of bouquet weaves follow; the last one in the group combines Danish medallion drawn up into small circles. The bottom band is gauze weave with heavy yarn wrapped to form a zigzag pattern. Woven by Zada Sigman. (Kent Kammerer.)

Gauze weaves: Those in which the warps are transposed (crossed, twisted). The weft passes through and holds the cross in place. When an all-over or large pattern in gauze weave is to be woven, the warps for the pattern can be controlled by an extra string heddle device, or doups. Gauze can also be woven entirely by the weaver's hands, with pick-up stick, sword-beater, and shuttle. Gauze usually means a textile of all gauze weave, with no areas of plain weave.

Leno: Leno is a textile woven in a combination of gauze weave and plain weave. It is called "fancy gauze" when more than one version of gauze weave is used for patterning.

Lace weave: This term should be reserved for the loom-controlled weaves that look like lace, with more or less open area and loom-controlled patterns.

Lacy, lace-like: Terms that can be used to describe the *look* of a gauze or Leno textile, not the construction.

Lace: Non-woven structures—needle-lace, bobbin lace, knitted, crochet, knotted, tatted, sewn, or embroidered over net (Carrickmacross and Limerick lace) and others.

Eyelet, slit: Wefts woven then returned, leaving a space open between warps —the *Kelim* or slit-weave used in tapestry and rugs. Usually, when woven as an openwork weave, just one color is used. If you do want more than one color, it is easy to change colors frequently, as in tapestry. The warps are not always completely covered. The eyelet, or small slit or hole, is made by drawing the weft in tightly, widening the space between warps at that spot. When eyelets or small slits are woven in profusion, you have a very "lacy" textile, such as Peruvian *Dema-desh*.

Bouquet, wrapped weaves: Groups of warp or weft are bound or wrapped to create openings between other wrapped, woven, or unwoven warps.

Spanish Lace, Spanish Eyelet: "Lace" is not quite as correct here as "eyelet." The weft is woven back and forth across the warp in small areas, leaving much warp unwoven. The warp is not deflected quite as much as in an eyelet. It seems to be something of a meandering inlay.

4-4. To prove that the gauze technique *can* be mastered, here are two examples woven by a new weaver, Sheila Demetre, one of Hella Skrowronski's students. Shown is a detail of a wall hanging in black linen, Leno, one-over-one, with an original use of two wefts over groups, and eyelets. See 4-5, next page.

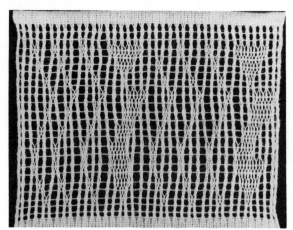

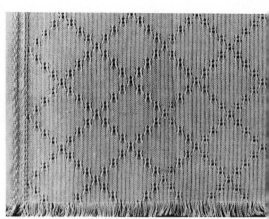

4-5. Tarascan lace in white linen. The subtle design is worked in one-over-one gauze twists, with angled lines created when groups are split. This is the top section of a long gauze-weave wall hanging. For the bottom finish see figure 4-14. Woven by Sheila Demetre. (Photographs by Kent Kammerer.)

4-6. Irish linen, Leno twist. Warp is fine white linen, weft is unbleached natural linen. Courtesy, Irma Robinson. (Photograph by Kent Kammerer.)

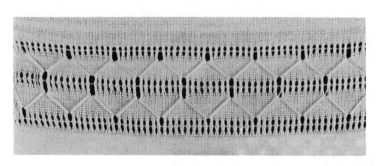

4-7. A clean-line geometric border, composed of Leno and a variation of Danish medallion. Woven by Zada Sigman. (Photograph by Kent Kammerer.)

Right:
4-8. Long narrow wall hanging. Bands alternate plain weave, narrow strips of inside cedar bark, and Leno. The end is finished off with macramé fringe. Woven by Patricia Wilson. (Photographed by Audio-Visual Services, University of Washington.)

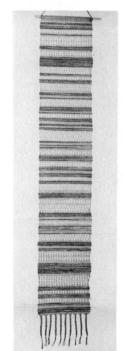

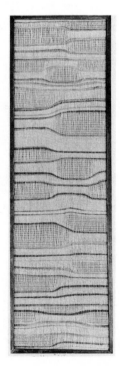

Far right:
4-9. Light control panel, precisely and perfectly woven and framed. Linen warp, cedar bark, and linen weft. The detail shows how the Leno technique compresses and opens, creating the gentle curves. Woven by Patricia Wilson. (Photographed by Audio-Visual Services, University of Washington.)

Tarascan or *Mexican Lace:* Intricate combinations of single and double twists, split twist, patterns laid in the weft sheds with heavier yarn. All were developed on the most primitive of looms. Peruvian, Greek, American lace, Tarascan, or Chinese are all related gauze and Leno weaves.

American Lace: Woven in early times, the patterns are in plain weave and one-over-one gauze. Sometimes the design was accented with an outline or double running stitch in heavy thread.

Danish Medallion: An extra, or pattern weft is woven in, hooked up and caught on the surface to make an enclosure around small plain weave areas. To make the most of the technique, the pattern weft should be heavier and/or a different color from the other weft. It looks a little like a honeycomb weave. It can be exaggerated into a scalloped effect with unwoven warps, a row or accent in an otherwise completely woven background, or worked along an edge.

TERMS RELATING TO WARPS

Crossed warps: Changing position by being twisted, transposed.
Deflected or *diverted warp:* turned aside or changing direction.
Deflected: a gentle shoving-aside.
Diverted: Swerving, arcing, curving, slanting.

HEDDLES AND DOUPS

For an all-over gauze weave it is well to prepare a heddle arrangement to pick up and cross a whole group of warps at a time. A doup is a half-heddle, no eye, just one loop taken over a dowel, under a warp, and back up around the dowel. Like heddles made on a back-strap loom.

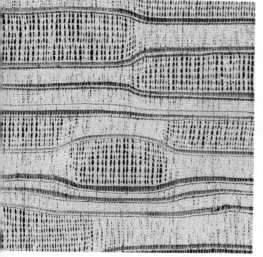

4-10. Detail of figure 4-9.

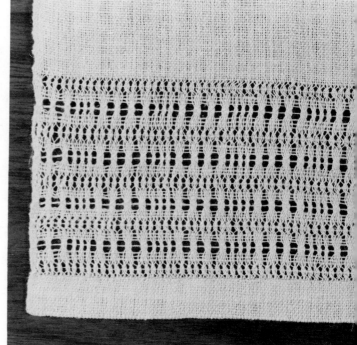

4-11. Neat repeat pattern of open and closed areas creates a wide border on a linen placemat. Woven by Noel Hammock. (Photograph by Kent Kammerer.)

4-12. Tabby motifs surrounded by gauze weave.
Note that each square has one small bouquet in
the center. Initials, symbols—almost any design
worked out on graph paper can be woven in this
fashion. The plain weave is laid in alternately
as you make the gauze-weave rows. Woven by
Bernice O'Neil. (Photograph by Kent Kammerer.)

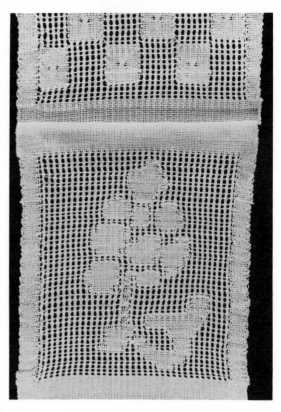

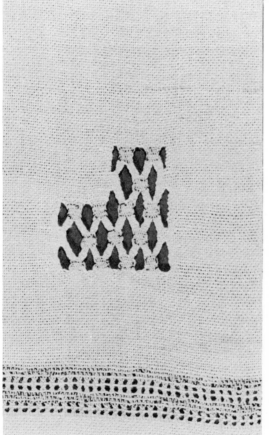

4-13 and 4-14 are from an interesting pair of
weavings by teacher and student. Figure 13 *left* is a
detail of a linen mat with a border of Leno and a
small inset of Peruvian lattice weave or Peruvian
lace. An extra color in very fine thread was
introduced at the spot where the warps are
divided and diverted. Expertly woven years ago
by Hella Skowronski, when she first became
intrigued with the open weaves and gauze techniques.

4-14 *below*. Hella Skowronski's student Sheila
Demetre, a new weaver, worked this beautifully
simple finish at the bottom of the white linen wall
hanging of gauze and Leno designs shown in figure
4-5. Done in the same Peruvian lattice technique
as the small insert in figure 4-13, but left open at
the end to become a tabbed fringe. Graceful,
and especially right in crisp white linen. (Both
photographs by Kent Kammerer.)

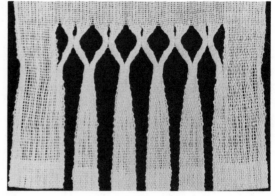

4-15. Open-work weaves on linen. *Top:* Bouquet weave on a linen mat, woven by Zada Sigman. *Bottom:* Openwork squares on a linen towel, woven by Gertrude Mortensen. (Photographs by Kent Kammerer.)

GENERAL NOTES

Tools

Only very simple tools are needed to help in weaving the openwork weaves: fingers, pick-up stick, sword beater, shuttles; a pick, pointed stick, or fork for beating small areas. The pick-up stick should be smooth polished wood, tapered at one end, and quite narrow. The sword should also be of smooth wood, tapered at each end and along one edge. The thin edge is used in beating; the thicker edge gives strength when it is placed on edge to make the shed. Shuttles will vary in size according to your particular project, but the flat rug shuttles with cut-out ends to hold the yarn are satisfactory—the thinner the better. Small, flat throw shuttles will work. Weavers are pretty clever at finding the right tool for the job. Knitting needles, tapestry needles of all sizes, crochet hooks, meat skewers, chopsticks, combs, forks, all are in our tool kit.

4-16, 4-17, 4-18, 4-19, 4-20. This group of pictures shows five divider sections between pattern areas of the long double-weave hanging that has so many different techniques referred to in other chapters. In figure 4-16 the two-color warps are used as threaded, and beads strung on the weft are woven through the cross. Note the one pair of warps that do not cross at the beginning and at the top, making a good transition from woven to crossed warps. In figure 4-17 the two layers of warp are twisted separately, the white woven with a double black weft, the gray woven with a bead placed to come in the open space between groups, with three extending out at the edge, for a little flip at the weft ends. Figures 4-18, 19, 20 show three variations on the same type of weft wrapping. The two layers of warp, white and dark gray, are separated and manipulated in different ways, making a secondary, very subtle design of warps. The black weft wraps them making an openwork band of bouquet weave. Black beads on weft ends add interest. Woven by Bernice O'Neil. (Photographs by Kent Kammerer.)

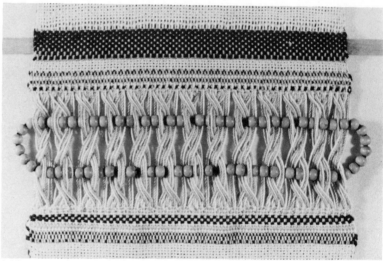

4-16

4-17

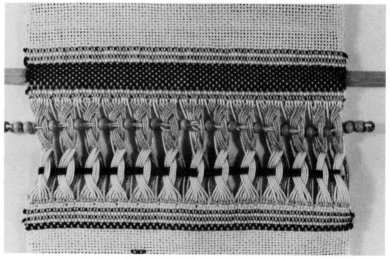

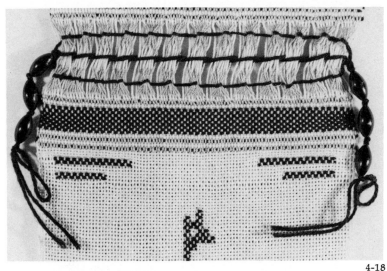

4-18

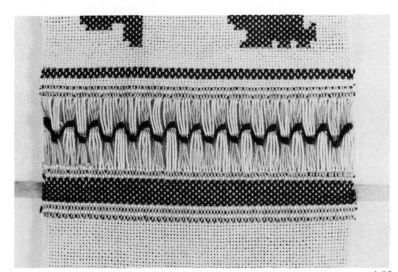

4-19

4-20

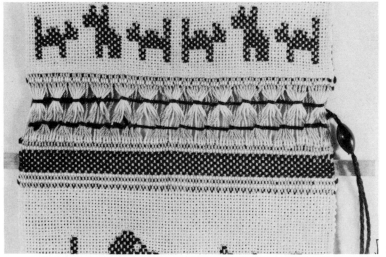

4-21

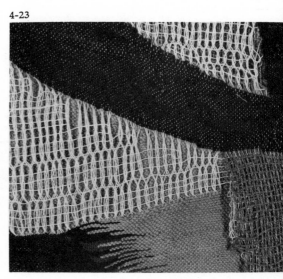

4-21, 4-22, 4-23. Betsey Bess uses Leno twists in very original and unexpected ways. On a small wall hanging, woven of very heavy handspun alpaca wools from Peru, in natural colors, "windows" of see-through widely-spaced Leno provide a strong contrast to the heavy, solidly woven wool. Figure 4-22 shows a detail. In another way (figure 4-23) she weaves areas of loose Leno in a many-layered warp tapestry. Extra warp layers are carried along, emerging to be woven solidly, or worked into a lacy layer. (Photographs by Audio-Visual Services, University of Washington.)

4-22

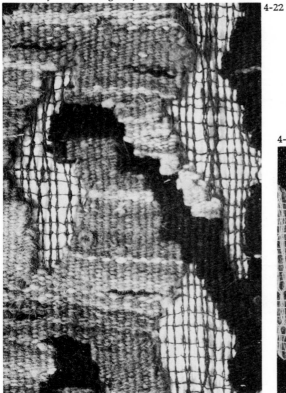

4-23

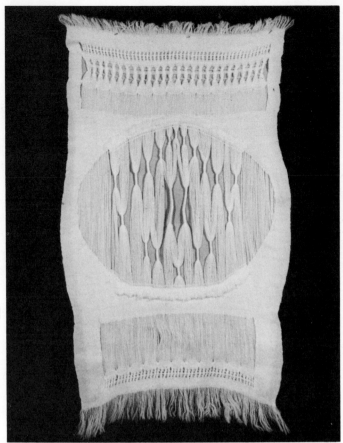

4-24. University teacher-student work. A sampler of techniques woven into a most attractive white-wool wall hanging. The weaving distorted the shape, but it was carefully controlled and possibly planned that way. *Starting from the bottom:* Leno, Danish Medallion, open warp, plain weave. Just under the central circle we see a little fringe of cut pile knots. In the circle, warps wrapped, divided, or left untouched are enclosed in a plain-weave tapestry border, smoothly shaped. The same techniques are repeated on up to the top, but a row of warp is divided and wrapped with a single weft before the finishing rows of Leno. Class of Richard Proctor, Assistant Professor, Art Department, University of Washington, and Betsey Bess, Associate Instructor. (Photographs by Audio-Visual Services, University of Washington.)

Kind of yarn

For best results, the warp should be a yarn that is somewhat elastic and resilient enough to cooperate with the lifting and twisting necessary to achieve this weave. Strength is important, and a smooth spun yarn will be most satisfactory for keeping a clean-cut division between open and closed spaces. Soft or textured yarns tend to fill in spaces and the structure becomes less distinct. The tension on the loom should not be too tight. Test out your particular warp to find just the right tension—enough to weave well and keep the rows even, not so tight that the twisting is difficult and a strain on the warp. The weft can match the warp in size and color, or be just about anything you want for the effect you are striving for. However, to appreciate the subleties of this technique you will find it most effective in matching color and yarn.

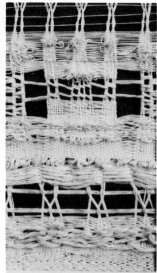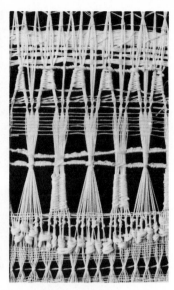

THREE THAT DEFY CLASSIFICATION—BUT THEY ARE OPEN WEAVES!

Small exercises to explore Leno constructions worked by a class of teachers learning to weave with Larry Metcalf, Chairman, Art Department, Seattle Pacific College. The assignment: Weave on a small frame loom. Use only white yarn. Composition and balance of over-all design as important as making a sampler of techniques.

4-25. Here we have a frenzy of loose weave, loops, pile, warps diverted, deflected, covered. A little Leno, some slits, and warps woven and wrapped in the manner of Peruvian lattice complete the piece.

4-26. Leno, both groups woven with one weft and groups, split and woven with several wefts in one shed. Also employed are Soumak-type wrapping of warp and passing around warp groups, plus plain weave, basket weave, and loops.

4-27. Leno, warp wrapping, buttonholed wefts and loose Soumak combined. (Photographs by Larry Metcalf.)

Planning

Unless very carefully planned, with a good knowledge of where the yarn will be going, a mixture of colors and textures will blot out your careful manipulation of twists and openings. Keep in mind that this weave is meant to create planned open spaces with a pattern of open and closed space, both equally important. Wefts should not fill in so much that these effects are lost.

LEARNING THE SYSTEM

When the author was first confronted with the gauze weave—reading the directions and looking at weavings—it seemed very confusing and complex. It seemed a lot to ask of a loom to produce crossed warps, open spaces—and plain weave along with it! I urge you to try it without an over-long perusal of directions. Weave a few rows of primary gauze, taking it step by step, and the system will be clear. Then, sample and experiment with the many variations of cross-overs, groups, and so on. Before you know it, you will be tossing off group-over-group, splits, left-handed Leno, and all manner of original-with-you variations on a theme. Every weaver discovers for herself more ways to divide the warps and combine other weaves with gauze weaves. Within the limits of weaving in and around the transposed warps, you will find endless possibilities.

HOW TO DO IT

Primary, one-over-one, or simple gauze twists

Work on an open shed. Start at right on the shed that raises the outside thread. With pick-up stick, pick up the first thread in the lower shed, at the same time moving the top warp threads slightly to the left with your finger tips. Bring the picked up warp to the top, letting one top warp move to its place under the stick. You have now made a cross, and the top warp is below. Pick up the next bottom shed warp; bring up and release the second top thread so it can move under the stick, making the second cross. Continue across until you reach the other selvedge, or until you have made enough crosses for your pattern. If your pick-up stick is wide enough it can be turned on edge to hold the shed; if not, put in the wider, beveled-edge weaving sword, turn on edge, and you have a pattern shed for your weft shuttle. Beat with a quick, firm beat. The sword or shed-stick can be turned flat and used as a beater, or it can stay in place and the loom beater used against it. For small pattern areas a fork or comb may be the best beater. Change sheds, beat again, remove the stick. Return the weft through this shed, from left to right. Beat. Now the warp has returned to its normal position, uncrossed. The spaces above and below the twist should be equal, and the open and closed spaces clearly defined.

Closed-shed gauze weave

Closed-shed is not as popular a method as the open shed but it is a quick way to weave bold gauze twists. However, since you work with all of the warp on one level, the twists are not quite as closely held and may tend to slip. The crossing method is the same as on the open shed: Pull the first warp group to the left; pick up the second group on the pick-up stick. The first group goes under the stick, making the cross. Continue by picking up the fourth group, put the third group under the stick, and so on. Beating and return of tabby is the same as in the open shed. If you are making a number of patterns across the warp you may find it convenient to use more than one pick-up stick so each pattern unit will stay in place and you can beat them all at once.

HINTS AND OBSERVATIONS

- Regular denting is easier to pick up than an irregular one.
- Use your left-hand fingers to help guide the threads over the pick-up stick.
- Unless you are left-handed, start the twists from the right-hand side of the loom. Most directions are written this way.
- In simple gauze, with the same number of warps in each twist, and the same warps twisted in each row, the open spaces occur in columns, one above the other. Observe just where and how the open spaces occur in relation to the woven areas in examples and photographs of these weaves. As a guide when you are designing, such observation will help you to plan a well-balanced, visually pleasing openwork weave.

• Remember that the void or empty spaces are just as important to your design as the areas filled with thread.

• In the various split, alternating, and grouped versions, the open spaces are staggered and are different shapes—ovals, round, almost square, hexagons.

• Gauze rows tend to pull in at the selvedge, so let the weft be quite relaxed, and be aware of the weft tension.

• A plain-weave border along the selvedge needs to be built up with extra rows, just as is necessary in weaving rows of knots and with some laid-in.

• Two basic methods of working, with slightly different results: on an open shed twists are more precise and tight and hold well; on a closed shed work is faster, twists are always done in groups of warp, and may have some tendency to move about. The other methods are variations of these two.

• The crosses occur above and below the weft shot that holds them in the transposed position. A tabby shot in the opposite shed must be made to put the warps back into their customary uncrossed position, ready for more tabby weave or more rows of gauze twists.

• A testimonial to the holding qualities of the gauze weave twist: Chenille yarn is made on a Leno weave. The twists enclose the cut pile, then the rows are cut apart and you have chenille yarn.

• The Harriet Tidball monograph *Two-Harness Textiles* is very helpful for learning about the many interesting ways to design and use these open work weaves.

HELLA SKOWRONSKI

This internationally-known weaver has developed ways of weaving and using Tarascan lace, gauze weaves and Leno to a high degree of good design. These weaves have almost become her signature. Figures 4-28—35 show a group of her openwork weaves. She employs the techniques in sheer casement cloth, and in weaves heavy enough for upholstery. Presently, she is intrigued with the ancient technique of Sprang or Egyptian Plaiting, a non-woven system of twisting warps. In this she has again brought her considerable design ability to a technique and is creating some remarkably interesting pieces. Regretfully, we could not wedge in instructions for this weaver-controlled technique, but we show two illustrations of Sprang in figures 4-36, 37. Articles in *Handweaver and Craftsman Magazine* and *Threads in Action* give an inkling of the possibilities. Another current interest of Hellas' is twining, and in chapter 2 you will see her "Twined Object."

Variations of the basic gauze-weave system are dealt with briefly in the notebook pages that follow. Directions accompanied by small sketches amplify the technique.

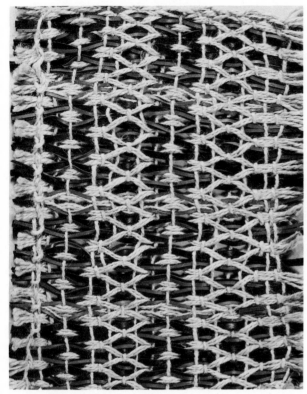

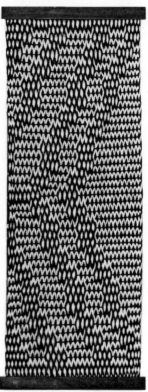

4-28. Calflace and jute. Contrast in color and smooth shiny leather against rough jute give great depth to this technique, where the warps surface, then submerge. Peruvian lace technique. An award-winner in the Leather-in-Decoration competition. (Photograph by Whitie Martin.)

4-29. Black-and-white wall hanging with a subtle diagonal pattern executed in Peruvian lace weave.

4-30. Peruvian lace weave. Note the barely perceptible squares.

4-31. Spanish lace, open weave, woven and unwoven warps form the design. (Photographs for 4-29, 30, 31 by Jack Dunn.)

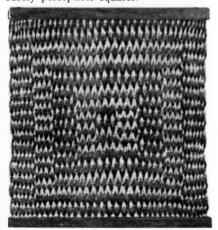

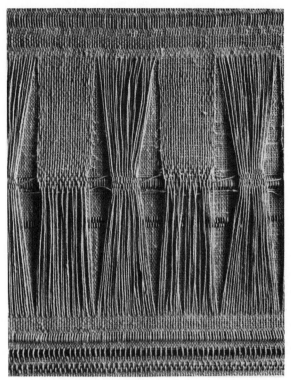

4-32. Double weave, with Spanish lace parting the unwoven warps. Background is plain weave with wood strips inserted. (Photograph by Don Normark.)

4-34. Gauze weave with regular openings made even more interesting by the use of a variety of linen yarns. (Photograph by E. F. Martin.)

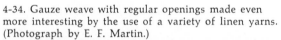

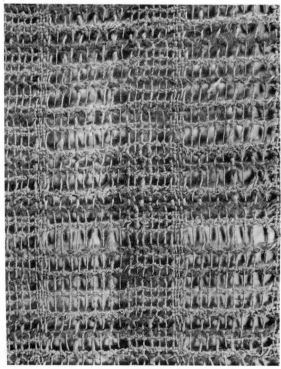

4-33. PERUVIA. Wall hanging. Each of the three panels is a combination of Tarascan Lace, gauze weave, and plain weave. Materials are natural linen yarns, copper and brass rods, and slats. (Photograph by Whitie Martin.)

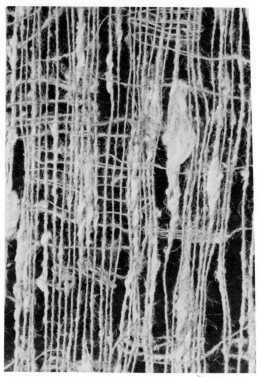

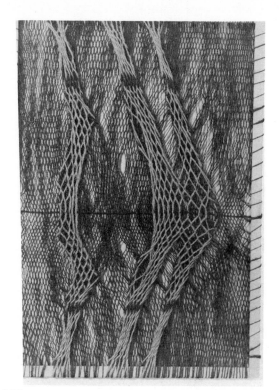

4-35. THIS WAY THE DRIFT. Detail of a wall hanging. Spanish lace worked in an extremely slubby linen. The wefts move around the large slubs, leaving them unwoven.

4-36

4-37

4-36, 4-37, Two framed panels done in Sprang technique—the non-woven, twisted, one-element technique also known as Egyptian Plaiting. (Photographs by Paul Gilmore.)

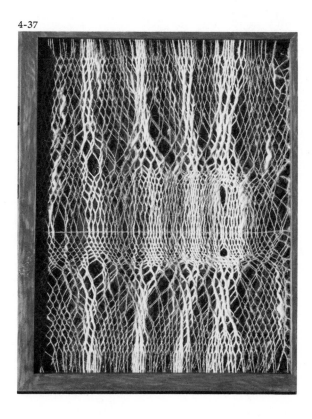

Notebook

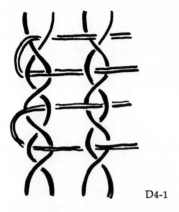

D4-1

Plain gauze (D4-1)

The system of plain gauze weave—the gauze twist, cross, or Leno twist. The direction of the twists can be alternated for different effects. For a larger opening and more curve in the twists, double or triple the number of warps twisted at one time.

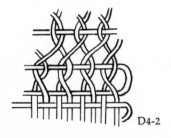

D4-2

Tarascan or Mexican lace weave (D4-2, 3)

D4-2. Single.

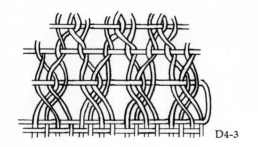

D4-3

D4-3. Double.

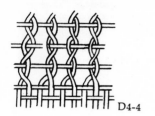

Simple vertical twists (D4-4)

This is found in Peruvian weaving, combined with pattern weaving.

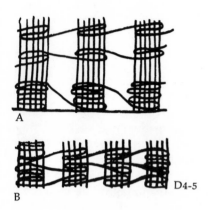

A

B

Spanish lace (D4-5)

A, in one direction. B, in both directions. This weave can be very open and lacy, or quite closely woven. When a very coarse weft is used, the curving lines will give a raised pattern.

Idea for use of Spanish lace (D4-6)

Shown here is an open-weave heading for the top of a drapery or wall-hanging.

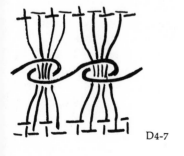

Warp wrap (D4-7)

The warp-wrap used in bouquet weaves.

Tapestry

A true tapestry is a woven textile with a patterned weave in which the design is identical on both sides. The wefts do not continue from selvedge to selvedge, but are woven as required by sections of the design, with many ways of joining the various colors. The warp is completely covered with a warp rib surface. Tapestry weaving has an awesomely long history, reaching back almost four thousand years—tapestries authenticated as made about 2000 B.C. have been discovered. The huge early-day tapestries with their infinitely fine detail, telling tales with photographic precision, give the most ambitious weaver pause. These remarkable productions almost make a potential tapestry weaver put aside loom and yarn in despair. But if this great art and craft is approached from the point of how to do it, you can sidle up and ease into it, for, after all, each piece began with a stretched warp and skeins of yarn in many colors. By bringing manageable segments into focus you can learn the methods, and then pursue any of the many avenues to pictorial weaving, on any scale you desire.

• To learn the various ways of covering a warp and joining the colors, we have instructions along with examples of the different techniques.

• To help you sort out methods used in making the familiar named textiles, a chart we made for our own information is included. This will help you recognize and reconstruct a look, a texture, a style.

• At the end of the chapter, in notebook fashion, there are briefed directions and sketches of the procedures.

DEVELOPMENT

The story of tapestry is an absorbing study with a vast body of literature well worth your attention. Clearly, there has been no one style, one technique, one use of the textile. Styles and uses varied with time and place. Originally, the huge picture-weavings were functional items, hung in rich folds over the cold stone castle walls for warmth. Being portable, they were taken along on journeys to warm and enrich a new environment. Slits were woven in for doorway openings. Later, walls and furniture were covered with woven-to-order pieces of tapestry, designed by artists, woven by groups of craftsmen. From miniature memorial portraits woven by the Copts to the immense story-telling Gothic tapestries, the opulent variety of the past has added to the richness of the craft today and provides us with inspiration and knowledge.

Fascinating as the whole subject is, we must content ourselves here with detailing selected techniques useful for present-day weaving. Tapestry weaving is done on looms of all kinds, from small frames to enormous vertical tapestry looms (see the Donegal loom in chapter 6, figures 6-15, 16.) Some kinds of tapestry are more easily woven on a loom with a shedding device, others are done readily on a flat warp. Each weaver must match up the loom, the weaving technique, and the type of tapestry to be made. Looms especially suitable for tapestry weaving are shown in figures 5-2, 3, 4. Our chart on page 91 will

Four tapestries woven by seventh-grade students. Egyptian tapestry knot technique. Designs from legends. Teacher: Roberta Barnhart, John Marshall Junior High, Seattle. (Photographs by Kent Kammerer.)

C-6. THE WHALE THAT SWALLOWED A PERSON. Woven by Laura Lowrie.

C-7. THE CRAB. Note the net-like overlay. Woven by George Anderson.

C-8. LEGEND OF THE RAM, THE SHEEP, THE THUNDER AND LIGHTNING. Woven by Timothy Quey.

C-9. THE WHALE. This whale with the baleful eye was woven by Todd Bell.

5-1. TACTILE GRID. Loop and knot techniques. Unspun and handspun wools. Design inspired by patterned fields. Woven by the author. (Photograph by Kent Kammerer.)

help in your selection. Sampling and trying out techniques will give you a direction. In our two previous books, *Weaving is for Anyone* and *Weaving is Fun*, in dealing with tapestry weaving we stressed the value of sampling on small looms, and we feel that there is no substitute for doing this.

TWO TYPES OF TAPESTRY WEAVES

There are two basic and different methods of weaving tapestry: (1) plain weave, (2) knot or wrapped. Within each type are variations. Both meet the tapestry definition of warp coverage, color changes, and the design being the same on both sides.

Plain-weave tapestry. This is the classical, under-one-over-one-warp plain weave. The warp is completely covered with rows beaten in close together. Variations are in the different ways of joining—or not joining—the different colored wefts that make the weft pattern, and the manner of weaving the background.

5-2. Tapestry loom. Shed A, made by standing ruler on edge. Blocks are lowered.

5-3. Tapestry loom. Shed B, made by standing blocks on end, raising heddles on bar. A strong, hardwood frame with brass nails holds the warp. Shedding device is two blocks and a dowel. Built by Mark Stevens. (Note tapestry techniques in progress, by weaver Melanie Chin.) (Photograph by Audio-Visual Services, University of Washington.)

5-4. A well-built portable loom with provision for four sets of string heddles. A series of dowels, fixed horizontally to the frame, allows a choice of warpings—forty inches to six feet. A fixed shed is made by raising the heddle bars and resting them on the groove provided. The photograph shows just two heddle bars in use. Manufactured by the Schacht Spindle Co., 656 Pleasant St., Boulder, Colorado. Availabe at craft supply outlets, along with their rope machine, inkle loom, and other weaving equipment. The weaver, Nancy Friend. (Photograph by Barry Schacht.)

Wrapped techniques. The wefts are taken around each warp, with variations in the exact method. Joinings are made or slits left at the color change points where the design requires. From these two basic methods, any number of mutations occur to create surface textures, open spaces, three-dimensional effects, combinations of the two. Departure is made from the classical type of tapestry. When tapestry techniques are used in new and different arrangements it seems more suitable to call these weavings wall hangings or constructions, saving the term "tapestry" to mean the classical style of flat, pictorial weaving.

5-5. Samplers of tapestry techniques to show the look of the different methods of making a color change, combinations of techniques, illusion, shadows. *At left, bottom:* Weaving on a slant and outlining. Dividing line, Oriental Soumak. *Middle:* Dovetail joining, plain tapestry, see-through look. Dividing line, Greek Soumak. *Top:* Interloop joining, slit, wrapped single warps.
Center, from bottom up: Shading, hatching, slant. Shadowing, interloop joining. Shadowing, with more contrast than previous one. Stepping up and over.
At upper right, from bottom: Grid stripes, shading down, pin-heads, diagonal and straight lines, triangles with broken edges, variations of hatching, spots, modeling, outlining. *At lower right across:* Modeling, shading, outlining on curving lines.

5-6A,B. *A,* small composition using the various methods shown in figure 5-5. *B,* different ways to cover the warp vertically by use of wrapping, knotting, dovetail joining, and slits over varying numbers of warp, with more than one color. (Photographs by Kent Kammerer.)

A   B

5-7. Single Soumak (Swedish Knot) tapestry technique employing short slits and single warps, to achieve a gently rolling surface. (Photograph by William Eng.)

5-8

5-9

Two tapestry technique samplers by teacher and student. 5-8, in greens and blues, all techniques, plus a fancy fringe, was woven by Louaine Collier Elke, teacher of Albany Adult Education Class, California. 5-9, woven by Ruth Holden, is an interesting patchwork in warm colors plus blue, black, and white. Note the skyline and bridge sketched in yarn on open warp. (Photographs by Louaine Collier Elke.)

A COMPARISON CHART OF TAPESTRY NAMES AND TECHNIQUES

The modern concept of tapestry weaving allows all techniques, added surface textures, and a wide range of fibers. The Soumaks are considered with tapestry techniques, and are used as such: Single Soumak, Oriental Soumak, and Greek Soumak. The usual weft is wool. It packs in the best to give the solid, complete warp coverage required in tapestry weave.

Tapestries are woven everywhere in Europe and, as in the Americas, each country has its own traditional designs, colors, yarns, and uses. Most are based on plain-weave tapestry, with color changes made with one or more of the interloop, interlock, dovetail, or slit methods. Specific European techniques are listed as such in the chart opposite.

The terms "high" and "low" looms mean this: A high-warp loom is a vertical tapestry loom; a low-warp loom is the usual floor loom where the warp is horizontal. The sheds on a vertical tapestry loom are made by pulling string heddles attached, involving the pattern areas to be woven.

THE PLAIN-WEAVE AND WRAPPED TAPESTRY TECHNIQUES

A brief explanation

(Also see our notebook sketches and directions at the end of this chapter.)

Plain-weave tapestry

While the basic method is plain weave, differences lie in the methods of introducing new colors.

Slit

A slit is made when each of two wefts in the same shed is returned around warp ends without joining. This makes a clean-cut edge, and when the wefts are not drawn in the slit will look like a smooth line. If the wefts are drawn in a bit, the opening will be wider and become a design element of space juxtaposed with weaving. If very long slits are created, they can be sewn together with invisible stitches. (See figures D5-1, 2, 3.)

Interloop and Interlock

We have chosen to call these techniques *Interloop* and *Interlock*, rather than grouping them under "Interlock." In fact, when the joining is made with wefts turned about each other it is an interlooping. When the turning involves wefts around warps, it is interlocking, and these more descriptive terms serve to identify the methods.

Dovetail joining (Interlock)

The dovetail technique of joining two colors results in a line that is toothed or serrated, with a slight ridge. Two wefts in the same shed are brought

TAPESTRY CHART

Type or Name	Loom	Usual warp	Usual sett per inch	Bobbins	Method of making color change	Slits	Comment
Plain-weave tapestry	Any type	Linen or cotton	8–12	Shuttle, small finger-bobbins	Interloop, single, double Interlock, straight slant Dovetail, single, multiple, slant 3-warp interlock	Yes, or not	Hatching blending, shading down, etc.
Coptic 3rd—7th C.		Linen or cotton	16 to 90+		Interloop, dovetail, interlock, slit	Small	As many as 150 weft per inch in some. Some low loops. Portraits, flora, fauna.
Gothic 12th—16th C.	High or low	Wool on wool	13–15 to 28	Small bobbins	Outlining, interloop	Yes	Only about 15–20 colors used. Much hatching, shading. Heraldic patterns, pictorial, mille fleurs. Root in Coptic weaving.
Classical, plain weave 16th-early 20th C.	High or low	Linen or hemp	7–26	Bobbins	As above	Yes, sewn	Pictorial, detailed.
Aubusson, mid-16th C.—18th C.	High or low	Linen or hemp	7–10	Bobbins, flutes	See above	Yes, sewn	Thicker warps and wefts. Weaving went faster. Designs more simple and fewer colors. 18th C. more colors and painterly details.
French, Gobelin 16th—17th C.	Low, later high	Linen	15	Special shaped pointed wood bobbins	On slant, stepped over, small slits	Long slits, sewn off loom	Hatching, blending, shading. More originality than others. Freedom of design.
"Contemporary" Early 20th C. to present.	Any type	Linen, wool, cotton	6–?	Finger-bobbins, small shuttles	All plain weave methods	Yes, or not	Use of modern painter's cartoons. Abstracts. Much color, texture, added methods—twining, open weave, wrapping, pile weaves, etc.
Rolakan Technique: Swedish Rolakan Norwegian Rolakan or Aklae.	High or low	Linen	10	Finger-bobbins	Swedish: double interloop Norwegian: single interloop	No	Woven from "wrong" side. Ridge is formed at color joins. Each type has it's classic pattern, one is Blixt or Lightning.
American Navaho	Upright	Hemp or linen	6 or 8	Finger-bobbins, shuttle. Short lengths laid-in	Slit, dovetail straight and diagonal, interlock, hatching	Small, inconspicuous	Traditional handspun-wool, colors, and patterns.
Chimayo, New Mexico (from Spain)	Low shed	Wool	10	Shuttle	Dovetail, hatching	No	Ethnic designs and colors.
Polish Kelim	Low or high shed	Hemp or linen	8	Small hand-bobbins	Mostly slits	Distinctive part of design	Usually in rugs, classic designs.
Peruvian	Backstrap	Wool, cotton	varied	Shuttles, finger-bobbins	Outlining, interloop slit, dovetail	Some	Intricate patterns—geometric animal, people, birds.
H V Swedish Half tapestry	Low shed	Linen	6–8	Shuttle	Pattern laid-in, interloop	No	Classified with laid-in, sheer and solid areas, pattern in fine wool and linen.

5-10. *From bottom:* Plain weave tapestry; dovetail and interloop joins. Single Soumak (Swedish knot) variations. Oriental Soumak, some squares all in one direction, some all opposite, and some countered.

5-11. *From bottom:* Greek Soumak variations. Plain weave with triangular hatchings, interloop and interlock joinings. Heavy Soumak, Gobelin type slits, and hatching.

Babette Joslin, a new weaver, student of Hella Skowronski, wove a long wool blanket-like sampler to explore tapestry weaves (5-10, 11, 12). Very colorful and useful as a reference for color combinations as well as techniques.

5-12. *From bottom:* Single soumak, plain weave tapestry with dovetail, slits, hatchings.

from each side to the change point, each one turned around a common warp, one above the other, then returned. With a very fine weft, this feathery edge is minimal and very useful when your design calls for a soft, blended joining of colors rather than the hard edge of the slit or interloop joinings. A handsome and distinctive use of this technique is to weave and return one color several times, then weave and return the second color several times. This is multiple dovetail and makes a definite zigzag line. Dovetail is also used on a diagonal.

Interlooped weft

An interlooped weft is the simplest and most inconspicuous of the joinings. The line looks slightly dovetailed, but there is no noticeable ridge. With a very fine warp and weft, the line looks quite smooth and straight. Interlooping is also done on a diagonal, but usually does not seem necessary since the stepping over and up makes a smooth line where no unusual joining strength is required. This method is done easily and quickly.

Double interloop

Each weft is interlooped twice. The result is a raised, conspicuous, slightly scalloped line. It is worked on the "wrong" side, so the line on the "right" side is straight and clean-cut. This technique departs from a true tapestry, because it is not identical on both sides. It is slower, and requires more weaving finesse. The result on the right side is not too much different from an interloop or a sewn slit. I like to reserve this method for a design on the top side, to emphasize a part of the pattern. Note the effect of this use in Margaret Collins' "Flags," figure 5-42, where she did this joining on the top as an effective change of line in her flat divisions. This method can also be woven on a diagonal. Do learn to do it, and add it to your store of techniques.

Three-warp interlock

This joining is of special use when strength is needed at the join, as when a tapestry of great size is woven to hang with the warp horizontal. The burden of weft turns is shared by three warps instead of one. (Detailed by Tadek Beutlich. See bibliography.)

Outlining

There are several traditional ways to outline a pattern or create a vertical line of a contrasting color. Some of these act as joinings between two pattern areas. A study of Peruvian and Coptic tapestries, as well as others, reveals the use of this device, employed in several different ways. See our samplers, figures 5-25—30, and notebook pages, for some of the ways to outline vertically and on a slant or curve. Also note how many of the photographed tapestries have more or less outlining. All outlining or limning is done as the weaving progresses.

Hatching

Also a part of the total weaving process are ways to weave the ground and patterns, creating a blend of color, shading, and perspective for more interest and design value, when you want more than a one-color ground.

Hatching is the traditional term for blending of colors. Hatchures were used extensively in the classic picture tapestries to depict minutely detailed folds and features. Yarns were split and blended, weaving rows were composed of many color changes. Alternating lines of weft were woven in and returned from different points to make blended areas and lines with uneven edges. Hatching provides color change and blending without the necessity of joinings or slits. It is used to give depth and perspective; to show roundness or form. The language of hatching is extensive and self explanatory.

• *Simple hatching.* Lines of differently colored weft are extended and returned in each row of weaving. The colors meet without joining, as they do in a slit weave, but the returns are made at a different place each time, so no extended slit results.

• *Triangular hatching.* Steep, broad, narrow, long, and short—triangular shapes are woven in regular rows, appearing like an exaggerated dovetail line, or casually, each one different; very effective in strong contrast, as a mirror effect, when dark and light areas alternate with the same shape. Just as simple

Work done by a University of Washington class of art teachers learning tapestry weaving (5-13, 14, 15). Taught by Richard Proctor, Assistant Professor, Art Department, and Betsey Bess, Assistant Instructor.

5-13. Partly double-weave, with areas woven in layers, along with modeled curves and added textures. Weaver, Lowell Hanson, Art Teacher, Chehalis, Washington.

5-14. Hatching and modeling. Unusual and effective, done with black and white wool plus a nubby gray, black, and white yarn. Suggests a mountain stream with stones.

5-15. Experiments with modeling, joinings, and outlining. Forms and ideas to pursue further. Weaver, Delpha Holden (Photographs by William Eng.)

5-16. A decorative hanging by a beginning weaver discovering how to do and to use tapestry techniques like slits, diverted warps, wrapping, loops, and others. Weaver, Kathryn Eyeler, student of Fritzi Oxley. (Photographs by Kent Kammerer.)

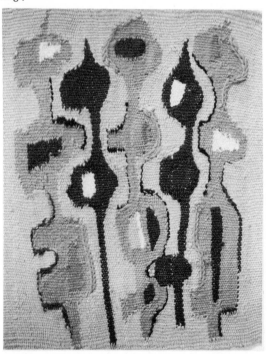

hatchings can be built up into rectangles, squares, and lines, so triangles can be woven in any combination and dimension.

• *Triangles with broken edges.* Spots and dots are woven at random, close to the point of the triangle.

5-17. Detail of figure 5-16. Shows the perky hanging-loop or finial.

5-19. Sheer, intricate lattice weaving overlays plain weave tapestry, which is also woven in layers. Brilliant colors against dark. See detail in color (C 10) on page 104. Figures 18, 19, weaver, Betsey Bess. (Photographs by Audio-Visual Services, University of Washington.)

5-18. A strong figure astride a background of modeling. A three-dimensional look achieved by use of color and lines.

5-20. Small tapestry with design of leaves. No interlocking; pattern is woven on its side, with selvedges at top and bottom. Silk and wool weft; hatching, modeled curves, shading and outlining. Weaver, Eva Anttila, Finland. From collection of Irma Robinson. (Photograph by Kent Kammerer.)

• *Lozenges, spots, modeling.* Triangular and simple hatchings suggest isolated areas woven in shapes or lines, and these are called lozenges or spots. When the shapes are larger, the procedure is called modeling. The wefts are eased into shaped areas with fingers or small beater, and are not necessarily at right angles to the warp, as the weft is, when the shape is made by joinings or woven slants.

• *Shading down, or Mottled.* Rows of alternating colors are woven closer and closer—from selvedge as a background, or in uneven rows as in simple hatching. For instance, start with two colors, four rows of each, alternating; then three, two, and one, until the colors are almost as one, and the effect is of a shaded area of closely blending color—creating the effect of a third color. This

5-21A. POMEGRANATE. Design by Marta Maas, woven in Sweden. Warm, golden tones in triangles, diagonals, lozenges, and spots. Fine wool on linen. Note the carefully finished, neat unfringed edge, with warp woven back into itself. Courtesy Irma Robinson.

5-21B. Detail of POMEGRANATE. Observe that warp shows slightly, and weft is packed in just enough to give a solid look. (Photographs by Kent Kammerer.)

5-22. Small wool tapestry in typical Yugoslavian design. Olive greens and reds. Note the similarity to the Swedish tapestry in figure 5-23, and to some Peruvian patterns. From the collection of Ann Johansen.

5-23. A traditional Swedish-style tapestry. Soft muted colors, fine wool on a two-ply linen warp. In Sweden, the weaver gathered natural materials and prepared the dyes. Plain-weave tapestry, interlocked joinings at color changes. Ground and pattern are blended in the weaving of many shades of brown, gold, blue, grayed green, and rose-red. Weaver, Gertrude Mortensen. (Photographs by Kent Kammerer.)

can be extremely subtle with similar colors, or bold and stripey with strongly contrasting colors.

• *Shading with the yarns.* Shading with the yarns themselves is another way to accomplish subtle color changes. Wind more than one color, in different proportions and color combinations in one bobbin, then weave with different ones in adjoining rows or areas. Plied tapestry wool can be separated, then two or more colors twisted or used together in one shed. If you dye your own wool, of course you are unlimited in scope. Going still further back in the process, if you dye the fleece, you can then card together whatever colors you wish for your own blends. It is also possible to card wools that have been quite loosely spun, and I have had some success combining and carding some commercially spun wools.

• In figures 5-18, 19, note the two bold tapestries by Betsey Bess. A number of tapestry techniques are used in unusual and fresh ways, woven on multi-layered warp on a large floor loom. Here are ideas for achieving a three-dimensional effect with color, and with warps woven in separate layers.

THIS PROBLEM OF NOMENCLATURE

I have no intention whatever of setting myself up as a Nomenclator, but it is an ever-present problem in this world of words to name techniques and methods. The accepted names of various weaving techniques are sometimes misleading, even inaccurate. In practice, it has been acceptable for an author-craftsman to re-name a technique if it seemed appropriate. For my own under-

5-24. Single Soumak (Swedish Knot).
Irish houses, piling up from the quay.
(Shown in color on the back of the jacket
for *Weaving is Fun.*)

standing and use I separated some of the tapestry color joinings into "Inter-loop" and "Interlock." This I have passed along as a matter of preference. The late Harriet Tidball in her many monographs and teachings made a point of calling methods as they are structurally, rather than by picturesque regional names. Lois Emery in her *Primary Structure of Textiles* has also classified them according to construction.

For years, textile experts everywhere have been working toward a common vocabulary. About a year before Harriet Tidball was lost to the textile world, she told me, with characteristic emphasis, that I had missed a rare opportunity to re-name a technique and end the perpetration of an inaccurate and mis-leading one. She impressed on me that I was obliged to do something about it at the first opportunity. Now—with a memorial salute to Harriet—I discharge the obligation and will perhaps make a small contribution to putting the language of weaving on a more accurate and descriptive basis. Her opinion was that the approach to and use of a technique described in *Weaving is for Anyone* was original enough for the change of name.

The technique under discussion is known as "Swedish Knot." Aware that the name was questioned, and the method rather obscure, I hedged a bit in my book by making a statement, then going along with the familiar name. Harriet told me how the mistaken name came into use. Years ago, a French weaver came to America to teach tapestry weaving. This was one of the methods she taught. In her explanation of its origin something was misunder-stood and it became known as "Swedish Knot"—although apparently not claimed in Sweden and technically not a true knot! It is really a wrapped technique, but worked from the back or "wrong" side. The weft is taken over the warp the same way as in the Oriental Soumak and Greek Soumak. The differences come in that Oriental Soumak is worked over and back on more than one warp while the Greek Soumak is worked with three wraps or knots over the same warp before proceeding to the next warp. Both Oriental and Greek Soumaks are woven with the right side up. In appearance the top side of the "Swedish Knot" is a warp rib, like the reverse side of Soumak. The reverse side of "Swedish Knot" is like the top side of Soumak.

Therefore—in view of the relationship of construction, and with the blessing of Harriet Tidball—in this text "Swedish Knot" has been re-named "Single Soumak." We hope this new name will be accepted and used.

ORIENTAL SOUMAK AS A TAPESTRY TECHNIQUE

Oriental Soumak is used both as a tapestry and as a rug technique. We have included it here with tapestries and also in chapter 6 on pile weaves. Not a true pile weave, it is related to wrapped loops, and traditionally is a rug weave. (See figures 5-10, 5-28, D5-7 in this chapter and figures 6-19, 20, 21 in chapter 6.)

Wrapped in the same way as the Single Soumak, but traditionally over four and back two warps. It may be taken over warps in different proportions, but always back on fewer warps than the journey forward.

THE WRAPPED TAPESTRY TECHNIQUES

Tapestry techniques are found in early weavings widespread around the world, and methods are so similar that all weavers seem to have worked it out independently and arrived at the same solutions for covering warps and joining colors! There are half a dozen or more ways to cover the warp with a wrapped technique. See the sketches and directions in our notebook pages at the end of this chapter.

5-25. Dark green trees silhouetted against an Irish bainen sky, seen when cruising down the Shannon River. Shown in color on page 33.

5-26. Reeds along the Shannon.

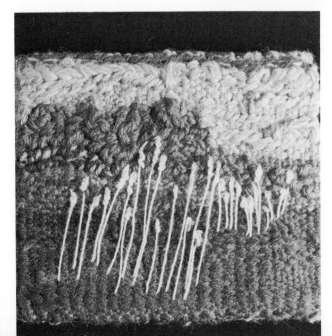

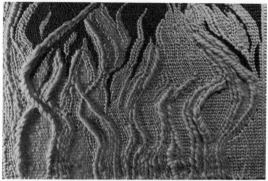

5-27. Irish fields separated by hedgerows are loop and Soumak texture. Shown in color on page 33.

5-28. WARM. The challenge of using mostly one color, one technique, is met by a try at capturing fireplace flames. Flame orange, with just enough red-purple background to set it off, was used. Greek and Oriental Soumak technique done in worsted and soft-spun Icelandic mountain sheep wool. It is still on its weaving frame.

5-29. STRATA. A small study of Greek Soumak, using from one to six strands of wool as a single weft. Weavings shown in figures 5-24–29 are by the author. (Photographs by Kent Kammerer.)

5-30. Greek Soumak with foam pillow form as the loom. Large Swedish rug-wool in brassy tones to yellow-green, accents of bright blue-green and red-orange. (For reverse side, woven of Ghiordes Knot, see 6-8 and 6-28A, chapter 6.) The author. (Photograph by Phil Davidson.)

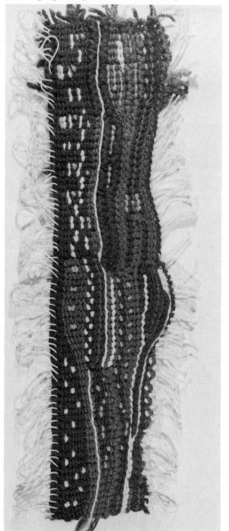

5-31. From a Canadian commemorative stamp, Gladys McIlveen wove a tapestry in Single Soumak and plain weave. White mountains, set off by olive-, dark-, and blue-greens, and purple-blue. The mounting, olive-green wool fabric with deeper piping. (Photograph by Kent Kammerer.)

Single Soumak (Swedish Knot)

Wrapped around a warp, but it is as secure as a knot since it is pulled down tight around the warp and to the previous woven row.
• A key to the different look in Oriental Soumak and Single Soumak, even though a similar method of wrapping is used, seems to be due to the pulling down of the weft after wrapping around a warp. In Single Soumak, this makes each wrap horizontal and tight around the warp, where in Oriental Soumak the wefts lie more on the surface, and at a slight slant. Even the ridged reverse side is not as tight and stiff as the ridged side of the Single Soumak.

Greek Soumak

Wrapped in the same fashion as the two other Soumaks above, but because three wraps are taken around one warp before proceeding to the next warp, a knot cluster is formed which makes the distinctive bumpy texture and holes between warps.

Egyptian tapestry knot

Similar to the above three but, although it is called a knot it is different in the way the weft is put around the warp. The result is the same ribbed warp textile as created by the Single Soumak, top side, and the reverse side of the Oriental and Greek Soumaks.

In Weaving is Fun we told about and included some of the Egyptian knot tapestries woven by Roberta Barnhart's seventh grade class at John Marshall Junior High, Seattle. In figures 5-32 and 5-33 are two we saved for this book. Also see color page 85. All these methods can be used in spot and small areas for a change of texture. Any one can be used to make an entire textile, or several can be combined in one weaving. All of them can be worked over more than one warp at a time. These techniques of covering the warp, added to the plain-weave tapestry with variations in joining and building pattern areas, will give you a rich source of methods to draw on.

5-33. Dragon and fish, detail of tapestry woven by Eileen Pierides. Roberta Barnhart, teacher, John Marshall Junior High School, Seattle. (Photographs by Kent Kammerer.)

5-32. Northwest Indian thunderbird and whale, woven by Lianne Hess. John Marshall Junior High School, Seattle.

• The selvedge of a tapestry woven in one of the Soumak or knot techniques is firm and good-looking, with a beaded edge when the rows are continued back and forth. Where the weft is brought around the outside warp and started in the opposite direction, a kind of knot is formed, parallel to the warp.

Identification with familiar named weaves and types

• Because Kelim rugs employed the slit weave as a part of the over-all pattern and method, this weave is commonly known as the Kelim weave.
• The slit weave is also identified with the ancient Gothic, and with Aubusson tapestries. Slits were allowed to form with no attempt at weft joining until they became very long; they were then sewn together after the tapestry was removed from the loom.
• Gobelin tapestries have their own recognizable appearance from the use of the slit in a different way. When rows of weft are stepped up and down on the diagonal, a very small hole or slit is formed, not large enough to weaken the fabric. More than two rows are woven in one color before stepping up and over to the next warp, adding a characteristic and interesting effect to the dividing lines between color areas. When only the minimum of two rows required to bring the weft in and return is woven, the hole is a tiny pinpoint, which can only be seen when you hold the fabric up to the light.

Two very fine examples of flat-weave tapestries with a great deal of depth achieved by use of color and forms are shown in figures 5-34 and 5-35. Hatching, steps, blending, shadowing. Both woven by Laurie Herrick, of Arts and Crafts, Portland, Oregon. (Photographs by Wes Guderian, The Oregonian, Portland.)

5-34. GREEN VALLEY. Courtesy of the owners, Mr. and Mrs. John D. Gray, Portland.   5-35. TRIANGLES.

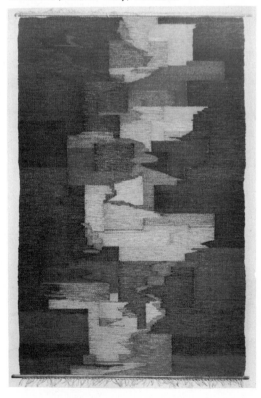

5-36. Detail of wall hanging OCTOBER, combining plain weave and open warp. Woven by Laurie Herrick. Courtesy of the owner, Dr. John Lang.

5-37. FRONTIER VILLAGE. Plain weave and stitchery. Weaver, Hope Munn. (Photograph by Kent Kammerer.)

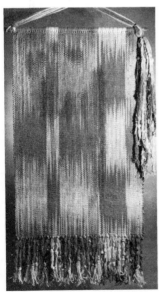

5-38. A shadowy pattern achieved with painted warp, plain weave. The deep, randomly knotted warp ends are repeated in the hank of knotted and painted yarns at the top. Note that the whole bundle is used as a hanger. Weaver, Hope Munn. (Photograph by Kent Kammerer.)

5-39. This stark tree was inspired by the storm-shaped trees of the Olympic Mountains, on the Northwest's Olympic Peninsula. Coarse natural linen warp and weft make the slightly open-weave ground. Colors are many subtle shades of gray, grayed greens, and blues. Note the well-finished edges, top and bottom. Plaited warp loops at the top, knotted fringe at the bottom. Weaver, Aletta Skille. (Photograph by William Eng.)

C-10. Detail of tapestry woven by Betsey Bess. Multiple warps, plain weave tapestry, and Leno. (See also in black and white, figure 5-19.) (Photograph by Audio-Visual Services, University of Washington.)

C-11. Small tapestry. An exploration of techniques. Adult student work. Teacher: Louaine Collier Elke.

5-40. Fanciful silhouette from Norwegian folklore. Plain weave tapestry, natural linen, and black wool. A perfect example of an emphatic dovetail joining which makes a toothed edge and gives character to the pattern. Both ends finished in an interesting knotted fringe. Weaver, Aletta Skille. (Photographed by William Eng.)

5-41. A tapestry skylight, woven for her home by talented weaver Luana Sever: blues, greens, and some orange, all cotton, on a white warp. The fabric was placed on a fiberglass mat soaked with liquid fiberglass; more liquid fiberglass was poured over to seal in the fabric. Edges were trimmed with a hand saw. The result is filtered light, shadowy pattern. (Photograph by Audio-Visual Production Services, for the Henry Gallery, University of Washington.)

• In Mexican weavings, particularly those with a flat, posterlike quality with no shading, the exaggerated points of dovetail joining are a major part of the pattern. The dividing line between two strong colors is sharp and bold.

• In Norwegian tapestries, dovetail joining is used with distinction when rows are tripled or more. (See figure 5-40.) In a wildly freeform weaving, this technique will serve you well.

• The most typical use of Oriental Soumak by Scandinavian weavers is the twill, or all stitches facing in one direction. The Oriental way is usually the chain or arrow effect, the result of alternating directions in the rows.

HINTS AND HELPS

• Refer to our chart for help in selecting the loom and technique best suited to you and your project.

• The tools you need will vary with the techniques chosen, the loom, your preference, and the yarns used. Some sort of beater is necessary. This can be a real tapestry comb, metal or wood, an ordinary plastic comb, dinner fork, smooth nails in a block of wood—any suitable toothed device—and, of course, fingers!

• Bobbins to carry your weft yarns also are many and varied. If you wish to weave in the classic Gobelin fashion, use the Gobelin or Swedish wooden bobbin, shaped with a neck at the top to hold the yarn, swelling, then tapering to a point, which is used to push the weft into place. Flutes, like those used in weaving Aubusson tapestries are like a slim spool, larger at each end, and yarn is wound in the center space. Not as picturesque, but handy and efficient are cardboard squares or rectangles with a notch to put the yarn through as they hang between uses. Fingerwound bobbins with yarn feeding out of the center are frequently used and quickly prepared. On small tapestries or in small areas, blunt tapestry needles are useful to hold the yarn, and the point serves as a small beater (also invaluable to pick out a mistake made in color).

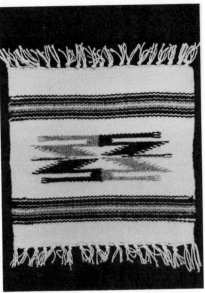

5-42. A study of tapestry methods in the form of signal flags, with the proper reds, blues, and yellows, but in the subtle shades of wool. Slits separate the blocks. Double interloop is done on the top side to show the double joining line. Weaver, Margaret Collins. (Photograph by Kent Kammerer.)

5-43. Woven in the manner of Coptic memorial portrait medallions, this small tapestry, surrounded by linen loops, is in the wine shades favored by the Coptic weavers, plus white and blue-green. Woven by author. (Photograph by Kent Kammerer.)

5-44. Chimayo weaving. A miniature rug. These weavers of northern New Mexico traditionally used natural wools and vegetable dyes; this piece is in natural grays, black, and white. As descendants of Spanish Americans, their weaving has its roots in Spanish rather than Indian techniques. Typically, the unit of design is repeated in the lower half of the pattern. Weft bands complete the design. Dovetail joining and hatchings make the familiar serrated edges along geometric patterns. Collection of Gladys McIlveen. (Photograph by Kent Kammerer.)

Plastic yarn needles are especially helpful—they are large enough to act as a one-point beater, and being somewhat flexible are useful for weaving in a tight place.

THE DESIGN—THE CARTOON

When you are a beginning tapestry weaver, and later when your designs become quite intricate, it is helpful to have a sketch or cartoon. You must know when a color change is due and prepare to make the joining, slit, or whatever your design requires. Sometimes only one row of weft or a pass over one or two warps is required before another color is needed. The traditional way is to make a detailed cartoon—either coded for color or in color—and fasten it to the back of your warp so you can follow it.

Weavers in Scandinavia are trained to make very detailed drawings and paintings before beginning to weave. Another way (see Donegal weavers, figures 6-15, 16) is to have a section of the cartoon before you as reference.

Still another way is to mark key lines or the whole pattern on your warp (with waterproof ink). If you choose this method, be sure the marks continue all around the warp, because the warps will twist and move in the weaving, and your design marks may be turned away from your weaving surface. As your skills in designing, technique, and vision increase you will probably be able to work with less elaborate cartoons, especially on freeform and spontaneous weavings.

Having tried all the different ways, my favorite one is to make a small sketch on graph paper, to scale, then work from that, keeping the weaving in proportion. It seems easier to refer to a sketch alongside than to have a paper attached to the loom or the warp. Where an exact dimension or proportion is important, mark a few guide lines on the warp with ink. It is impossible to simulate the exact look of blended colors in a cartoon on paper, so this must be done in the actual weaving, which gives the process a certain freedom and off-the-yarn-pile spontaniety. However, it is also important to have worked out the balanced color and pattern plan in general, and perhaps enough of a sketch and bits of yarn placed together to hold the thought and the color scheme.

In planning the jacket tapestry for *Weaving is Fun*, "The Yarn Bearers," certain limitations on color and shapes were present. I wanted to include specific creatures, woven in their own yarns, so it was a design problem of sizes, shapes, colors, and textures in a very small area, and it had to "read" well as a book cover. After dozens of sketches on tracing paper and a few cartoons in approximate colors, I tore rough shapes out of construction papers in colors close to the yarns, and had a game of moving the creatures. They finally fell into places that seemed right, and the little tapestry was woven with an occasional look at this last cartoon.

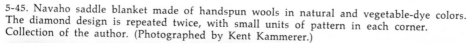

5-45. Navaho saddle blanket made of handspun wools in natural and vegetable-dye colors. The diamond design is repeated twice, with small units of pattern in each corner. Collection of the author. (Photographed by Kent Kammerer.)

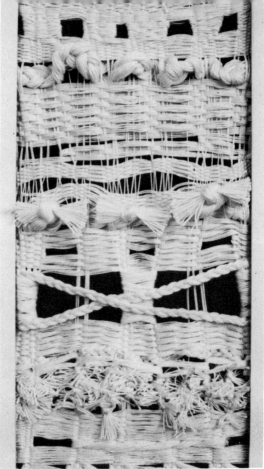

5-46. REDWOOD II, a wall hanging woven by Laurie Herrick, Portland. Double weave, with many layers of woven and unwoven warps, laid-in wefts of yarn, and long leaves. Courtesy of the owners, Mr. and Mrs. John D. Gray, Portland.

5-47. Adult student weaving. Study of a number of techniques. Slit weave widened to make open areas, chained and knotted wefts, Soumak, and plain weave. Class of Larry Metcalf, Director of Art Department, Seattle Pacific College. (Photograph by Larry Metcalf.)

COLOR SKIPPING ON THE BACK

In most tapestry techniques, it is best not to skip over more than two or three warps, at most, to begin another area in the same color. It is much better and more correct to finish with a color, cut it off, then start in again. In the Single Soumak, for instance, where a dot of color on one warp is put in, it can be cut, leaving at least half an inch, and stay safely in place. It is entirely acceptable for the back of a tapestry to be filled with short ends—many of them could almost be used as pile fabric!

WRAPPING OR KNOTTING AROUND THE WARP

More about these ways of covering individual warps will be found in chapter 9, "Fringes." Useful in weaving free-wheeling wall hangings and open warps. • Wrapping is just that—simply take the weft around and around one or more warps as necessary for your design.

5-48. Ogee forms woven at the bottom of a long black hanging has the shapes outlined in heavy rope; pile, plain weave, and unwoven warps.

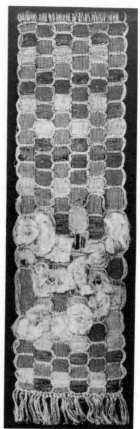

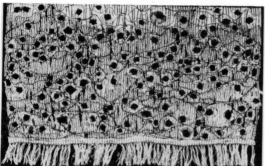

5-50. Caged seedpods are silhouetted and held by a fine meandering weft and lacy bands of warp.

Three wall hangings by designer-weaver Judy Thomas are shown in figures 5-48, 49, 50. Triple and double weave. (Photographs by Paul Thomas.)

5-49. Encircled like jewels, ovals of plain weave and unwoven warp against a layer of plain weave burst into a mass of fine fibers, held in by one layer of warp.

• Knotting is a series of half-hitches, or buttonhole stitch around warp, which gives a ridge of small knots. The column will spiral, if worked always in the same direction. Alternately changing direction keeps the warp from twisting.

WEAVING DIRECTIONS

How many warps per inch

In our modern versions of tapestry we want the weaving to be fast and not too finely detailed. From eight to fifteen warp ends per inch is satisfactory, with a warp of cotton or linen about the size of carpet warp or string. This will allow for some quite fine detail and is a good warp for learning. Then as your skill grows, you can weave a detailed and blended tapestry with a close-set fine warp and a fine wool weft.
• I almost always work with warp in pairs. Then you have the option of working over one or two warps, interchangeably; over one warp for a finer detail.

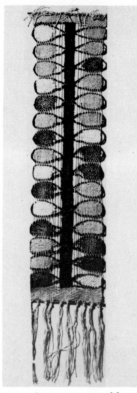

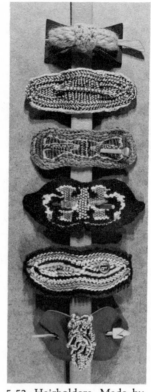

1) Finger-woven tube of rug wool and crocheted band on leather.

2) Silver satin cord to complement Navaho silver and turquoise barette.

3) Plain weave and slits, in shades of green, with a brass pin.

4) A real tapestry, black, white, and gray, with silver and turquoise pin.

5) Soumak with wool warp cut as a soft edge, and grandpa's gold stickpin.

6) Gold satin cord on suede leather, with wooden pin.

5-51. A narrow tree-like hanging, with woven areas regularly confined and outlined by heavy black weft. Adult student work. Teacher, Louaine Collier Elke, Albany Adult Education Class, California.

5-52. Hairholders. Made by and for the author. A variety of techniques are displayed. (Photograph by Kent Kammerer.)

How to begin a new weft

Plain-weave tapestry: Weave the new end over and under a few warps, as you do at the edge when starting a new weft. Any ends can be trimmed off later if desired. Wrapped or knotted tapestry: Put the new end down through the previous wrap on the last warp, to avoid a slit. If a small hole left for only one or two rows is acceptable, the new weft can be tied around the warp with a simple knot. Always be sure, in either method, that the tail hangs straight down so it will be out of the way.

MORE USES FOR TAPESTRY WEAVES

A weaver can find a use for, and inspiration for, only so many wall hangings and tapestries. Here are a few suggestions for different ways to use these weaving methods. After you have done your small sample weavings and have learned the techniques and methods of weaving a good structure, so you can even build three-D weavings that work and can turn out craftsmanlike flat weavings, sharpen your tapestry-weaving skills on some other projects. Not only will you learn a lot about weaving small details, but you will also learn effective uses of the different methods and what works best where.

We made a batch of "hair-holders" or barrettes, and picture them for you in figure 5-52. Numbers 2, 3, 4, and 5 were woven and shaped on the loom. We used a size and shape to fit the hair style. Slit weave made space for the pins to go through. Edge finishes are Soumak, plain weave, or a needle buttonhole-stitch done off the loom. Felt glued to the back gives body, and covers the turned back cut warp ends. The pins should match your materials— elegant or casual. Small weavings like this are excellent exercises in making weaving techniques really work.

How to weave small shapes such as our hair-holders

A warp ten or twelve to the inch, about five inches wide and twelve inches long is ample to weave at least two pieces, and have plenty of warp ends long enough to knot or turn back. We used a small frame, but you could warp up a floor or table loom and weave several on one warping. We cut a paper template for each one, placed it in the warp and wove the beginning rows to shape, modeling and pushing into place. You can put your paper pattern behind the warp, or mark an outline with ink dots on the warp. In chapter 7 on edge finishes, you will find ways to secure the warp ends. On number 5, we just cut the wool warp ends and left narrow fringe.
• Weave a dozen hat bands with small tapestry patterns like the narrow Mexican hair bands (figure 7-34). Use Greek Soumak for texture.
• Luana Sever, a weaver with skill, imagination, and a flair for creating something unusual, has combined leather and weaving in many rich ways:
• A bedspread of buckskin leather in natural shapes was put together with woven areas filling the spaces between skins. The woven sections were done on cardboard looms. The strips of buckskin and the wool sections were joined together by crochet. Result—a handsome abstract pattern of wool and leather.
• A leather-and-wool cape in adapted ancient Peruvian Scaffold Weaving (see Raoul d'Harcourt) was made of wool woven on small cardboard looms and joined to the leather during the weaving by stitching through the leather. Wool sections were joined to each other as the weaving proceeded. Also note the fabric and plastic sandwich Mrs. Sever made for skylights in her home (figure 5-41).
   At this writing, old-fashioned chokers of fabric, ribbon, chains, and beads are very much the thing. These weave up in a hurry, with minimum warp and weft and maximum imagination. You can make one in less time than it takes to shop for the just right one!
• Weave collars and necklaces. The shape is made by nails on a board or pins on a thick foam pad. Warp is taken around the pins. Add richly elegant yarns to beads and knot techniques.
• Weave a shaped background for a smashing pin, clip, or string of beads.
• Weave bracelets of leather and yarn. Margaret Collins wove two for us to photograph (Figure 5-53.) She used the cut and shaped leather as the loom, putting the warps through the leather with a needle. Plain-weave tapestry, outlining, slit, and Ghiordes Knot were all called on to make these miniature tapestries. One has "warp beams" of quills! This same idea can be used for making a wide watch-band.
• Weave a belt using plain-weave tapestry, Greek Soumak, wrapped warps, and slit. Apply warps to a leather belt either by putting through with a needle, or on heavy leather, wrap the warp around it. Ties for fasteners can be knotted sinnets or narrow woven tapes.

5-53. Two bracelets made of suede leather, wool tapestry, and pile weave. Weaver, Margaret Collins. (Photograph by Kent Kammerer.)

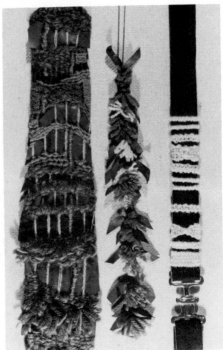

5-54. Leather and wool. *Left.* Pile weave, wrapped warps, Greek and Oriental Soumak. Shaped pieces of leather laid in. *Middle.* Two-warp Oriental pile weave. Strips of leather and wool knotted with Ghiordes Knot over two warps. *Right.* A heavy suede belt wound with wool, then weaving over these little warps. Dark green leather, lemon-yellow wool, brass buckle. The author. (Photograph by Kent Kammerer.)

• Weave a band of open warps, wrapped and knotted, then thread leather strips or woven strips through the slits.
• Several tapestry techniques adapt to or are used in rug weaving, such as plain weave (Navaho), Oriental Soumak, Greek Soumak. (See chapter 6.)
Three suggestions
• Keep your designs and patterns simple and direct.
• Depend upon richness of color and texture of your materials.
• Line with felt, where suitable, to give firmness and a neat back.

These small weavings-to-wear are perfect spots to try patterns from other cultures—a typical African design in their rich red or ochre with black and white; a delicate Japanese crest symbol; a wild little Peruvian personage figure; a Mexican flat stamp pattern; a Northwest Indian eye. These make small studies for a larger work—"thumbnail sketches."

Some of these suggestions for accessories are high-style and "in" as I write. We include them just as hints of what you can do with weaving beyond yardage and wall decor. What is wild and splashy fashion one season can be modified and toned down another. You will always find new and different uses for tapestry techniques.

Notebook sketches and tapestry weaving directions for reference follow.

Notebook

HOW TO WEAVE TAPESTRY

• Try this way of sampling on a small frame loom: Divide warp into three sections, and explore different tapestry techniques, paying attention to balance, color, and over-all design. (See figures 5-5, 5-6A,B.)

PLAIN-WEAVE TAPESTRY COLOR CHANGES

Slit (D5-1A,B,C)
Vertical

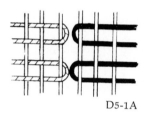

D5-1A

In the same shed, bring the two colors from opposite directions, turn each one around adjacent warp ends and return, leaving a space unwoven between the warps. Change shed and repeat, turning the wefts around the same warps until the slit is as long as you want. The wefts should be relaxed enough so the warps are not pulled out of alignment, but pulled enough so the edge is smooth. If you want an open weave, the wefts are pulled so the warps do move further apart, to make eyelets or long slits. Slits can be made deliberately long, then sewn together later. If slits are woven and left open at one end, you have woven fringe. A maximum amount of open weave is achieved by wrapping single warps or weaving only two or three together, with rows of weaving to close them at top and bottom. (See figures 5-6A,B.) You have the choice of all these ways to weave the slit—from a tiny pinhole to a fringe-like open weave. (D5-1A.)

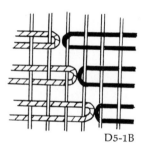

D5-1B

Diagonal

Wefts are turned around adjacent warps as in the vertical slit, but advance or recede on the next pair of warps to make a diagonal joining of colors. (D5-1B.)

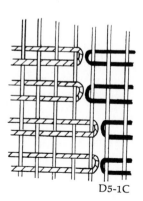

D5-1C

Diagonal in pairs

The same as above, except that the same warps are involved twice (or more). This method is used extensively in Gobelin tapestries, with the minute slit and stepped edge giving them a distinctive look. (D5-1C.)

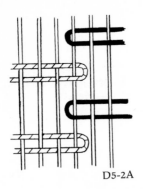

Dovetail (D5-2A,B)
Vertical

The two wefts are woven in and back, from different directions, and turned around a common warp, alternatively. The wefts can be woven and taken around the warp two or more times before weaving in the second color, to make a more pronounced toothed joining. (D5-2A.)

D5-2A

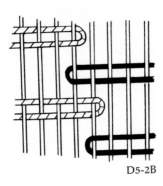

Diagonal

Dovetail joining can be made on a diagonal by stepping over one warp in either direction in succeeding rows. (D5-2B.)

D5-2B

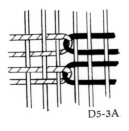

Interloop (D5-3A,B,C,D)
Vertical

Weave in pairs of shots, and loop the two wefts together where they meet. The loop involves only the wefts, being made between two warps. (D5-3A.)

D5-3A

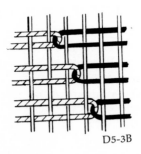

Diagonal

The pairs of weft are looped between adjacent warps, stepping over from right or left. A wavering or sawtooth line can be woven by gradually shifting the interloops over several warps, then back and forth. For a sharp line, try to center the looping, with tension the same each time, especially in vertical interloop. (D5-3B.)

D5-3B

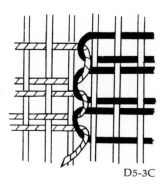

Double interloop
Vertical

Each weft is interlooped between warps twice. Start the two wefts in the same direction, in the same shed. It sounds confusing, but look at the sketch, and try it step by step, and it will come clear, we promise! Look sharp and be sure that you keep the right sequence of your plain weave over-under as the second color continues to fill out the row. (D5-3C.)

- Left color from left to right, let hang at change point.
- Put right color in shed here, take to right, then left, and hang.
- Left color around hanging right color to left, then right, hang.
- Right color around hanging left color to right then left. This is the complete sequence. Repeat as many times as needed.

D5-3C

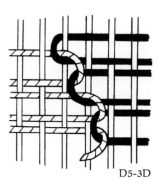

Diagonal

Follow the same sequence, but move over one warp each two rows. (D5-3D.)

D5-3D

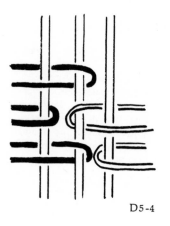

Three-warp interlock (D5-4)

Something like the slit weave, as the wefts just meet and return without looping; a little like the dovetail, as the alternate turnings around three different warps create a slightly toothed joining line.

- Wefts are brought into the change point, in the same shed, turned around adjacent warps and return. The next pair turn around a different pair of warps. The third pair turn around the same warps as the first. Continue alternating, first around warps one and two; then around two and three; then one and two, and so on. The slit is so minute it does not matter.

D5-4

D5-5A

OUTLINING (D5-5A,B,C)

There are many ways to outline an area of pattern, and you may invent one to fit the weaving of the moment. Here are a few to give you some ideas.

• Outlining weft is woven over and under, following the slant of the pattern.

• Two rows of weft can be laid into the shed following the already-woven pattern, and pushed into place to follow the shape. Two rows are necessary for a definite line—one row will give a very fine, uneven line. (D5-5A.)

D5-5B

A Peruvian technique, called Limning

The outline weft is carried up and over the warp as it travels up to follow the pattern, like an embroidered stem stitch. One row is sufficient, but a smoother line is made with two rows. More than two creates a very wide outline, almost like a pattern section itself. A wide and narrowing outline can be made by using one, then two, then three, and diminishing again. A single row is slightly wavy. (D5-5B.)

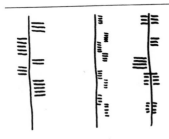

For interest and emphasis of an outline

• Alternate colors in short hatchings, maybe only two or three warps in width.

• Offset blocks of alternating colors, a few warps wide.

• Add hatching, blending, spots, beside the outline weft.

• Outlines with texture: The Greek Soumak wrap (D5-8) is very adaptable to use for an outline with a raised surface. It can be worked and pushed into place to follow the pattern; tightly knotted for a small, bumpy line, or loosely pulled in coarse yarn, or many knots on one warp for a deep hedge around a flat pattern area. (D5-5C.)

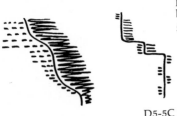

D5-5C

WRAPPED TAPESTRY WEAVES (D5-6—5-9)

To do these correctly, follow the arrows in the sketches.

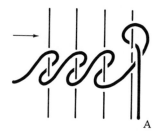

A

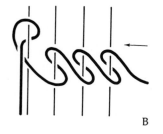

B

Single Soumak (Swedish Knot) (D5-6A,B,C)

- Work over one warp (or group, as one).
- Work with "wrong" side up.
- Weave from either or both directions. The top or ridged side will look the same. The reverse will look like a twill, if all from one side; like knitting, if directions are reversed each row.

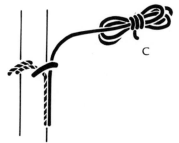

C

- Starting a new color.

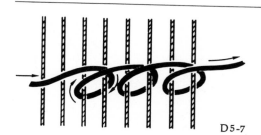

D5-7

Oriental Soumak (D5-7)

- Classic method is over four warps and back two, but number of warps involved can vary.
- Work from the top side.
- Work from either or both directions. In the same direction each row, the result will be like a twill weave, with all stitches at the same slant. Alternating directions gives an arrow or knitted look. Note: It is sometimes desirable to weave a row of tabby between the Soumak rows, if firmness is needed, as in a rug. A very fine weft can be used and it will disappear between the Soumak rows.

D 5-8

Greek Soumak (D5-8)

• Classic method is three wraps or knots on one warp before continuing to next warp, but number can vary.
• Work from the top side.
• Work in either or both directions.
• When changing directions, reverse the wrapping.
• Size of holes is made larger by using coarse yarns, or several strands at one time; or not pulling the knots down as tightly; or setting the warp further apart.
• Size of the knots and nubbiness of the textile is controlled by the size of yarn used in warp and weft, as well as how tightly the knots are pulled in and down to the previous row. This technique works as an open, bumpy textile or a tight, grainy surface, heavy and stiff enough for a rug. (See chapter 6.)

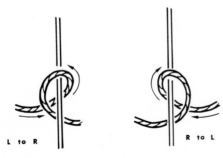

L to R   R to L

D5-9

Egyptian tapestry knot (D5-9)

• Work from the top side.
• Work from either direction, reversing the wrapping so the working end of the weft comes out on the correct side of the warp in the direction you are weaving.
• The spacing and size of the ribs is controlled by the size of the warp and number per inch.
NOTE: In all these wrapping and knotting techniques be sure to reverse the direction of working when you change direction of the row.

Now, in the next chapter, on to the pile weaves, other methods you can add to your growing store of ways to cover warps and create exciting textiles and objects.

Pile Weaves:
Knots and Loops

It must be that perhaps thousands of years ago a primitive weaver, wondering how to produce the shaggy warmth of animal skins in a woven fabric, worked out a method for making a pile weave. This creative weaver of long ago discovered that by weaving a foundation and adding knots, loops, tufts, tags, or cut lengths of yarn by inserting them into the weft, he had a warm furry material. One very early example, found in Iceland, detailed further along, has much the same appearance as long-haired fleece. As time went by many ingenious methods were devised to construct a woven material with surface depth and texture. While the first attempts at this kind of fabric were probably made primarily for warmth, later examples seem to use the loops and knots for interest and enrichment of the design as well. Today we use these pile techniques as a part of design and to add long-wearing qualities to such articles as rugs.

DEFINITIONS OF A PILE WEAVE

Loops or ends of yarn forming a raised surface over a ground weave are called pile weaves. This is a compound weave with a basic weft used throughout, plus a supplementary pattern or pile weft. Often the foundation weave is completely covered, but pile weft can be introduced in small areas and isolated units of pattern. Pile weave creates a three-dimensional fabric.

There are two major structures of pile fabrics: (1) knotted or wrapped and (2) picked up loops, with minor variations in methods of construction and a myriad of design possibilities. Some established names of pile weaves are not accurate according to structure. For instance, the Single-warp Spanish Knot is really wrapped, not knotted. We decided that a weaver looking for a new pile weave would be more interested in look and performance so in our sampler pages we grouped the cut pile weaves, then the loops. Of course, some can be either, and this is shown or mentioned.

Uses

At first thought pile weaves make us think of rugs. But there are other uses for knots and loops. Wherever a change in texture or a contrast of flat weave and raised surface is desired, you can use one of the many knotted, looped, or

6-1. A sheep is a Ghiordes knot loop weave, done in his own handspun wool. Woven by author. (Photograph by Kent Kammerer.)

6-2. Ghiordes knot, cut. Detail of an evenly-cut pile rug woven of handspun yarns in natural white, through grays, to black. Pattern is based on squares with large plain squares repeated in the border. This was an award winner at the Henry Gallery, University of Washington. Weaver, spinner, Mildred Sherwood. (Photograph by Audio-Visual Services, University of Washington.)

6-3. Picked-up loops from Mexico. Natural black, white, and gray wools picked up in low loops form geometric designs on the flat-weave ground. Locally called *Cobiha Chiva*. Courtesy of Gloria Huntington. (Photograph by William Eng.)

wrapped weaves. Since loops and knots are used again and again in the same way, we have brought you some of the less well-known ones. Security is a Ghiordes knot!—but try some of these other ways to achieve a durable, handsome pile weave.

SOURCES FOR IDEAS

Archeological and anthropological journals are wonderfully rich sources for finding out about true textile techniques. We have done some enthusiastic research for you, but our excerpts, notes, reconstructions, and adaptations are just a small bit of the available material. You go on from here—you will find it rewarding. Although meticulous details of measurement, locations, and analyses in scientific works may seem a little formidable, you can nevertheless visualize what the original craftsmen did and then weave your own interpretation. Mention of an effect, a small photograph or description of a textile will conjure up an idea of how to construct something like it. Perhaps our reconstructions and adaptations would not be recognized by the ancients, but they do provide us with variations on the familiar theme of pile weaves, and the other techniques, too.

Here is an example of how this works. In the *History of Costume*, by Blanche Payne, there is a small photograph and short description of a fringed Bronze Age skirt, found in Denmark. This immediately suggested a way to make a fringed edge on a bedspread or poncho. An interpretation and reconstruction of it was woven. Later, *Costumes of the Bronze Age in Denmark*, a beautiful book on the finds in Denmark, came along and in it is a large photograph of the

6-4. Ghiordes knot—shaggy cut pile. Reminiscent of early pile-weave mantles, Bonnie Meltzer's luxurious shag coat is spread to show the pattern on the back and some of the heavy flat weave at waist and front. The sleeves are crocheted, with some pile weave, from shoulder to wrist. The wide, shaped neckline is also of crochet. In richly-colored yarns, deep reds and purple-reds with contrasting yellow-green, this coat is high-style and elegant—completely designed.

6-5. Detail of back of shag coat. (Photographs of coat by William Eng.)

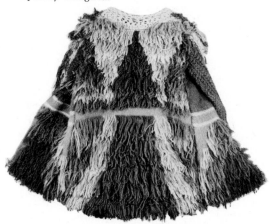

6-6. Idea from a carved garment on a Sumarian statue. It suggested a shaped, petal-like pile. Woven by the author. (Photograph by Kent Kammerer.)

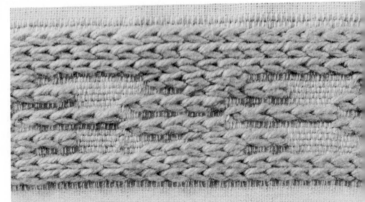

6-7. Soumak combined with plain-weave. The rows are worked from left to right, and right to left, resulting in the "knitted," "arrow," or "chained" look. Woven by Zada Sigman. (Photograph by Kent Kammerer.)

same skirt and a detailed drawing of the construction. Our interpretation happened to be about right, so we included it in chapter 9, on fringes, (figure 9-59). This is one of the joys to be found in searching out what those ancient weavers were up to! Another example is a sheared woven-pile idea (figure 6-6) from a carved Sumerian statue. See directions in the notebook pages at the end of the chapter.

PILE WEAVES BY OTHER NAMES

Tufts, flocks, tags, wool-tufted: These are short ends of unspun or lightly spun wool, laid in with ground weft. The Greek Floccata rugs with shaggy pile are an example.

Woven pile: Supplementary wefts introduced into the ground weave; velveteen and corduroy (machine-made); cut weft floats (laid-in pile).

Supplementary or extra warps that make the pile: Terry loops, on one or both sides; velvet, plush, Brussels carpets.

Knotted Pile: A form of wrapping. The so-called "rug knots"—Ghiordes, Spanish, Tibetan, Sehna, Icelandic, Egyptian. Cut or left in loops.

Pile-loops: A supplementary weft, raised above the ground weave in loops.

Soumak: A wrapped weave with the weft going over and around the warps. Some techniques appear to be border-line in their classifications; for instance, a Soumak weave almost becomes a looped pile when woven in a very large rug yarn; one of the Coptic loops, if pulled tight, becomes a Soumak weave.

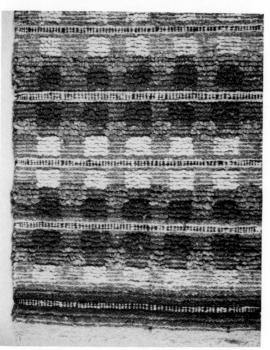

6-8. Pillow woven of Ghiordes Knot loops. This is the reverse of the Greek Soumak pillow shown in 5-30. The two sides are related in color, have the same yarn and design. Woven without a loom—warped around a foam pillow form, weaving done on both sides and the edges. (See *Weaving is for Anyone* for this on a round pillow.) Woven by the author. (Photograph by Phil Davidson.)

6-9. A rug from Mexico, similar to the one shown in figure 6-3. Handspun wool, natural grays, browns, black, and white. Picked-up loops. Rows of plain weave alternate with rows of loops raised from the background in geometric patterns. Rich and luxurious. Courtesy Viola Patterson. (Photograph by William Eng.)

KINDS OF PILE WEAVES

Knotted pile

Supplementary wefts are wrapped around warps securely, so they can be cut to form the pile. Some are wrapped, rather than truly knotted, but through centuries of usage we call them knots. Because this method is used to make pile rugs, the familiar name is "rug knot." Rug knots can be made with a continuous length of weft yarn, or short pieces cut and worked in. When knots are made with continuous weft they can be cut or left in loops. Long, dense cut pile can be sheared and shaped into contoured surface designs, sometimes called carving. Firmly fastened around the warp, further held by the ground weave, the pile will stay in place. Some methods of knotting form a heading above the loop that can be a part of the design if left exposed (Egyptian cut-pile knot) with flat weave between the rows of pile. A firm pile fabric will take the severe wear required of a rug.

Woven pile

Weft-loop pile: Extra weft is laid into the shed, pulled up to the surface, between the warps, to form loop pile. Loops do not encircle the warp. The foundation weave is a background for and independent of the loops. It is necessary

123

to hold the loops in place with firmly beaten tabby rows. Because the pulled up loops are not attached to the warp, it is not desirable to cut them. However, if the design requires a combination of cut and uncut pile, it can be quite safely done when the warp is set very close and the rows can be beaten with extra firmness. Loop weft is usually carried through the shed for the width of the fabric, whether loops are pulled up the entire distance or not. A gauge may or may not be used.

Weft laid in: Cut ends form the pile. This method results in a flat, combed-looking pile, contrasted to the knotted pile, which tends to stand at right angles to the ground fabric (Eigg, Highland Guatemalan). Short, cut wefts can be laid in with the ends on the surface. Almost the same effect is achieved by weaving overshots, then cutting them (corduroy weave). Of course the depth and density of pile will vary with the kind of yarn used, the number per inch of warp and weft, and the number of yarns used as one weft element.

WEAVES RELATED IN LOOKS OR STRUCTURE

• A pile-like effect is possible when long floats are woven in, overlaying the ground, then cut. This type is usually woven in a loom-patterned overshot weave.

• *Tufts:* In weaving, tufts are understood to mean bunches of unspun or slightly spun fiber, wrapped or laid into the foundation weave. They may be of several strands of spun yarn put in as spots of texture. A familiar use of tufts is in candlewick or tufted bedspreads, where clusters of tufts are put into the plain weave to form patterns or an over-all pile.

• *Nap:* Pile and nap are not synonomous, although sometimes the terms are used that way. Nap refers to the surface quality of a fabric, or a finishing process that has been used to "give it a nap," such as teaseling or brushing of blankets, brushed-wool coating, etc. Pile refers to the structure or weaving technique that gives the fabric a nap, such as an rugs, velvet, etc.

• *Warp-faced pile:* Warp-faced pile weaves are woven with extra warp beams and two or more sets of warp. One warp is slack, the other tight. These are loom-controlled loops or pile weaves. We are only concerned in this text with the finger-controlled weft-face pile weaves.

WEAVING A PILE TEXTILE

Because the pile in a knotted weave is more secure than a loop or inserted ends, choose the method best suited to the planned use of the fabric. For example, in a carpet subject to hard scuffing wear, you would use a firmly knotted technique. For a small design unit in a firmly woven piece, you could use a loop or inserted cut ends. In a decorative piece, such as a wall hanging, where wear is not a factor, you can work with high and low pile with loose globs of yarn, and you can play with loop and tuft effects. There is excitement about adding cut and uncut loops or knots to the foundation—anywhere, any color, any shape. Unlimited color play is possible. It's a little like painting, adding a dash of color here, graying down an area there. The knotting techniques are especially adaptable for experimentation with color and depth of texture. Remember that cut pile in any given color will appear to be a different shade (darker) than a loop of the same color. Shading can be accomplished by cutting some loops and leaving others uncut in the same piece. You can see this clearly if you hold a clutch of looped yarns and one of cut ends together, upright.

6-10. Looped rug from Greece made of very soft, silky hand-spun white wool. The soft-twist wool is used double, on linen warp. Note how the geometric motifs are worked out at the edge. The loops are always raised over the same warps—very even and regular. The treatment of the hem is simple, and right. Courtesy of Irma Robinson. (Photograph by Kent Kammerer.)

6-11. A paper project— Ghiordes knots. Two units of a wall hanging. Judy Thomas, a weaver with great imagination and talent in the use of unusual materials, used paper for wefts and covered warps. The Ghiordes knot loops are made of paper gift-tie. You will recognize the warp covering as printed papers and ring-binder reinforcements. Straws divide the design panels. (Photograph by Paul Thomas.)

6-12. A narrow wall hanging is enriched with rows of Ghiordes knot loops. Several different yarns are used, and bits of shell are attached to some of the loops for further interest. Woven by Patricia Wilson. (Photograph by Audio-Visual Services, University of Washington.)

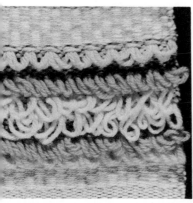

6-13. Weave a fancy pocket. This one is bright yellow and orange, with Ghiordes knot loops of different sizes and different spacings —a kind of layered loop fringe. By the author. (Photograph by Kent Kammerer.)

Here we describe and illustrate for you the classic or traditional ways of weaving pile, and also include suggestions for variations and adaptations. Some may be new to you, as they were to me when I discovered them. We hope you will be inspired to invent variations of your own. Loops—knots—tufts—texture —high pile—low pile—pattern in relief—call them what you will and use the appropriate method to achieve the effect you want. These are all part of designing and creating a fabric with depth, texture, and character.

TWO-WARP PILE

To prove that this Oriental knot on a two-warp loom can produce a planned design, and does not have to be hit and miss, we show the beginning of a carefully designed floor pillow or small rug. Each strip is knotted to complete the design of a grid with combination of yarns in the different areas. The

6-14. Formally, this is called an Oriental two-warp pile weave, but we call it a portable pile weave, because you can fasten the two warps and knot cut wefts over it without using a loom. It can even be worked on a small piece of cardboard. This much was done by the author while flat-out in a hospital bed! (Photograph by Kent Kammerer.)

strips of pile are sewn together. This is a joining project as much as a weaving one, because you are assembling a larger textile from woven strips (figure 6-14). Refer to *Weaving is for Anyone* for more about this technique, including a box arrangement for a loom, and directions on how to make the knots over a continuous warp.

DONEGAL CARPETS

Two views of the huge upright looms at the Donegal Carpet Company, Killybegs, County Donegal, Ireland. We watched these girls work, and their speed is incredible. The need for teamwork and keeping up is paramount, and they scarcely dare to visit much. The great loft-like room has dozens of these looms, with an enormous rainbow pile of rug wool in the center. A walk through the supply rooms with aisle after aisle of shelves, ceiling high, filled to overflowing

6-15, 6-16. Highly skilled workers weaving hand-knotted carpets at the Donegal Carpet Company, Killybegs, County Donegal, Ireland. Ghiordes knots, cut precisely, are clipped with scissors that become an extension of the trained fingers. (Photographs courtesy of the Donegal Carpet Company, Dublin.)

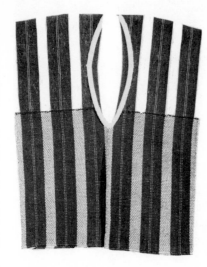

6-17. A delicate row of loops across the front of a Naga jacket (India) is the boundary line between the plain woven stripes and the stripes with an overlaid weave. In chapter 2, figure 2-19, see the handsomely decorated back view of this jacket. Courtesy of the Costume and Textile Study Collection, School of Home Economics, University of Washington.

with pure color, all in gorgeous top quality rug wool is a weaver's dream of heaven! (We experienced this dream several times—in the tweed-weaving mills, too.) Each girl has a section of cartoon to follow, the newer weavers being given areas with mostly one background color. The Donegal carpets are woven for castles and embassies, stately buildings and great homes. Most patterns are extremely intricate and ornate, with much symbolism. Even though the weavers produce quite an even finish, the carpets are run over a large shearing machine. A smooth, perfect surface results. The pile is deep and solid. In another room, a girl was preparing small samples by giving them a shave with an electric clipper! They also mend valuable old tapestries and rugs here, and someone was at work on one when we were there. All this, and a charming waterfront town, too.

GENERAL NOTES ON PILE WEAVES

• Unless otherwise stated, all the techniques discussed are woven on a standard twill threading (1, 2, 3, 4) with plain weave, twill or basket weave grounds. Some are woven on a closed shed, some on an open shed.
• The density of a pile fabric is determined more by the warp sett, number of knots per inch, size and number of yarns in a weft element, than by the method of knotting.
• For a full rich pile, the weft for knots or loops can be made up of several strands, up to about twice the diameter of the warp yarn. Multiple strands provide an opportunity for subtle colors, giving a lift and interest to the design.
• If you choose to weave with just one color, the foundation and pattern weft can be the same, all in one shuttle.
• When cut ends of yarn are used, pile does not have to be put in one row, in exact order. All of one color can be knotted in along the width, then other colors filled in, in any order before the next row of foundation is woven in. Sometimes you may want to blend colors as you go.
• When knots are spotted or put in isolated units, begin and end each pattern weft at the selvedge. Interesting color effects happen in the ground weave.

6-18. Detail of Ghiordes knot made with thick and thin hand-spun white wool, for a bedspread. The ground weave is copper-colored linen and off-white raw silk. By the author. (Photograph by William Eng.)

• A gauge is not always used. A slight unevenness in the size and height of the pile is a desirable characteristic of this method. It is quite easy to regulate the size without a gauge as your fingers learn the feel.

• Unless you want a really precise pile, do not trim. To avoid a definite line where the ends of the pile fall, make the two ends of each knot a slightly different length.

• Motifs or areas can be sculptured by cutting a narrow, deeper furrow around as an outline. This works on a very closely packed pile, quite deep, so there is enough rise to accommodate the levels.

• Knots can be placed with different spacings—over different numbers of warps than the usual or classic method. The way of wrapping or looping is the same.

• Note that some of the lace weaves, and others, depend upon knots and wrapped weaves.

• If, when an area of knotted pile has been woven, you want to add a bit more color or make an area more dense, this can readily be done by inserting additions with a large tapestry needle.

• Cutting of loops is usually done row by row, before the gauge is removed, but it is possible to do all of the cutting, trimming, shearing, or shaping after the weaving is off the loom. Sometimes, with rugs, this is the best way, and perhaps a new idea for surface texture will emerge, with some loops left uncut. Try both ways.

KNOTS USUALLY USED FOR RUGS

Ghiordes, Sehna or Persian, and Single-warp Spanish Knot are customarily used in rug weaving, but can be used wherever a spot or area of knotting is required, in any piece of weaving. Instructions are on pages 133-135.

General Suggestions for Knotting Rugs

• 6 to 8 dent reed is best for rugs.

• Linen or cotton seine twine warp is preferable. May be sleyed double for heavy rugs. Single or double cotton carpet warp is satisfactory.

- If some flat weave will be used, or warp will show, be sure it is color-blended with the weft yarns. A white or too light warp may intrude on the design and color of the rug and spoil the effect you want. It is very important to carefully plan the warp color and number per inch when a warp fringe is to be left at the ends.
- Be sure your warp has an even number of ends when you are using a knot that involves pairs of warps.
- Double the number of warps in each dent at each selvedge, several on each side. This is desirable for strength. It also helps in weaving a firm, even selvedge which is so important in a rug.
- No knots are worked over the two outside warp pairs. The edge of the rug will roll under if the knots are carried too far out to the edge. The pile will usually cover over this flat-weave selvedge. If a fringe is to be added along the selvedge, plan the number of unknotted warps as necessary.
- The ground weave is built up at the selvedges where required, when the knotted rows do not fill the space out to the edge.
- Warp tension should be quite tight, so the warp is taut when weft knots are pulled down into place, but must be relaxed enough so the wefts can be put in and around them.
- Particularly on a wide or especially heavy rug, it is desirable to use a stretcher to keep the width even. Some weavers insist that no rug should be woven without one. This adjustable device of wood has teeth at each end to grip and hold the rug to an even width during the weaving. It must be moved every few inches, so is a bit of a nuisance, but it does help.
- Beat with a drawing squeezing motion rather than a sharp slamming beat.
- Beat each row with both a closed and an open shed. On a frame, or a loom with no shedding device or beater, use some kind of a sturdy fork or wooden rug beater. Strong nails pounded into a piece of wood is crude, but adequate.
- Arc or bubble the foundation wefts between knotted rows, so the warp will be well covered and edges will not be drawn in.
- Good idea: Put a row of twining on either or both sides of a tufted, knotted or wrapped pile row or area to help support it.
- Put some kind of a measuring device along the selvedge when you are doing a large rug that will be rolled around the beam. Sometimes I pin a cloth tape-measure at the heading, moving it along and keeping track of the inches. Other times a length of measured warp yarn, a pin or a bit of bright yarn tied in the selvedge at the edge, every yard, serves the purpose.

ORIENTAL SOUMAK AS A RUG WEAVE (SOUMAKH, SUMAK, SUMAKH)

Traditionally, Oriental Soumak is a rug weave. Not a true pile weave, it is related in construction to wrapped loops. (Figures 6-19, 20, 21, D6-15. Also see figure 6-7.) It is also used as a tapestry technique, and included in chapter 5, "Tapestry," (see figures 5-10 and 5-28).

The technique

An ancient rug weave, classically woven over four warps and back two (D6-15), this is also done in other combinations. All warps are always encircled.

Soumak is "something like" so many other techniques that it can be grouped

6-19. Soumak weave for a rug. Spots of pattern can be made in this technique. Note the vertical pattern that occurs along the selvedge where the yarn is returned to go back across, which is an added design element. By the author. (Photograph by Kent Kammerer.)

D6-15. Oriental Soumak.

and compared with a number of methods. In *Weaving is for Anyone* we put it with the tapestry techniques. Here, we have placed it in both the tapestry and rug-weaving sections. It is like a stemstitch or overcast in embroidery. It is similar to Single and Greek Soumak. It is related to the wrapping method in bouquet and progressive warp-wrapping weaves, where it is drawn up to bunch the warps. It is part of some loop weaves. It is called "Soumak Inlay" when a small area or raised band is woven with a flat weave. Color changes are made as in the interloop and other tapestry methods.

The stitch is always slanted. Rows worked back and forth produce an arrow or look of knitting. Rows always started from the same side slant in the same direction for a twill look. These characteristics should be considered in your designing.

The Soumak weft can be the only, or major weft; it can be a supplementary or pattern weft with tabby between rows. For a durable, firm rug, several rows of plain weave between the Soumak rows is most satisfactory. The plain weave packs in under the Soumak rows and tends to raise them from the ground weave. The filler rows can be the same yarn as the Soumak, or finer, or a different color. Soumak allows leeway in color, flat or raised pattern. Soumak rows can be taken around curves, pushed into molded contours, or woven into vertical stripes. It is smashing when a large bundle of weft is used for a really thick

6-20. Oriental Soumak rug, Rows are woven in both directions. Pattern is woven in areas, vertically, joined so that there are no slits. By the author. (Photograph by Kent Kammerer.)

6-21. Unspun-wool rug. Oriental and Single Soumak are woven in white and gray, units joined. By the author. (Photograph by Kent Kammerer.)

row of Soumak in a wall hanging or a ridge in a rug. Many more ideas are waiting for you to pursue or discover.

Oriental and Single Soumak Rug

The Plan: To weave a bedroom carpet from unspun wool, white and gray. Units woven on a 20-by-20-inch frame loom, linen warp, then joined inconspicuously. A meandering water pattern echoes the view of the bay from the window. Some units have varying amounts of pattern—some have none. (Figures 6-20, 21.)
Use of the techniques: To create a flowing, non-directional effect and pleasant, soft texture. Reversible, since the warps are completely encircled. The section shown is two units, joined.

MORE PILE WEAVES: KNOTTED, WRAPPED, LAID-IN

There are a number of other pile weaves that do not fit easily into either of the above classifications. Each has its own individual construction and a classic or best use. They are interesting to know about and experiment with for weavings that are a little different from the familiar ways. These are shown and directions given in our sampler section that follows.

6-22. Curly, kinky mohair yarn is lifted into loops against a plain-weave ground. By the author. (Photograph by Kent Kammerer.)

6-23. Stripes burst into loops toward the selvedge. Idea for a pillow, bedspread, mat, or shawl. By the author. (Photograph by Kent Kammerer.)

6-24. Weave a loom-controlled pattern, then add something special of your own for the handcrafted, one-of-a-kind look. Give a traditional pattern a modern-day lift by weaving a row or two of weft loops, picked up to outline a unit of design. They frame, and make a nice shadow line. By the author. (Photograph by Kent Kammerer.)

6-26. Boutonné weave, from Quebec. Border on a finely-woven linen tablecloth. The center has a star-like motif. This method, where the weft is lifted into a loop to make a pattern, is adaptable to rugs as well as fine weaving. In Quebec they weave Boutonné rugs in flat weave with mosaic-like patterns of loops. Typical designs are stars, squares, hexagons. Courtesy of the Study Collections, School of Home Economics, University of Washington. (Photograph by William Eng.)

6-25. A pillow full of raised polka dots—the weft is brought up in loops, caught down with the weft. Also see chapter 2, on chaining. Weaver, Mrs. Earl Dome. (Photograph by William Eng.)

6-27. Boutonné technique in a rug of handspun white wool. The tufts are natural gray unspun wool. By the author. (Photograph by Kent Kammerer.)

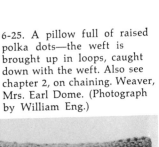

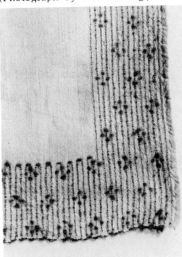

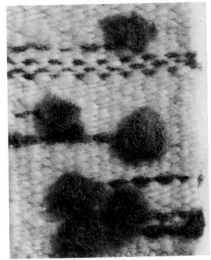

SAMPLERS

In this section we show 16 examples of knot and wrapped techniques, both loop and cut, each woven so you can follow the path of the yarn and see how each one looks. To help you, we include detail sketches (also grouped in our notebook for handy later reference). We hope you will learn these less familiar techniques. Then, when you want a certain density or appearance in a pile weave, you will have more choice. For instance, if you want a rather sparse, random pile weave, you can choose the Icelandic cut pile instead of adapting the old faithful Ghiordes knot to your needs.

As a reference and a help in *seeing* the different appearance of these many ways to weave pile, why not make a composition of units woven in these techniques in various yarns and colors. We recommend this as an exercise that will result in an attractive wall decoration and at the same time be your own "picture encyclopedia of pile techniques."

Ghiordes Knot (Figures 6-28A, D6-1, 2)

The classic favorite, most often used by weavers everywhere, it carries the yarn over two warps, and then the ends are brought up together between the two warps. Ghiordes knot is used in the following named types of rugs:
Flossa: Standing pile. Rows of tabby between pile, but rows are closely spaced so no background shows. Cut or loops, any length. A gauge is used, either a stick, dowel, or a special Flossa bar with a groove in it for running a knife along to cut the loops. Weft is wound into small flat hanks for continuous weft.
Half Flossa: Design combines flat ground with standing, full pile areas, in rows or spots; cut and/or loops. Use gauge or flossa bar.

D6-1A

6-28A. Ghiordes knot. *Left:* rows of cut pile (like Flossa) worked with pre-cut wefts. *Right:* Loops worked over a gauge with continuous weft.

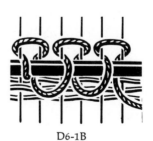

D6-1B

D6-2A

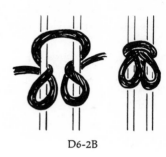

D6-2B

Tricks a Ghiordes Knot can do

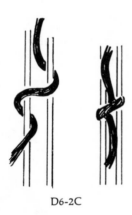

D6-2C

D6-2D

Rya (Figure 6-28B)

Flat, combed down pile. Tabby rows between are covered by the cut pile, two inches long, or more. Uses fewer rows of knots (less yarn). A gauge is used with continuous weft, or cut pieces may be knotted in.

Sehna or Persian Knot (Figures 6-29, D6-3)

Right hand or left hand. The cut weft is put around either the right or left warp in a pair. The two ends emerge facing in different directions. Two rows of plain weave ground are woven between the knot rows.

6-28B. Rya. A rug style, made with Ghiordes knot.

6-29. Sehna (Persian) knot. Right-hand Sehna or left-hand Sehna. *Left:* rows of pile, and the knot—left-hand Sehna. *Right:* rows of pile, and the knot—right-hand Sehna.

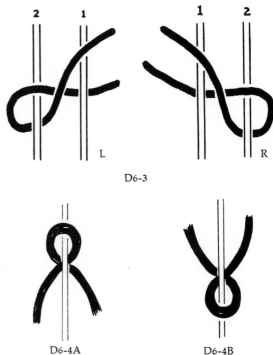

6-30. Single-warp Spanish knot. Rows of knots offset by one warp.

Single-warp Spanish Knot (Figures 6-30, D6-4)

Unique, done on a single warp, good for using up thrums and short lengths of yarn. Try two or more fine yarns as one weft, for interesting blends of color. Always a cut pile, the wrapping makes it secure and durable, but it must be firmly beaten. Advantages: Rapid, easy, with great design flexibility.

Suggested uses for Spanish knot: Rugs, wall hangings, borders on clothing, drapery, textured spots in drapery, texture in tapestry. Very good where high and low pile surface is desired. Combines well with flat weave. Can be used in combination with other knots, tufts, or loops.

D6-6

6-31. Egyptian cut-pile. Single pile weft around four warp pairs. Ground is basket weave.

Egyptian Cut Pile (Figures 6-31, D6-6)

Our example was woven in cotton, with single pile weft so the method would show. This kind of cut pile was woven about 2000 B.C. with a coarse, slubby linen. A shaggy pile results, which can be smoothed flat to cover the entire background. The ground is basket weave. When rows are placed close together, and cut quite short, the pile will stand up supported by itself. Pile rows can be close and dense; pile can be put around the same warps, or offset each row.

Icelandic Cut Pile (Figures 6-32, D6-7)

In 1959 an exciting discovery was made at Heynes, Iceland: A fragment of fabric, apparently part of a cloak or mantle, was unearthed. Research proved that it must have dated back to about 1100-909 B.C. On a twill weave ground, strands or locks of wavy wool placed in the shed create a fleece-like shaggy material. Cut pieces of weft are worked over five pairs of warp, with ends left hanging.

6-32. Icelandic cut-pile. Done over five pairs of warp. Background is twill weave.

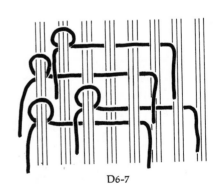

D6-7

6-33. Isle of Eigg cut-pile. Flat pile on plain weave ground. Two rows are woven between pile rows.

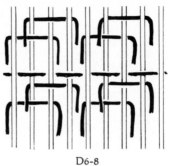

D6-8

Modern versions: Use several strands of spun or unspun wool for each tag; several colors together for a shaded pile. Weft ends will still be safely held if only an inch long. For a casual texture, cut pile in uneven lengths. Knots can be spaced apart, or close and dense for a solid shag rug. Design possibilities are excitingly varied, as locks are put in separately. Suggested uses:
• Try a room divider with some surface texture on both sides, using this method.
• A rug, background of twill weave, scattered high and low cut strands.
• Coat or jacket material using low cut shag on the inside for a warm lining. Some shag used on the outside for trim on hem, fronts, collar or cuffs.
• Bedspread, using areas of cut pile and foundation of twill weave. Make in strips and sew together as original mantle was constructed.

Isle of Eigg Cut Pile (Figures 6-33, D6-8)

This method of making a laid-in pile surface material, probably for cloaks or mantles, was discovered on the Isle of Eigg, west of Scotland. It is a simple one to weave, and results in a satisfactory well-covered flat pile fabric. Here are a few notes on this technique:
• The ends can be cut as short as one-half inch and still make a practical fabric, if beaten in firmly.
• Because the ground is a plain-weave, it is best to use a loom with a shedding device and beater. A two-harness loom is adequate.
• For the background, you will need yarn in a shuttle. For the pile, work with cut ends of yarn in an open shed.
• Three warps are involved in one pass. One unit of the technique consists of two rows of pile, separated by two rows of plain-weave ground. Each pile row is made in the same shed as a row of ground weft.
• Work from the right or the left, whichever is most convenient.
• A warp is skipped between each pile insert.
• Determine what length you wish for the laid-in pile. For instance, if pile is to be one inch, cut pieces should be about two and one-half inches long, when the warp is set at eight to the inch.

6-34. Highland Guatemalan cut-pile. Cut lengths laid in. In center section, note vertical striped effect.

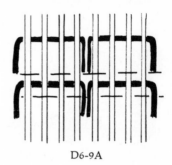

D6-9A

D6-9B

Highland Guatemalan Ways with a Laid-in Pile (Figures 6-34, D6-9)

This pile weave is fun to play with, there are so many ways of combining pile and·any of the flat-weave backgrounds like basket weave, or a loom-controlled pattern. Color is unlimited, as each insert is separate. Ground is plain weave, so a loom with shedding device and beater is desirable. One version gives a vertical shaggy stripe.

Czechoslovakian Shepherd's Cloak Shag. (Figures 6-35, D6-10)

A shepherd's cloak was woven in a shag weave, using a method of inserting cut ends. It sounds somewhat involved, but the result is good, as the cut ends criss-cross each other to give a variation in texture from the usual cut ends that hang down straight and give a brushed look. The ground is plain weave. Between two rows of tabby, for each unit of pile, three insertions are made in the same shed with six cut ends hanging to make the pile, occuring at different places because they emerge from between different warp ends. An all-over pile fabric made in this manner will be dense, flat, and smooth. The groups of insertions can be offset for best coverage as the weaving progresses. They are not required to be put in at any specific spot.

Tibetan Rug Knot (Figures 6-36, D6-11)

Woven over pairs of warp, worked over a rod, with continuous weft. A true

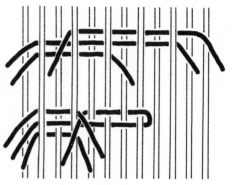

6-35. Czechoslovakian shepherd's cloak shag. Cut ends laid in shed, brought out at different warps for uneven shag. *Bottom:* One of three ends is laid in, wrapped, and brought out; the other two are just laid in. Repeated each row. *Top:* Three ends laid into the shed, emerging at different points. Pile ends offset in rows.

D6-10

Tibetan rug is woven with high-grade handspun wool, vegetable-dyed in strong shades of many colors. Typical geometric designs have their base in both India and China (figures 7-27, 28). A 32-page booklet, *Warp and Weft from Tibet,* by William King, is devoted to the method of weaving this pile technique, along with many directions for the proper loom and warping, design, motifs, color, some history. Available in a second printing from Robin and Russ, McMinnville, Oregon. We worked out a slightly simplified way to do it, and it has become one of our favorite ways of weaving a cut pile. Here are some notes on the Tibetan rug knot:
• This is something like the slip loop. The pile weft is wrapped around pairs of warp, and a loop is brought over a gauge.

D6-11A

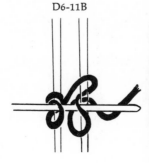

D6-11B

6-36. Tibetan rug knot. *From bottom:* Loops. Two warps skipped in between for clarity. Row of cut pile. Open warp example, one loop over gauge. Cut and uncut.

- The process lends itself to an easy rhythm. We found that the weaving goes more rapidly than some other pile techniques. A firm, long-wearing cut-pile rug is the result.
- Color changes are made readily, so shadings and design units are possible.
- Traditionally, the end finish is a warp fringe. Choose a warp that will be right for your design, if you do leave a fringe.
- The warp is completely covered, with weft going around all warps.
- Two shuttles are used, from opposite sides, in the same shed, for the rows of background weft. The pile weft is wound into a small ball or hand-hank.
- Peter Collingwood, in his rug book, calls this the "Sehna Loop" (D6-3).

Don't let our directions or anyone's scare you off. The operation will be done almost simultaneously with both hands. When you master the sequence, it really is a rapid way to make a pile rug.

Slip Loop (Figures 6-37, D6-12)

A fast loop method. Weft is put under warp, pulled out in a loop. The weft crosses the warp on the way to the next loop, and a neat heading is made. Because of this continuous line, the slip-loop is a good choice when spaced rows are woven. It looks complete, much like practice-penmanship rows of connected o's. It is similar to the Tibetan rug knot, but is made without a gauge. Three warps are involved before the next loop is begun under the fourth wrap. All warps are covered. It can be quite a casual, random loop-pile, as each loop is simply pulled out, with no attempt at measuring it.

D6-12

6-37. Slip loop. All warps are covered. Shown in two sizes of loops.

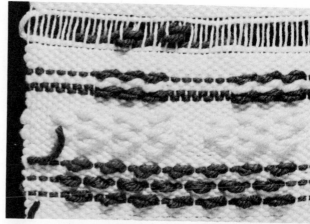

6-38. Spanish Confite, or *Granitos*. Double loop around four warps, second loop offset. Sampler rows show classic white on white pattern, a row in two colors, on open warp to show passage of weft over warp.

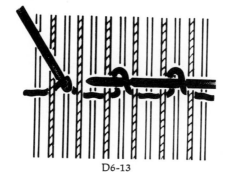

D6-13

6-39. Picked-up loops. Raised over a gauge. *From bottom:* Three rows of loops over every other warp. *Left:* Twisted before putting over gauge. *Right:* No twist. In groups and rows, woven left to right, then right to left.

Spanish Confite, Granitos, or de Confite (Figure 6-38)

We prefer the name *Granitos*—small grain—because it is so descriptive of the "grainy" surface texture. Composed of two loops, slightly offset one above the other, pulled in just enough to lie quite flat, but still raised above the background. These flat little loops have a texture with a bit more interest and change than single picked-up loops. Do not confuse Spanish Confite with the Spanish single-warp knot (D6-4). Spanish lace is a relative.

Traditional use: Granitos loops are most often found in cotton coverlets, but are also seen in old Moorish wool weavings. Typically, designs were pictorial, or with loops spelling out the names and dates of a Spanish wedding—part of the bride's dowery. Traditional colors varied with the location—blue on white, all white, or multicolored. Size of the loops are variable, large, small, far apart, or set close in clusters. The spreads were made in three strips, sewed or laced together with handwoven tapes, sometimes crocheted to join, and fringed on all sides. Another good example of multiple techniques in one article.

Picked-up Loops (Figures 6-39, D6-13)

Loops are raised above the foundation weave either from the main weft or an extra weft. They are formed over a gauge, or lifted up by fingers, hook, or a pick. No knotting or wrapping is done. A gauge evenly measures the loops and holds them in place during the beating. Rows of plain weave must be put in before and after loop rows, to hold them in place. Loop weft can be picked up between all warps, or spaced in bands, rows, spots, or areas of pattern. Frequent change of color is workable. Wefts of several colors are carried along together and lifted separately into loops at will.

Notes on designing and weaving with loops

• For a textile with looped motif, yarns for pattern and ground must be in sizes that work well together.

The pattern weft becomes part of the background when not lifted into loops. Therefore, when the size or color differs from the foundation yarn, it becomes another element of the total design and must be considered.

• Purpose of the looped textile is important in deciding the kind of yarn and sett. A wall hanging may have dramatic big loops, eased into place in open warp. A rug must have strong close-set warp, low loops to avoid heel-catching, and be beaten very firmly.

• Different sizes of yarns in pattern and/or ground weft will give more variety of texture and pattern.

• Loops are usually made with continuous lengths of weft on bobbins, hand-hanks, or shuttle.

• If very heavy yarns are used for small areas of loops, special care in beating the rows is necessary. The loop weft causes a thicker section to build up and finer background yarn will slant at the selvedge and in flat areas. It may be necessary to build up the edges with extra weft shots, as in rugs. Or the slanting wefts modeled around the heavy looped spots can be a part of the design.

• Twisting loops before putting over a gauge gives a still different look, and the twisting holds them in more securely.

• Loops picked up from left to right have a different slant than those from right to left.

Color change with loops

The smoothest, simplest way is to have one color for background weft, another for the loops. Alternate rows of plain weave and loops. At the extreme opposite, effect a color change at every loop. Complications of tucking in loose ends or a build-up of background is solved by designing these extra yarns into the whole plan.

• Great care must be taken to beat the weft in very closely as loops merely lie in the rows with no wrapping around the warp.

• Loops may very easily be pulled out, if:

There are too few warp ends per inch.

Foundation rows are not beaten in tightly, both before and after loop rows.

Loops are too high from the background where catching is a hazard such as in rugs or unholstery.

If yarn is slick and slippery.

Other threadings for loops

• Looping can be done on threadings other than twill, basket, or plain weave. The one constant requirement is a firm background. Try raising some of the pattern units up into loops when weaving a loom-controlled pattern.

- Loop some rows of tabby to divide the flat patterns. See what you can do with both color and texture. (Figure 6-24.)
- Use loops to outline a unit of design, in matching color or a contrast. Obtain shadow line and depth by use of light and dark outlines in loops on opposite sides of a design segment.
- Try high and low loops for emphasis in outlining.
- In a room divider, where both sides will be seen, do loops on both sides.

Length of loops

Loops, unless extremely long and of very soft yarn, will not droop over and cover the background. If you wish to have a solidly covered loop fabric, the rows must be firmly beaten, the weft yarn sized to fill the space fully between the close-set warp. The loops will then stand in close formation, supporting each other.

Loops in rugs and upholstery

- Picked-up loops can be used in rugs or floor mats if the back of the rug is thoroughly covered with liquid Latex, as a good anchor for the loops, creating a firm rug that will not travel on a slick surface.
- Low loops in upholstery are satisfactory when back of the yardage is painted with the Latex liquid.

Clipped loops

Picked-up loops are not too satisfactory if clipped for a cut pile, since the loop weft is not attached to the warp. Best to choose another technique. Within the following limitations, it is possible to clip them and still have a fabric that will stay together:
- If the ground is *very* tightly woven with loops high enough not to slip out easily.
- If the yarn is wool, which tends to cling to itself.
- If woven of cotton, washed before use, with some matting and shrinkage.
- Or the liquid Latex treatment, as mentioned above.

Loop techniques from other lands—early days

Similar looping techniques are found in almost every culture. Each has its own variation of color, designs, yarns used, use of the fabric, and actual method of picking up the loop. Loops are found in Coptic medallions adorning shirts, in early Egypt; in cloths for covering marriage chests in Sardinia; in American Colonial counterpanes, Scandinavian wall hangings and rugs, Bulgarian covers, Mexican blouse fabric, Boutonné rugs from Quebec, Peruvian bedcovers and shirts.

Mexican picked-up loops (Figure 6-40)

There is a Mexican technique of making loop designs, using a cactus thorn or some similar pick to quickly lift small loops. The subtle change in loop sizes gives interest to the slightly uneven, grainy texture, and does not look mechanically woven. These fabrics are usually of fine cotton, often all white. Be-

6-40. Mexican picked-up loops. The traditional white on white.

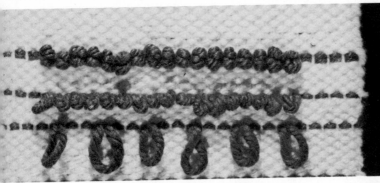

6-41. Chivas (Mexican, Guatemalan). Plain weave ground. *From bottom:* Long loops, spaced. Single row of loops picked up, no gauge. Row of double loops, each a separate weft but in the same shed.

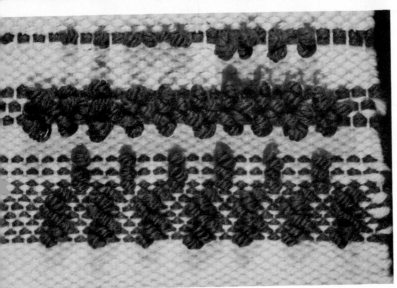

6-42. Coptic plain loop. (See figure D 6-14, Coptic Soumak loop.) Loop weft in same shed with ground weft. *From bottom:* Loops in zigzag pattern, ground showing. Loops one above the other, space between. Two wefts in the same shed, raised up in pairs of loops. Alternating in rows, one skip between, for a dense looped surface. One row to show single and double.

D6-14

D6-15

cause of fine yarns, firm beatings, and some shrinkage after washing, these fabrics will stand hard use even though the loops are not knotted in.

Guatemalan *Chivas* (Figure 6-41)

A Guatemalan version of loop-pile on plain weave is called "Chivas" because it resembles tightly curled pelts. The loop yarn, carried along in the shed in a second shuttle, slightly loose, is hooked out into loops wherever wanted. The pattern yarn is brought along outside the selvedge, then put through the shed when needed again. Loop rows are staggered, looped between other warps in following rows. Sometimes it is woven with two single loop yarns in the shuttle. Each single yarn twists and becomes a separate loop, thereby making many fine loops. When loops are put above each other in rows you have a stripe of loops. (See two rugs, figures 6-3, 9.)

Coptic loops (Figures 6-42, D6-14)

The distinctive Coptic roundels and bands from ancient Egypt are discussed and shown in chapter 5, "Tapestry"; see our version of Coptic-style medallion and linen loops in figure 5-43. Some combine tapestry insets with loops filling the background, surrounding the central tapestry. Natural linen was the usual choice for ground and loops, but many were woven in wool. The little portrait or memorial tapestries, wool on linen, with colorful low loops, are expertly shaded. Supposedly, these were likenesses, woven in their own unique style, featuring huge eyes.

Oriental Soumak (Figure D6-15)

This traditional rug weave is fully discussed and illustrated on pages 129-131.

Boutonné (or *Boutoné*) (Figure 6-43)

A French-Canadian method of picking up loops to make patterns, usually regional geometric designs, woven on a plain ground. The contrasting pattern weft is rather like a dotted line punctuated by an oversize dot. Very effective when just two colors are used, as in the typical white on a dark blue ground. They may be composed as isolated design units or all-over pattern.

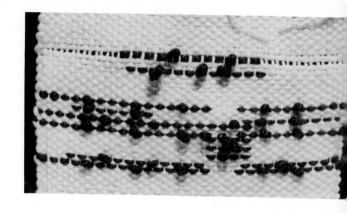

6-43. Boutonné. French-Canadian. Line and loop combine to make pattern.

D6-16

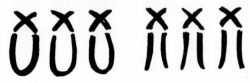

D6-17

KNOTS AND LOOPS MADE WITH A NEEDLE
(Figures D6-16, 17)

In the realm of embroidery there are some stitches that make a pile fabric. These can be adapted and put into the web as it is woven, or added as needlework after the fabric is off the loom. Another way is to weave a few inches of cloth, go back and put in the pile stitches with a needle, weave, add more pile, and so on. These stitches are useful for adding surface interest to your weavings. If, on completing a piece of weaving, you find it needs further texture emphasis, the needle stitches can be added.

By any other name . . .

Fair warning: When you delve into the relationships and names of needle-made pile stitches and woven pile, you will find a mass of different names for similar methods. It is an interesting study. We feel these stitches enrich a weaver's store of techniques. Here are a few. Perhaps your interest will be caught and you will want to dig further into old needlework books, new books, and other sources of information on embroideries from all over the world.

Ghiordes Knot Needle Stitch

This knot can also be done with a needle on fabric or canvas. In the Scandinavian manner, weave a background of closely-beaten wool weft on a linen warp and every half inch or more—depending upon the amount of pile you want—leave one row unwoven. After the fabric is removed from the loom, the pile knots are worked along the empty warp rows with a needle, following the same procedure used for a woven knot.

Turkey Work (See D6-1)

The looped stitch called "Turkey Loop" or "Turkey Work" is a needle-made version of the Ghiordes or Smyrna knot. Originally, it was done to imitate the Turkish carpets woven with this knot making the pile.

Berlin Work, Plush Stitch

These stitches are an imitation of Turkey Work—which is an imitation of the woven Ghiordes or Smyrna knot!

Still more needle-made versions of these knots are Single and Double Maltese Stitch, Single Knot, Candlewick, with the added confusion of several stitches called "candlewick," but that employ slightly different methods with a different result. All are called candlewick stitches. (Figure D6-16.)

Single Maltese stitch (Figure D6-16 *left*)

Much like a small, flat tassel caught at the top with a horizontal stitch. Short cut ends hang at the bottom.

Double Maltese stitch (D6-16 *right*)

This looks like a small, flat, fat bow tie with stubby cut ends spread at each side and a low loop in the center.

Candlewick—origin and use

The name "Candlewick" apparently comes from the weft yarns, which were either a soft, lightly spun cotton roving or the many-stranded cotton that was used for wicks in candles.

To begin with, candlewick textiles were handwoven, usually bedspreads. Technique was the picked-up loop over a gauge on plain weave (see D 6-16). Patterns were geometric, limited by the right angles of warp and weft. Later, the designs became more curvy and fanciful, when the spreads were needle-worked on muslin. The completed work was washed to make it shrink, thereby securing the tufts or loops. When the spreads were washed, dried, and briskly shaken, the cut ends of the stranded cotton fluffed out into what we think of as typical candlewick tufts.

Modern-day Candlewicking

A later method of needlework for ladies-in-a-hurry is used today. Inexpensive cotton muslin or sheeting—*guaranteed to shrink when washed*—is the background. The design is simply basted on—long, short, or combinations of stitch lengths worked with many strands of cotton in a large needle. The stitches are put in with relaxed tension. Cuts are made in the center of the stitches, just like cutting an overshot or float weave. The washing, shrinking, and fluffing with a shake are still important to the total process.

Velvet Stitch (Figure D6-17)

This pile stitch, derived from the cross stitch, can have a cut or looped finish. It is a charming one, with a little cross stitch holding the loop at the top. Especially nice to use in a spot design with the cross a part of the total effect. It could be used in a rug, with proper ground weave. Space the rows so the crosses show. If you want dense loop pile, the rows of crosses could be alternated or combined with closely-spaced plain loops. There is one little area of this stitch in the stitchery sampler shown in color on page 202.

Other embroidery stitches

Most of the knot stitches in embroidery can be considered as needlework pile. They can be worked on your fabric as you weave, or added later. Worked in bunches they will cover an area just as the woven pile and loop methods do. Try this use of the French Knot, Pekin Knot, Coral Stitch, Bullion Stitch. There are many more that are worked on the surface of the fabric.

Below we briefly discuss additional techniques that may be unfamiliar.

MORE PILE-WEAVE IDEAS

Just a mention

A pile weave from Greece. Floccata (*Flokati*) rugs are a remarkably soft, thick felted textile with shaggy pile. Until you know how they are woven, you wonder how the long lengths of pile are put into such a close background. Long narrow strips are loosely woven on a wide-spaced wool warp, with weft of the same natural white wool. At intervals, cut pieces of wool are laid into the shed. The yardage is cut from the loom, then sewn into pairs or four pieces, ready for the drastic finishing process:

The fabric is shrunk and felted, usually by immersion in a waterfall or whirlpool, which does the work. A less picturesque way is by immersion and beating to felt it. Sometimes piece-dyed, but more often left in the natural white with stripes of natural brown and black wool. We saw one small sample with sparsely placed single ends of brown pile on white for coating material, with pile worn inside.

From Crete—Couscousis technique

This is a unique and very sensible use of dense looped pile. Narrow fringed and tasseled strips woven in a solid loop surface are made to protect the blouse from the water jug carried on the shoulder. Of wool and cotton, many colors and yarn sizes. Another example of a craft being put to use for utility and beauty.

From Peru

• A Peruvian method of putting loops into a textile, different from the usual method of lifting loops up between warp ends: Lifting the loop directly above alternate warp ends, alternated in the following rows.
• Rep weaves with patterns have been found, with the animal figures woven in very fine, low loops, simulating fur.
• Tapestry weaves with crinkly loops emphasizing some of the patterns are also in existence. The Peruvian ways of making the loops resemble Turkish towelling (terry cloth) and the Coptic methods of loop weaving.

Early American counterpanes

The very old white counterpanes show an interesting use of fine cotton woven in a loom-controlled pattern with design units raised in low loops. In old directions these were called "tufts," the supplementary weft, "tufting weft." Loops were picked up on wire. To insure very even small loops, four gauges were used in rotation, with three kept in place until the fourth picked up loops; the tabby rows were woven and beaten in, then the first wire was removed and used.

Variations on knots

(Note: Sketches referred to appear in the sampler section and notebook.)
Knots, even the classic Ghiordes knot (figure D6-1), need not always be made over the prescribed number of warps, or facing in the same direction. Figure D6-2 shows the Ghiordes knot upside down, loops pulled through instead of the cut ends, the ends pulled in different directions, and a figure-8 double header!
• A dense pile can be made by overlapping—each warp with a part of the next knot on it.
• The Sehna knot (figure D6-3) can be crowded for a thicker pile by starting the next knot on the unwrapped warp of the previous knot.
• Figure D6-5 shows a one-warp French knot used in the Middle Ages. Hint on the procedure: Double your cut weft, with the cut ends to left, a wide loop at right, put under warp. Bring the topmost end over the warp (to the right) and down through the loop. This is like the Egyptian Cut Pile (D6-6) but on just one warp.
• An Araucanian way with Ghiordes knot short-pile rugs is to distribute a few very, very long lengths of pile throughout. One row of filling is woven in between pile rows, which are of many colors. Sometimes fringed on all four sides.

From a photograph of a statue

Be alert for design ideas everywhere. *Two* ideas are suggested by a photograph of a mantle worn by the subject of a carved Sumerian statue, dated about 2500 B.C. It looked like a woven pile sheared into a pattern. Because it was wrapped to and covered only one shoulder, the rows of pile slanted.

Idea 1: Weave rows of pile on a diagonal, then shear into petal-shapes (see figure 6-6). On a plain weave ground, work Ghiordes knot pile rows, beaten on a slant. Pile should be long enough to cover the ground after clipping and shaping. Once the correct proportion of background to pile was worked out for our example, the weaving proceeded as fast as a regular horizontal row.

Idea 2: Weave straight rows of pile, long enough to cover the ground weave after leaf-shapes have been cut. Or weave pile rows, trim them into leaf patterns, in rows with ground weave showing between.

These ideas could be used for a shaggy jacket, cape, or coat; an unusual pile rug, or areas in a wall hanging.

Tri-colored picked-up loops

Weft: Three colors in one shuttle. Ground weft in second shuttle. Throw several rows of plain weave, beat in tightly, then put in the three pattern wefts, lift loops of separate colors, or all in one. The background is composed of the ground weft and the three colors in a single shed. An attractive selvedge appears where colors scallop out around the plain weave rows and into the pattern row. A stunning rug can be woven in this way, with a very decorative edge finish built in. Try it on a placemat or runner, with a large center area of plain weave for the plate, and a border of low loops and scalloped selvedge. More than one color or weight of yarn can be carried along and lifted up into a multi-colored loop. No technical problems here, of having to change colors. Each unit of design or each row can be different. Example: One strand each of three shades of white. For a surprise color change, add one strand of color in some rows or areas. The basic colors will give you a common denominator of color so the flow throughout will be smooth and subtle.

• Try a very dark background with the loop design in white and a very light shade of the ground color.

• Light and dark colors can be reversed in rows of background and loops for striped effects, borders, or bands, either horizontal or vertical.

In our following notebook section we have grouped the detail sketches, along with briefed directions, to provide quick reference for procedures.

Notebook

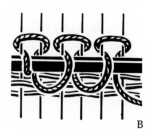

Ghiordes Knot (D6-1)

A. Made with cut weft.
B. Continuous weft, over a gauge.

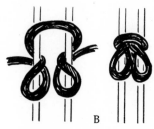

Tricks a Ghiordes Knot can do for you to give a pile fabric a slightly different look (D6-2)

A. Upside down.
B. Ends pulled out in loops.
C. One end up, one end down.
D. A figure 8 with ends going out in opposite directions.

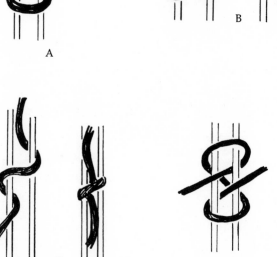

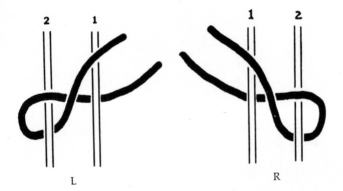

Sehna or Persian Knot (D6-3)

L: Left-hand knot.
R: Right-hand knot.

A   B

Single-warp Spanish Knot (D6-4)

A. The usual method. This knot is only wrapped, so must always have a tight ground weave before and after the knots. Worked on alternate warp ends.
B. Upside down.

Single-warp old French Knot (D6-5)

Egyptian cut pile
(D6-6)

Woven on basket-weave ground, over pairs of warp.

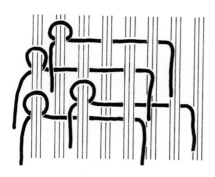

Icelandic cut pile
(D6-7)

Woven on twill ground, over pairs of warp.

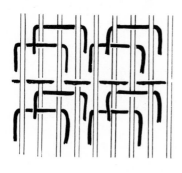

Isle of Eigg cut pile
(D6-8)

One unit consists of four rows of pile, with one row of tabby between the first two rows and the last two. Plain weave ground.

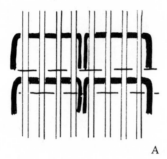

Highland Guatemalan cut pile (D6-9)

A. Pile under four warps, plain weave on either side of pile row.

A

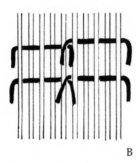

B. Pile woven in, ends crossed where they meet.

B

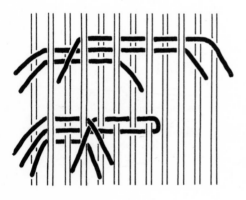

From a Czechoslovakian shepherd's cloak (D6-10)

Two methods are shown. *Top:* The three rows of pile are woven over a total of nine warps, and the ends left hanging. *Bottom:* The three rows of pile are woven over seven warps, with the middle weft taken around the seventh warp, woven back in, with all cut ends left hanging.

A

Tibetan Rug Knot (D6-11)

A. The sequence of putting the weft over and under pairs of warp ends, then pulling down in a loop over the gauge.

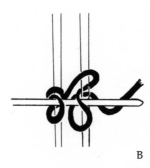

B

B. Shows one loop tightened up, the next one in process, and end of weft on the way to the next.

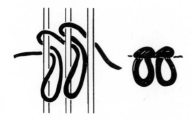

Slip loop (D6-12)

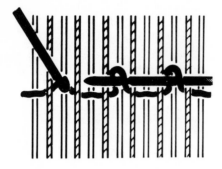

Picked-up loops, over a gauge (D6-13)

The system is the same, whether a gauge, the fingers, or a pick is used.

Coptic Soumak-style loop (D6-14)

The Coptic weavers also used the plain picked-up loop, sometimes long and hanging, sometimes short and close together, as in their small portrait weavings.

Oriental Soumak (D6-15)

Full directions are on pages 129, 130.

L   R

Needle-made pile stitches (D6-16, 17)

Left: Maltese, or single knot.
Right: Double Maltese stitch, or candlewicking. (D6-16)

Velvet stitch (D6-17)

Left in loops, and loops cut.

Edges, Hems,
Bands, Belts

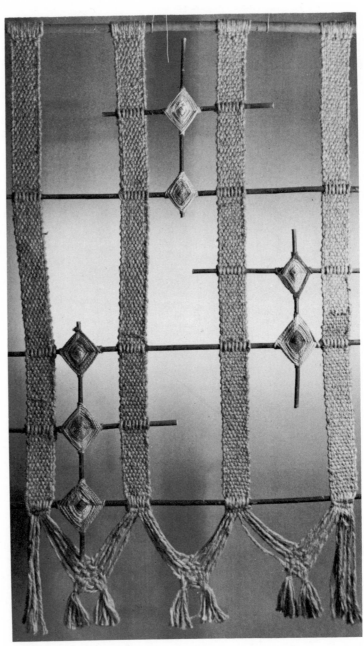

7-1. Wall hanging, all woven bands and fringe in heavy gray-green tow linen. Bands are held apart by sticks. The "God's Eyes" are woven in warm colors; Indians of the Southwest weave this little symbolic diamond as a legendary protector. Hope Munn placed them perfectly for a well-balanced composition.

Edges of fabric are always with us. Every time a piece of weaving is created there are those ends waiting for some kind of attention. Always four sides to consider: two selvedges, two warp ends. You must think through to the finished product, and decide whether the edges will be fringed or hemmed; whether selvedges will be cut off, turned in, joined to another, ornamented—or? Edge finishes of handwoven fabrics are especially important. This orphan area of design is often ignored or forgotten, when it should be an integral part of the whole handmade article. Too often a beautifully woven textile may be casually finished with a machine-stitched edge, an indifferent selvedge, or a fringe having no design relationship. In these past few years, however, designer-weavers have become more aware of total design in handcrafts, and most pieces seen in publications or in exhibits show the result of thoughtful, complete planning. It is a challenge, but the result will be an integrated, satisfying accomplishment. You will need to learn a few other crafts, such as sewing, embroidery stitches, knotting, to achieve certain of these edge finishes. Then your handwoven dress, for example, designed with all edge finishes planned into the whole, will be lifted from just another stitched-up dress to a creation obviously worked out with care.

CATEGORIES

Edges, fringes, joinings, hems, trims—anything that might be done to a selvedge or warp-end edge—are difficult to separate into neat categories. A finished edge may be a part of a preface to the joining of two pieces; a fringe may be made separately, then applied as a trim; a selvedge may be woven a special way for a finish, or extended into a weft fringe by use of a skeleton warp. We have arranged these finishes in what seems to be a logical sequence, but remember that an edge finish can include a hem, a joining plus applied trim; a fringe might involve special edge preparation, embroidery stitches, a knot technique, and braiding. Don't necessarily consider the ideas in the next three chapters in solidly fixed relationships. Mix, match, shuffle, and rearrange as you will, always remembering that your finish should be suitable to the over-all design and material, and the use of the textile.

WHAT WE MEAN BY . . .

So you will know exactly what we mean in this text, below are terms defined as we use them.

Braids and Bands: A woven band is often called a braid. Peruvian decorative bands are called braids. Commercially woven bands for trimmings are often called braids. This is confusing, because "braid" is also the technique of braiding or plaiting—a construction—the interlacement of yarns, as hair is braided.

Braid (or *plait*): The structure, as used in braided fringe, etc.

Band: A woven strip used as an applied trim or a unit by itself.

Belt: Sash, girdle. To tie or buckle about the waist, like a band, therefore the terms "bands" and "belts" are interchangeable in use. Could be plaited, woven, knotted.

Tape or *Passementerie:* Tape. A narrow band. To be applied as decoration or used for ties. (See Japanese scarf tie, figure 7-31.) Passementerie is highly ornamented, jeweled, embroidered, etc.

Cord: Knotted, twisted, or knitted yarns. Used as belts, bag handles, trims.

All photographs in this chapter are by Kent Kammerer, unless otherwise credited.

Binding: A band that is folded and sewn over an edge to front and back.

Border: A row or rows of pattern, woven as a part of the fabric, as a decorative treatment on or near an edge. Sometimes called a "woven band," meaning that it is in the weft. When a warp-wise pattern is woven it is usually called a "stripe."

Edges: Any of the four boundaries of a piece of fabric; ends, hems, headings, selvedges. The term "edges" is usually qualified by the addition of a specific term—selvedge edge, warp-end, cut edge, and so on.

Ends: Usually refers to the cut edges or the warp-end edges.

Hem: Usually refers to the cut end that is turned in and sewn to prevent raveling, and to give a finish. However, a selvedge edge can be hemmed, too.

PLANNING

It is such fun to work with an edge—all those warp ends to manipulate, that lovely firm selvedge to do something more with. While it is as important to plan the finish as it is to plan the main fabric, resist the temptation to do too much; be discriminating and don't use all your techniques on one project. But do make a hanging or shawl that is *nothing* but fringes and bands. (Figure 7-1.)

Know . . .

• When to stop!
• Invisible or inconspicuous finishes as well as the ornate ones.
• Some embroidery stitches. Learn new ones that complement the weaves.
• When the best choice on a textile, lovely in itself, is to turn up a hem and sew it invisibly, or when a single, simple row of hemstitching is enough.

After deciding what you are going to weave, ask yourself these questions as you plan your project:
• Selvedge. Will it show?
• Is it an important design element?
• What preparation must be made for the finish?
• Is it to be joined, hemmed back, have more added, for instance, bands or fringe?
• Warp ends. Will they be hemmed, knotted, or fringe? This is an especially important part of the over-all design for items such as wall hangings.
• Hemstitched? On or off the loom?
• Special rows of weaving at each end for hem? Pocket for a rod hanger? Decorative treatment woven in? A warp-protecting row of knots that must be done on the loom, under tension? Or do you want a length of warp left empty at the beginning, to be dealt with later, off the loom?
• At the beginning and the end, do you need special preparation for fringe, such as Soumak, hemstitching, or Leno to divide the warps into groups for later knotting?

Your answers to these, and other questions, will influence the color and kind of warp you use, the length of fabric woven, the warp ends left, and perhaps the type of loom you use. For instance, four selvedges are possible on a backstrap loom. A warp on a frame or primitive loom will give you loop warp ends instead of cut ends, if you want. Edges may need to have no-nonsense hems and good straight selvedges, or they may be a dominating, flamboyant design element. Decorative possibilities of edges, considering the design and plan of a finished piece, follow. Two different kinds of edges must be considered, each with its own set of problems.

SELVEDGES

The selvedges more or less take care of themselves, since they are a finished edge that will not ravel. The problems there are in the weaver's skill in handling the wefts, beating, and choice of warp. If your selvedges are to be enhanced with an edge treatment, it becomes even more important to weave them well. You can't count on a fancy decoration to cover poor craftsmanship. We will have more to say about selvedges as a design element further along.

HEMS

The hem ends, or warp-ends of the fabric, present an immediate problem the moment the warps are cut. They must be fastened in some way, to secure the weaving. In "Fringes," Chapter 9, are more ideas about how to treat these ends. Here, we explain what to do immediately as protective measures.

Secure the cut warp ends

Of prime importance are practical ways to keep the woven area from loosening up or ravelling out. Before the warps are cut and the weaving removed from the loom, secure the ends even if by temporary means.
• A thin line of a white glue preparation (Elmers, No-So, etc.)—IF—it won't spoil the edge for further finishing. Try it on a sample first. It will leave a slightly stiff line, be shiny, and should be used only if the glue line will be covered or turned back into a hem. If possible, run the line of glue on the back of the edge, a half inch or more from the finished edge. It could be cut off later, after serving to protect the warp ends until all work is finished.
• An overcast stitch, with needle and thread, fairly loose so it can be pulled out later, will protect the weaving. This can be a part of the finishing, done on or off the loom.
• Several extra rows of weaving, which will be pulled out as the final finishing is done. Strips of cardboard or "throw-away" yarn may be put in.
• Cut just a few warps at a time, tie the groups together in a loose over-hand knot, cut and tie a few more, and so on, across the warp. On or off the loom. You will find other ways, suitable to your weaving.

MACHINE STITCHING

A row of machine stitching is often needed to hold the woven part or to strengthen it for better wear. Remove the fabric from the loom carefully, and stitch immediately. Stitching is also necessary on cut pieces for a dress pattern or other raw edges. Preferably, machine stitch only if you plan to cover it with a decorative stitch or band, or if it disappears within a hem or seam. A zigzag stitch or straight stitch in a matching color will disappear in a textured or pattern weave. Hand-threading, matching or contrasting, will turn a necessary stitched line into a good-looking handcrafted edge finish with little added time or effort. If an article is worth hand weaving, it should be worth the little extra design for a finish that is suitable and hand done.

WARP AND WEFT PROTECTORS

A whole group of the warp and weft protector techniques are especially useful on rugs, because they are firm and wear-proof. Not limited to rugs, these protectors can be used on almost anything where they accomplish the needed finish. Some can be just a hem-like plain edge, or the heading for a fringe. We have put this group in chapter 9, on fringes, but remember to look at them when you are choosing an unfringed edge. If extended, some of them almost become a fabric. Others can be made into wide borders.

WHEN YOUR EDGE FINISH IS A HEM

Hems are an integral part of the woven article. There should be complete harmony between the woven piece and the hem. Consider the purpose of the article, the best width of hem and best method of doing it. Unless the hem is planned as a showy part of the over-all look, it should be as inconspicuous as possible. The proportion of the hem to the article is important, and if wrong could very well spoil the looks of the weaving, especially in a small unit like a placemat or towel. Nothing is more elegant than a linen placemat or runner with a generous hem, mitered at the corners and beautifully sewn by hand. While the sewing is kept nearly invisible it must still be sewn with strength, to withstand frequent washings.

Notes on hemming placemats, and such

• When designing the article, note that it sometimes makes hemming easier if a heavier thread or narrow pattern row is woven in where the hemming is to be sewn. This will help to hide the stitches in an otherwise plain area.
• Hemming should be done on the same weft thread across the width.
• The turning point for the hem can be marked during the weaving with a row of colored sewing thread, to be pulled out later.
• On a patterned fabric, the hem should be sewn into the edge of a pattern row, design area, or stripe, if possible. If the fabric is checked, hem to the edge of one row of the checks, not in the middle. Hem to one edge or the other of a patterned border, not somewhere in between—for the best design, the hem should not be turned up in the middle of a pattern.
• Rows of plain weave will make a flatter hem than pattern weaving. To reduce the bulk in the hem, especially if the body of the weaving is heavy, weave a heading of fine yarn, matching in color, for the first turn-in, or enough for the whole hem. This will also serve to mark the turn-in and provide a straight line.

KINDS OF HEMS

Books on sewing will show you how to do ordinary hems. We show you a few hems that may be less familiar and are especially appropriate for a handwoven fabric. Others to look for: Damask hem, French hemming, top or over-sewing, slip-stitch.

STITCHED HEM

This is a modestly decorative hem, like an ordinary hem, but turned up on

7-2A, B. *Top:* Stitched hem turned up and stitched on the top side. *Bottom:* Herringbone hem in several variations, closed and open.

the right side of the fabric and fastened with a kind of back stitch. A precise line of stitching along one line of weft is necessary for a smart look. Use a thread that is heavier or doubled either in contrasting or matching color. Our example is on a placement woven of coarse nubby and smooth cotton, two grays. The stitching is white mercerized cotton, doubled in the needle. (Figure 7-2A.)

How to do it

Draw a thread just above the first turning. Your stitches will be made along this fold. Turn once more and stitch along the drawn thread, through the three thicknesses of cloth. Sew a back stitch, being careful to put the needle down just where it was drawn out after the last stitch. The back stitches should be very even, each stitch up to the other, with no space between.

HERRINGBONE HEM

This is a good hem to use if your material is bulky or if you have insufficient material to turn a regular double hem. The hem is turned back just once; herringbone stitch covers the raw edge. Rows of machine stitching keep it from ravelling and act as guidelines for the needle stitches. The herringbone side can be a decorative right side, or you may work it so the top side is the single line of backstitching that occurs on the reverse (and looks like the stitched hem). Use matching or contrasting thread, fine or heavy, for the effect you wish. (Figure 7-2B.)

How to do it

• Machine stitch three rows, close together, at edge. Trim warp ends close to outside row.
• With wrong side toward you, turn up a single hem below the third row of stitching.

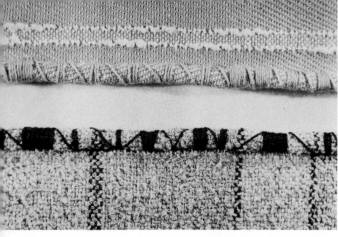

7-3. Rolled hems with decorative stitches.

• The top and bottom stitched rows will be your guidelines for the herringbone stitch. Work from left to right, making the stitches only one or two warp threads apart, depending upon the coarseness of your fabric. Keep the stitches close together for good coverage. The needle always points toward the stitch just taken. The points at top and bottom meet. You are making what looks like a double row of crosses. The stitches are taken alternately along the upper and lower stitched lines. Each stitch passes back to the top raw edge, catches the hem edge and the body of the cloth. This makes the continuous stitch line on the other side. Along the lower line, catch only the top layer of cloth so none of these stitches show on the reverse. The machine stitching will not be noticed when the hem is finished. (See figure D 7-1 for progression of stitches.)

ROLLED HEM

The rounded look of this hem is attractive. Roll the edge of the material until the cut edge is well covered. You can hem or slipstitch it inconspicuously at this point, or make a rolled hem, ornamented (figure 7-3).

While a rolled hem is usually associated with delicate fabric, such as fine handkerchief lawn, it may give just the appearance of bulk and accent you need on a coarsely woven mat. It is a secure hem, too, for long wear.

How to do it

Roll the edge of the material toward you, until the cut edge is well covered and you have the size roll you want. For maximum emphasis, roll it up on the right side of the material as we did in our examples. Overcast, Cross Stitch, or a combination, can be sewn around the roll to hold it. Sew around the hem and through the cloth. On a striped fabric, or an all-over pattern, your stitches can be spaced to extend the lines or between the stripes, as we did, by using black thread to echo the black stripes.

EMBROIDERED HEMS—GUATEMALA

This is a favorite Guatemalan and Mexican way with hems, using many colors, changing every inch or so. On a narrow, rolled or turned hem sew a zigzag or cross stitch. Make the crosses by sewing in one direction, one color, all slanting in the same direction. Then return, making the other leg of the cross using another color. Or change colors every few inches. (Figure 7-3.)

HEM ON A GREEK RUG

A simple hem on a white wool looped rug is easy to do and adds a little something to an otherwise plain finish. Suitable for any weight material. Weave about an inch or so of plain heading below the last pattern row. Turn up a narrow hem, and sew. Then, the special touch, about every five or six inches sew a group of yarns through, tie in a simple knot. You have a widely spaced tassel fringe. (See figure 6-10, chapter 6.)

SCALLOPED HEM

A scalloped hem, quickly made, is an old-fashioned lingerie finish. My first introduction to it was in sixth-grade sewing class—which goes back a long time! We have tried it now, on different weights, and think it is a useful edge for you to know and experiment with. Depending upon the width of your hem and spacing of stitches, you can make a gathered edge of tiny scallops or a wide, slightly waving edge with just a slight tension on the threads. Try this out on different materials; each one seems to accept this edge in a different way, and it may not always be suitable. The running stitches can be inconspicuous, small and matching, or quite large and of a different color.

Our scalloped hem examples in figure 7-4

Three fabric weights show some of the effects possible. *Top:* We like what happened to the straight lines in a loose, soft wool twill weave. The stitching and extra over-sewing at the dip was done with wool worsted yarn. *Middle:* Light-weight fine wool. Heavier yarn is threaded through the stitching on the left, and there is a long, single chain stitch at the dip, only slightly tightened, to suggest a scallop with little distortion. *Bottom:* Fine, nubby cotton tightened into gathers forms very shallow scallops. This is more like the original use of this hem. On sheer or soft lingerie fabrics the tiny scallops can be gathered at a neckline, or used flat as a hem. The running stitches can have added top stitching as shown and more rows of stitches, plain or fancy, can be added to the scalloped line, widening into a pretty border. It tends to round a little on a heavy material, so try it as a top edge finish on a flat shoulder bag.

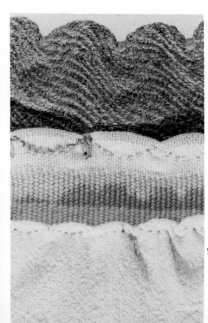

7-4. Scalloped hems, on fine and on heavy fabrics.

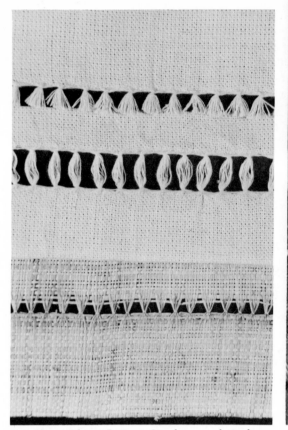

7-5. Hemstitching. *Bottom:* Simple row of single hemstitching at the hem. *Middle:* Hemstitching done on the loom between mats. One row of simple hemstitching finishes the edge. Enough warp is left unwoven between mats to provide short hemstitched fringes. *Top:* Hemstitched row cut. All from the Philippines.

7-6. Three examples of fancy hemstitching worked by Shirley Shapley, Seattle. *Bottom:* Square Hemstitching. This is not quite as open as the other two, but can be drawn slightly tighter than our example. The reverse side of this stitch is a double row of crosses. *Middle:* Ladder Hemstitch. Vertical bars of warp, with hemstitch holding them apart, top and bottom. *Top:* Trellis. Weft threads are drawn to the width desired for your hemstitched row. The simple hemstitching stitch is worked over a group of warp threads on one side for the width of the row. Along the opposite side, the warp threads are grouped to form V's as you work the stitch across.

7-7. Picot hem from Perugia. Courtesy Zada Sigman.

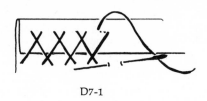

D7-1

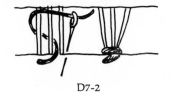

D7-2

HEMSTITCHING (Figures 7-5, 6, 7 and D7-1, 2)

Hemstitching is classic, elegant, and satisfying both practically and esthetically. A hemstitched hem shows that the craftsman went one step beyond the necessary hemming and spent time, thought, and skill. Often a single row of hemstitching will lift a plain linen mat or napkin out of the ordinary. This technique can be done on the loom or after the fabric has been removed from the loom. Worked on warp threads exposed in a woven fabric by drawing out threads, or on unwoven warps on the loom. (Figure 7-5.)

NOTE: Hemstitching on the loom is a very good preparation for fringe. If the stitching seems too heavy for your purpose, a very good substitute is pseudo-hemstitching, which is a row of Leno weave (see Gauze and Leno weaves in chapter 4.) A line or two of these techniques will make a good row to hem to, or a heading for a fringe. Work with tight tension on a flat warp.

Variations are many (figure 7-6). It is often identified by the country of origin, such as Italian hemstitching, which is usually worked on beautiful linens along with drawn and cutwork. Hemstitching is one of the openwork or insertion stitches, related to faggoting, and as such it is useful as a joining stitch. Because it is so much a part of the sewing and embroidery culture and directions are easy to come by, we take space here to mention only some of the less known kinds. We refer you to Theresa de Dillmont's *Encyclopedia of Needlework* for a number of interesting and unusual hemstitch methods.

A picot hem

Our example in figure 7-7 is from Perugia, on hand-loomed table linen with a border of dull gold on natural ground, the pattern taken from the Renaissance patterns of Umbria. This simple but effective edge finish provides a handmade look without competing with the loom-woven pattern of fabric and border. To make this hem: Before rolling the edge into a small firm hem, a row of picots are worked about half an inch from the raw edge, at intervals of about two inches. Then, when the hem is tightly rolled and sewn, the little rings are all around the edge. To make the picots, a buttonhole stitch in the gold thread of the woven border is worked around a thread. This technique can be used in many ways—it can be applied or worked on any edge, with no special preparation, and it can be on almost any scale of boldness or delicacy.

EMBROIDERY STITCHES FOR EDGE FINISHES
(Figures 7-8, 9, 10, 11)

Handwoven fabrics are naturals for hems and edges enhanced with needlework. Many stitches are workers, to hold the hem in place. Others are purely decorative, to cover machine stitching or to add richness. Relating the edge finish to the fabric is easy—just use the same yarns as warp or weft. Many pattern weaves suggest a complementary embroidery stitch.

• A buttonhole stitch on a checked material, with the spacing keyed to the check.

• An exaggerated overcast on the same slant as a twill weave.

• A "Y" stitch on a diamond pattern, and so on.

Basket-weave—over and under two warps with two wefts—suggests an edge finish of double blanket stitch. Just one unit of the woven pattern can be emphasized with stitches, or an enlargement of it embroidered on a plain-weave hem.

Embroideries at the edge

On a length of yardage for drapery, skirt, scarf, or towels, plan and weave a little something extra as a hem finish. At the beginning and end of an all-over woven pattern, weave a band in plain weave, using the same weft. You will be embroidering on this plain area, so make it the width you need for the design, plus another inch or two for turning back a hem, or other finish. When just two colors are used, one for warp and one for pattern weft, stitchery shows to the best advantage. Briefly, the design idea is to extend the woven pattern into a border, by embroidering it on the plain band. Double or triple the yarn for emphasis of the design. Choose stitches that echo the weave. A much heavier yarn, but still in the same weft color, could be used. Our example is Norse Fret pattern, in blue and off-white (figure 7-8). Try this idea on just one or two panels of drapery. Or embroider a wide border at the bottom of a long evening skirt. Perhaps on a pillow, use a band of the woven pattern and one of the same pattern stitched with textured yarn. Lots of possibilities! A variation on this theme: If your woven pattern is large, with spaced units of pattern, stitch over some of them, making them more important, and raised. Do this as an accent here and there, a medallion effect, or as a border.

7-8. Enhance a hemline or border by emphasizing the woven pattern with embroidery on the plain-weave hem. Norse Fret, loom pattern, blue on a white warp. Units of the pattern are stitched in two shades of blue in Outline, "Y", and Seed Stitches. The narrow fringe is secured by a row of blanket stitches over and between each warp end. Only partly done, so you can see the plain-weave band below the woven pattern.

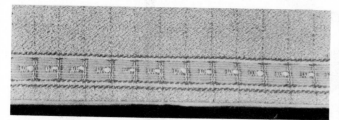

7-9. Woven band at the hem. An overshot pattern woven and laid in, spacing related to the fine warp stripe of the lightweight wool fabric. Enough plain weave was continued below it to be turned up for a hem.

7-10. Wide band of stitches, row on row, fill the space between a woven band and the bottom of a long skirt. By the author.

More ways to emphasize a hem end

• While weaving, double or triple the weft for a few inches at the ends.
• Add other colors to your weft at the border.
• With a pattern weave, do a border by fragmenting the pattern—weaving a few rows of tabby between the pattern shots to separate and elongate them.
• Lay in a long overshot design (figure 7-9).

Showcase for stitches

Sometimes a weaving becomes a background and showcase for embroidery. The skirt shown in figure 7-10 was planned to have a long and useful life. Of plain-weave deep-blue mercerized cotton, a top and skirt were woven with two-inch bands of textured white. A little copper was added for sparkle. The hem was a deep one, planned to be let down ankle length later on. We did this, and could not resist the lovely open spaces between the woven white band and the hem. So here is our banded skirt, rows and rows of simple embroidery stitches, all in different white wool yarns. Hard to detect, but near the top is the original woven white band.

Philippine skirt from Baguio

A joining and an edge finish appear on this example (figure 7-11). Shown at the top is the edge, worked with an up and down blanket stitch, in alternating red and black wool with points of the stitch kept within the woven white stripe. At bottom is the joining, in the same yarns and blanket stitch, moving from side to side making the join, much like some of the joinings used in Mexico and Guatemala. Skirt fabric is navy, blue and white stripe.

NECKLINES AND ARMHOLES (Figure 7-12)

Embroidery stitches, different hems and trims are sometimes needed for an armhole or shoulder. Figure 7-12 shows how the side seam joining-stitch on a *huipil* is continued on around the armhole. Dull red stranded cotton in plait stitch is worked so closely that a thick, ridged edge is formed. (See more of this Mexican *huipil* in "Joinings," chapter 8.)

7-12. The joining stitch up the side seam in this Mexican *huipil* separates to become an edge finish around the sleeve. See more of this *huipil* in Chapter 3, on laid-in. Courtesy Mr. and Mrs. Fred Hart. (Photograph by William Eng.)

7-11. An edge finish and a joining on a striped skirt from Baguio, the Philippines. Courtesy Irma Robinson.

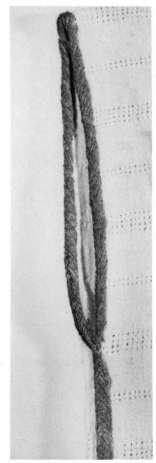

7-13. Naga technique for reinforcement of a "V" neckline slit.

Reinforcing a neckline slit (Figure 7-13)

The need for a reinforcement at the bottom of a neck slit, or a slit at the side of a shirt or skirt, can be turned into an attractive trim. The Naga hill-tribe people of India stitch an elipse of plait or buttonhole stitch for a few inches at this spot (see "Laid-in," chapter 3.) We did two examples—one in a heavy wool, the other in a very fine cotton.

How to do it

Turn back a narrow hem. Sew on the back, invisibly, or sew on the top side with an ornamental stitch. On the edge, at the bottom of the cut, buttonhole around an inch or so, or as far as needed to cover the narrowing turn-in of the hem. This can be done, as we did, with a contrasting thread or a fine, matching one. The buttonholed bar is made by putting two or three strands of thread across, then buttonholing over it—much like making a picot loop or an eye loop for a hook-and-eye fastening.

Top. On soft stretchy wool, twill weave, which ravels readily, one turn back was made and basted for a hem along the sides of the slit. At the bottom of the slit closely spaced buttonhole stitches were sewn in a half-circle with twisted silk thread. When the bar is put across, as shown, be careful to have it exactly fill the space, without drawing up or being too loose. An outline stitch holds the hem and outlines the whole edge.

Bottom. The same method was used as that on the coarser material above, but the edge was hemmed back on the reverse side with three-strand embroidery floss.

ESKIMO LACED EDGE (Figure 7-14)

Named for the Eskimos and Aleuts who use it on the seams of their seal parkas, this stitch is decorative, and also practical to secure a hem. It is done in two parts—first a running stitch, which holds the turned hem in place, then the lacing stitch, which goes over the edge to the other side, through the running stitches. Being the same on both sides, it is an excellent choice for the edge of a scarf, poncho, pillow, or anything where both front and back will show. Try it on a room divider or curtain that is seen from both sides. It can be quite fancy. Experiment with colors. You can use a large or textured yarn for the lacing, since it is not taken through the material. More detailed directions and suggestions for color are found in *The Stitches of Creative Embroidery*, by Jacqueline Enthoven. For a daintier version see Mrs. Enthoven's sampler shown in chapter 8.

Briefly, this is how it goes:

Baste the hem. Sew a running stitch close to the folded edge. Be sure that the first running stitch is on the top side of the cloth. Space the stitches according to the size of the yarn and the depth of the hem. Do just one stitch at a time, so each stitch will be relaxed enough to put the lacing through. Lace with a tapestry needle to avoid picking up any fabric. Work from back to front, from right to left, with the edge away from you. Turn the edge over and back as you work.

Start lacing at the back by putting a beginning knot inside the hem. Come up under the first running stitch, without catching into the fabric. Lace over the edge and up under the first running stitch on the other side. Continue lacing under stitch, up over and to other side. Two lacing threads will be side by side under each running stitch, both back and front. Both sides are identical.

OTHER STITCHES

There are so many kinds of suitable stitches that we refer you to the excellent books on embroidery listed in the bibliography. Paintings and drawings from past centuries, when costumes were elaborately embroidered and edges were ruffled and frilled, provide a rich source of ideas. Books on costume and folk arts are full of details that will suggest embellishment and finishes.

Special Hem Problems—Special Solutions

Not enough hem allowance for double turn-in? Use herringbone hem, which requires only one turn. The stitch covers the raw edge. Or apply a band over the raw edge after one turn. Fabric too heavy for a double turn? Use the Herringbone or closed buttonhole.

Magic Edge (Figure 7-15)

Warps are darned back into the edge. Result? A kind of pseudo-selvedge, magically inconspicuous, especially in a textured textile, as shown here. This can be done on or off the loom. It is a smooth, secure base for further treatment or additions. It can be folded up and hemmed without the bulk of the extra turn. Works well on a heavy textured fabric, but may show on a fine one.

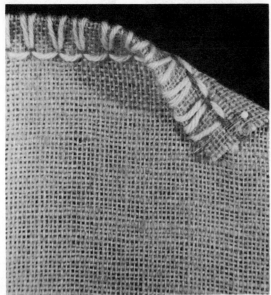

7-14. Eskimo laced edge. Worked in large scale, with the corner folded over to show identical reverse side.

7-15. The "Magic Edge." Now you see the warp ends, now you don't! Each end is darned back up over and under a few rows of weft, then cut. Especially successful on a heavy, textured or multiple-warp weave.

How to do Magic Edge on the loom

There is an advantage to doing it this way, while there is still tension. Cut the warps, one by one, thread the warp end into a needle, then darn back into the cloth at least half an inch or more to the right of the next warp. Cut, darn, cut, all the way across. You will have a smooth, flat, nearly invisible finish. Ends can be trimmed close after removal from the loom.

Off the loom

Place material so the edge hangs over the edge of a table. Weight it with books or covered bricks to prevent it from skidding. If necessary, ravel a few rows for enough warp length to work with. An inch and a half is enough—more is easier. Weave the ends back into the fabric as above, taking them in order. Clip the ends close. This sounds slow and involved, but it really isn't. It is worth the effort, when this is the only or best way to finish your material.

The problem of turning a bulky hem can be solved at the preweaving design stage in this way:
• Plan in a hem woven of matching fine yarn, which will be turned up, or . . .
• Weave a few rows of fine yarn where the crease will come at the turn. The hemming can be done along the raw edge with a close overcast, blanket stitch, or one of the methods described earlier.

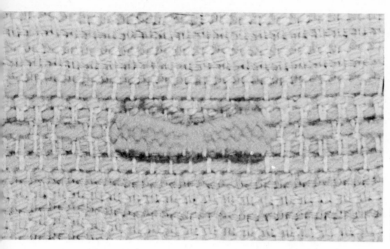

7-16. Embroidery Weave.
Detached needle-woven motif
is part of a woven border.

PLANNED REMODELING

As this book is being written, a tempest is stirring about skirt lengths—dropping from mini-short to midi-knee to maxi-ankle length. When a hem is too narrow, add a strip of fabric to lengthen, and cover the seam with rows of stitchery. A tell-tale line where the hem had been creased can be covered by decorative stitches discreetly matching or in an all-out splash of design and color. (See figure 7-10.) Or apply a handwoven band over seam or line. Experience has taught me that it is wise to keep remodelling in mind on handwoven clothes. The cloth never seems to wear out! Put in deep hems, wide seams, and some day you may have a whole new design problem to solve.

NEEDLE-WOVEN MOTIF (Figure 7-16)

An extra hand-crafted effect in a weft pattern band is where a detached needle-woven motif is made as shown. A woven row with a few of these raised patterns will greatly enhance table linen edges, with a matched single motif added on the napkins. A group is effective on a yoke for a blouse or dress, at the bottom of a skirt to ornament a hem. You will find many places for this technique. It is surprisingly easy and fun to do. Margaret Burlew, an accomplished weaver, uses this idea and calls it "Embroidery Weave," the motifs "butterflies." She tapers the needle-weaving to look like wings, in toward the center, where it is caught to the ground fabric. Plain weave sets it off best.

How to do it

• Weave plain for the length needed.
• Lay in or weave a simple overshot weft pattern, alternating with tabby shots. At least three pattern wefts are necessary for the woven motif, but make them the size you want. At intervals, skip the pattern weft over the surface in a long overshot, weaving it in again. Repeat more than once in the width if you wish. Then, with tapestry needle threaded with matching or contrasting yarn, weave over and under these wefts (which now become your warp). A

stitch at the center through to the ground weave will not be noticed, but you may want to do the catch stitch in another color. Weave the weft pattern rows at intervals in the plain weave and scatter these needle-woven motifs at random, or make a precise repeat pattern.

PLANNING, DESIGNING, AND WEAVING SELVEDGES

Complete design of a fabric will include treatment of the selvedges, too. Consider the finish of the warp ends, and have all sides harmonious. Selvedge preparations must be planned for before warping the loom because the required warp ends must be put in. We have separated the types of selvedge treatments into those requiring work while weaving and those completed after the cloth is off the loom. Some of these are fringes, and will be found in chapter 9.

Weaving a good, straight, firm selvedge is a sign of a careful weaver. We have been more concerned up to now with ways to enhance the edge, but please never lose sight of the importance of constructing a good textile. No amount of fancy banding or fringe can disguise sloppy weaving.

On a rug, to make it durable and straight, so it will stay put on the floor, warp and weave the selvedge properly, with double warps at the edge, building up the weft where necessary between heavy rows of knotting or extra pattern wefts. (See Coptic double selvedge, figure 7-19.)

If you are counting on the selvedge as part of the over-all design, plan and weave it with special care. An edge that will be the background for a fringe must be firm and suitably prepared.

Extra weft at the selvedges

Particularly in heavy rugs, where knots or loops stop short of the selvedge, it is necessary to add extra wefts to fill the space. There are no set rules on when to do this, but you will know when your selvedges show uncovered warps.

Navaho rug weavers use two floating warps (usually in a heavy wool like the weft) woven in, but twisted after each row. This makes a cord-like twined edge. Because these two ends become tightly twisted after a few inches of weaving, they are tied to the upper and lower cross bars where they can be easily unfastened, untwisted, then tied on again. Look for other ways of compensating for empty warps at the selvedge. Collingwood's rug book has many detailed directions on how to cope with this problem. Look for floating, Navaho, Argatch, wrapped, woven, or a combination of techniques.

Woven-in decorative selvedges

Here is an ornamental selvedge, with no extra work: Put in several warp yarns on one or both edges. Contrasting or blending colors, heavier or nubby yarns in spaced extra warps will all make a distinctive stripe down the sides.

Scalloped selvedge (Figures 7-17, 18)

A weft of coarse and fine yarns in different colors may be utilized to weave a striking and unusual scalloped edge. The coarse yarn can be brought out at regular intervals at the edge, making a shallow loop. The fine weft makes a straighter edge between the loops. If you have a stiff weft, like flexible

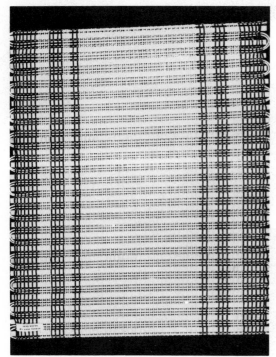

7-17. Scalloped selvedge placemat. A fine example of weaving material dictating the design. Flexible reed turns in natural arc. Courtesy, Henry Gallery and Audio-Visual Services, University of Washington.

7-18. Scalloped selvedge in two colors.

basketry reeds, mats can have a wide-curving, handsome edge (figure 7-17).

Planning carefully with color and sequence of weaving—beginning both wefts from the same side—it is possible to have scallops on one edge of color A, the opposite edge all color B (figure 7-18). Directions are given below. Effects are limited only by your yarns. This idea would be grand for a flat-weave rug, a narrow belt or band, as well as for placemats or runners. If you want to use only one color for the same effect at the edge, use two wefts as above, both the same color.

From the notebook of Noel Hammock, of the Seattle Weavers' Guild, here are the directions for achieving scallops of different colors down each selvedge.

How to do it

1. Enter color A on tabby shed, beat, change shed (very firm beat).
2. Enter color B from *same* side as color A in step 1, beat and change shed.
3. Return color B, bending smoothly to scallop of size desired at edge. Beat, change shed.
4. Return color A, bending smoothly around scallop made in step 3. Beat, change shed.
5. Return color A, forming scallop, beat, change shed.

Continue, making certain that there are two shots of each color before changing the color. Be particularly careful to turn one color around the other so that the loops are the same size. Beat firmly. One edge should have loops of color A and the other edge should have loops of color B.

Coptic double-woven selvedge

A reinforced woven selvedge is found in some Coptic weavings. On a fragment of a narrow patterned Coptic band, the wool ground weft was seen to be woven over two outside warps, between the regular rows. It is so closely packed that the edge appears to be finished with a needlework border. The weft is woven in a figure 8 several times around a few warps, before the next full width shot is woven. We have tried this in several weights of yarn, over different numbers of warp, and have adapted it as a decorative border. (See figures 7-19, 20, 21.)

Using the distortion as a design element

One bonus element that occurs can be planned for. Because extra wefts are put in, the edge of course becomes more dense than the body of the fabric. This is the reverse of the selvedge warp-filling problem in pile weaves. With a fine weft, put in just once between full rows, it will pack in with little or no distortion. The additional wefts, especially in a heavy yarn, will cause the selvedge to become slightly wavy. If heavy yarns are doubled and woven in the figure 8, an inch or more in width, you are creating an interesting border. With variations in pull-in and beat, you can weave a gently scalloped edge with an integral heavy border (figure 7-20). With planned color in warp and weft, you can weave an edge that is durable and ornamental.

Patterned Selvedges

On our sampling warp, in trying different ways of weaving the Coptic selvedge, we explored new ways as we thought of them—weaving the extra wefts in a pattern, introducing more colors, twill and basket ground weave, looping the extra wefts. And this is hardly a start on the many possibilities.

SAMPLERS (Figures 7-19, 20, 21)

• We began with three rows, expanded, to show the way the Coptic weavers used this method. One extra weft shot between full rows, taken around two outside warps in a figure 8. (Our warps are used in pairs, as one warp.)
• The classic way, on plain weave. You can feel the firm ridge, more than see it on this one-color weave. (Figure 7-19.) Then we began improvising . . .

7-19. Coptic double-woven selvedge. Bottom area shows the Coptic way, expanded to show weft woven over two warps between full rows. Top area, in two colors, shows weft over four warps for a heavy, wider selvedge.

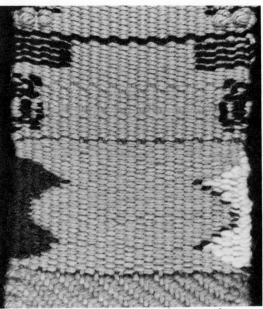

7-20. Bottom area shows double weft, wide double-woven Coptic selvedge, the irregular edge woven by pulling in and relaxing the wefts. Top area shows diagonal twill weave of heavy rug wool, the extra selvedge wefts forming a slightly eccentric edge with a bumpy texture.

7-21. Double-woven Coptic selvedge as a design element, on both selvedges, is a good idea for a rug. From bottom up: Points in two colors. Casual pattern—the extra weft is in a different color. Flat rows, then loops.

• Large size rug wool, a second color, is introduced in a wide selvedge along one side. Good idea for a flat-weave rug. The color can move from side to side or be taken along on both edges.

• The scalloped edge. Woven in white worsted yarn, beaten so the orange warp shows in the center, the selvedges are solidly packed. The distortion comes from a combination of the tension in the weft at the edge, and the beating.

• Twill weave, large rug wool. The extra weft around two warps, every fourth shot. A very good solution to the problem of a good selvedge on twill. In this large scale, it also makes a little raised bump regularly along the edge. Good idea for a rug or blanket—makes the selvedge stable and full. (Figure 7-20.)

• Next sampling, a logical progression—why not a pattern at extra weft? Triangles laid in, two more colors, a good idea for strength and pattern in a rug. Basket-weave ground.

• Then, experiments with beating the ground fabric—some warp left uncovered, some packed in. This has great design possibilities, playing with warp color and different wefts. At the edge, black wefts were laid in for different effects, then some loops were lifted in the background color. (Figure 7-21.) The end of our sampling warp was the only thing that stopped us here. But below are more ways we thought of. Some are for a practical strengthening of an edge, some are for both ornamentation and reinforcement:

• On rugs. Selvedges exaggerated by yarn size and/or color.

• On long lengths of drapery, fine weave, to strengthen the selvedge.

• On bands or belts, either inconspicuous or as part of a border detail.

• On blanket, poncho, or rug units to be joined, to give you good firm edges to sew together.

• On a selvedge where fringe or bands will be applied.

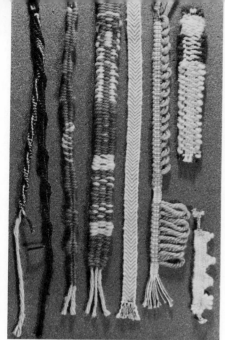

7-23. A colorful band of orange and blue, sewn on a black cotton cloth: the edge from an ancient skirt. The pattern is built with twisted cord, laid and coiled into a design. Courtesy Irma Robinson. (Photograph by Kent Kammerer.)

7-22. Tapes and cords. From left to right: 1) On one warp, with one other strand, a buttonhole or half hitch; two spirals, one black, one gold, mesh together for a round cord. 2) On two warps: Wool, shaped as it is woven over two warps, back and forth, pulled in, then relaxed. 3) On three warps: Wool, different effects woven with two colors. 4,5) Two tapes on very fine warp: Gimp, for upholstery trim in Chevron pattern, very fine wool weft; firm and tight. Gimp with loops along one side. These two by Noel Hammock. 6) Wool band. Color-play in warp and weft, with relaxed edges that almost loop. 7) A tiny experiment with Peruvian saw-tooth band. Points are woven, then drawn in. At the bottom, one point is left unwoven in a loose pattern. See directions in the notebook section.

BANDS, TAPES, AND CORDS

Like some of the fringes in chapter 9, weft bands can be woven at the same time as the body of material or they can be fabricated as separate strips to be applied. They can be woven, knotted, or plaited. They can be attached with embroidery stitches. You can achieve an all-of-a-piece effect by crocheting a band to an edge or selecting an embroidery stitch that seems to belong.

Weft bands made on the loom

At the end of a warp, especially when you are weaving wide yardage, weave some rows of patterned bands. Make them wide enough so you can turn the edges in and sew on as trimmings. You might turn in one edge and leave a knotted fringe on the other. Then you can add a woven fringed band to a poncho, skirt, blouse, or curtains.

• With a needle, weave some of the band wefts back into the body of the weaving, unevenly spaced and uneven lengths as in a laid-in meander.
• Try a band of monochromatic colors, blending with the fabric, no pattern.

Bands made off the loom

Bands and belts can be woven off the loom in almost any fashion, just so you can put some tension on the warps. Fasten your few warp ends to something solid and weave across. Being in a hurry for a 40-inch long woven narrow belt of knitting worsted yarn, and with all my looms full, I once strung a warp between two chairs and wove the belt in jig time! Plain weave, nine warps, three shades of orange wool, enough warp at each end to braid for a finish, with three strands in each braid.

• Knitted cord applied all around a plain-weave pillow makes a handsome edge trim. Our pillow is off-white wool and mohair, the cord is chartreuse rug wool. (See figure 7-26 and directions on page 183.)

• The Peruvian weavers made bands to be applied, or woven in as part of the textile. They went still further, and wove tapestry patterned tabs like a fringe. (See chapter 9, "Fringes.")

Tapes and cords (Figures 7-22, 23)

Narrow, firm tapes are sometimes needed for trim (in the fashion of Scandinavian and Lapp applied rows of tapes). Upholstered furniture is often trimmed with woven tape on the seams. This is called "gimp." Weave matching gimp with the same yarns as the handwoven upholstery material. Our illustration of an assortment of these done in a number of techniques shows only a few of the variety of possibilities. As you can see, a tape can be woven on only two warps, or on three warps, or on many fine ones. A very stiff, firm tape results with very fine warp and weft, packed in, making a crisp selvedge. Just about a minimum is the single-warp sennit, with a single knotting cord.

Weaving on two or three warps

Weave over and under, back and forth with one color or more. With two warps in tension you can pull the wefts in or let them be relaxed, and create a very interesting narrow tape with contours. This one is fun to play with— you can make hour-glass shapes, triangles, ovals. Our example is wool worsted on linen warp. You can make loops or have cut ends along either or both edges. (More about this in chapter 9.) Just be sure the construction is sound, by putting rows of weft between loop or cut-end rows, making a selvedge to secure it.

If you need several yards of narrow tape, it is sometimes better not to use a regular loom. Instead, work on warp coming directly from the spool. Fasten each end so it is tight enough to weave on. Use the same idea as the Oriental Two-Warp Loom or the principle of the backstrap loom, fastening one end of the warp to a door handle or anything solid, the other end to a belt around your waist. (See *Weaving is for Anyone* for these loom types, and directions.)

Weaving more than one tape at a time

In chapter 9, on fringes, weaving two strips of fringe at one time is discussed. You can use this same method to weave two, three, or more simple tapes at the same time, the only difference being that each tape must have a selvedge, therefore you will not be weaving a fringe weft across.

7-24. A narrow band, woven first, then two wider ones using the same idea.

Narrow and wide bands (Figure 7-24)

The narrow band was made on a sampling warp for a study hour on edges and trims. We liked it enough to try it on a wider warp. The first and second ones have doubled white worsted for the wandering weft that divides the jewel-like blocks of color—bright red-orange, yellow, and green-blue. Oriental Soumak is worked across, carried up to the next row, framing the colors on three sides. The colors are plain weave, basket weave, and twill. Another version is wider, with dark gray outlining light yellow. Where the weft travels up the edge, it is wrapped and loops out slightly. A lot of ideas from a tiny ten-inch by one-inch strip! Try it with leather and jute in a belt.

TWO PERUVIAN-EDGE BANDS

Undulating-edge tape

An illustrated description of this ancient Peruvian technique in Lila O'Neale's *Textiles of the Early Nazca Period* inspired me to reconstruct it as a band. Used by the Peruvians as an applied decorative border, woven separately, it was a challenge to see if it could be woven along with the cloth as a border finish. Either woven on, or applied, this scalloped, raised edge would be suitable for a place mat, pillow edging, on cuffs, drapery edge, bottom hem of a skirt or jacket, vertical band along the front closing of a coat or jacket. Pulled in firmly and quite flat, it would be a handsome rug finish along the selvedge. Or a really smashing edge on a wall hanging, in bold yarns and colors. Try different yarn sizes and color-ways. Complex looking, it becomes a fairly simple procedure when set down step by step. You do have to keep the yarns in correct order. The result is an unusual reversible band or border. If you weave this either like the original, over two warps, or make a wider band, it can be sewn invisibly to an edge. Use matching yarn. Put the catch stitch through between the alternate rows of tabby—the same way it is fastened in when woven along with the fabric. If you want to enlarge the width for a wide decorative band, sew it on and add rows of embroidery stitches that complement the lines of the edging. The unique line design of this undulating braid is more effectively seen when the two outside pairs of yarns strongly contrast with the center pair. Each of the six yarns can be a different color. The reverse side is a different pattern—a long half-oval appears. (See figure D7-3.)

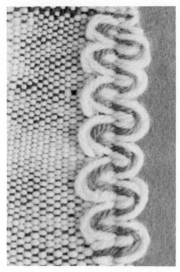

7-25. Adaptation of a narrow woven Peruvian tape with undulating edge, woven as an integral part of the fabric. By the author. (Photograph by Phil Davidson.)

Adaptation devised by author (Figure 7-25)

If you weave this band along with your fabric, it can be made on either or both edges; the border is finished when the yardage is taken off the loom. Width of the border can be controlled by the number of warp yarns used, and the size of the yarn. For directions see D7-3, notebook. Also see frontispiece.

Peruvian saw-tooth tape (See figures 7-22 and D7-4)

Tapes such as this were woven, cut to size, and sewn onto finished garments. It is a kind of early-day rick-rack, in a tapestry weave. Directions for weaving this as a separate banding, and how to weave it along with the cloth will be found in our notebook pages at the end of this chapter.

BRAIDING AND KNOTTING (Figure 7-26)

Again, because there are good books full of directions on the subject, and combinations of braiding and knots are almost limitless, we can only list names and describe a few selected examples. These braids have so many uses—as belts, handbag handles, applied trims on seams and edges. Using the proper yarns, you could even braid a rug, going a few steps beyond the familiar braided rag rug. Mats, runners, bags—all can be made of braids sewn together.

To braid more than three strands

A brief basic rule for braiding four or more strands into a flat braid: When braiding an even number of strands, the outside strand on one side must be started under. The outside strand on the opposite side has to be started over. When braiding an odd number of strands, the outside strands on both sides are started over the next strand, then under. This may help you until you can look up some of the fine sources for braiding and knotting suggested in the bibliography.

Here are names of braids, plaits, and cords you will want to look for and learn to do:

Three-strand braids: Three-strand, Three-strand Solid, Zigzag. Vertical Half-hitch, which puts ridges on top and is flat at the back, is a good one to apply to cloth.

Four-strand braids: Tied, Spiral, Square, Flat, Over Double Strands, Four-in-Hand or Osage Indian, Round, English Sennit, French Sennit. Binding, half-hitches over core.

Five-strand: Greek plaited braid.

CORDS

Aside from the usual crocheted, braided, and twisted cords for bag handles or applied edge finish, here are two more ways to make them.

• Coxcomb Braid, or double-wrapped cord.

Over two cords (large-size jute or twine) weave a third cord or yarn in a figure 8. Push the rows very close together, so the core cords are completely covered. This gives a slightly flattened cord. It can also be sewn together in rounds, ovals, or strips for a rug or mat.

• Cover a bundle of cords with tight half-hitch, blanket, or buttonhole stitch.

Knit a round cord, slim or full

A similar cord can be worked on the fingers. Both are called "Idiot's Delight" and each one is fast, fun, and useful. See it on the pillow in figure 7-26 and centering a hairholder, in chapter 5, figure 5-52.

How to knit the cord

Double-pointed sock-knitting needles are a necessity. Cast on three stitches. Knit row one. Slide to opposite end of needle and knit three stitches again. Firmly pull down on the cord after each row. The working end of the yarn comes up from the bottom stitch, which aids in drawing into a round cord. The cord is always on the right side of the needle. The pull-down settles the stitches into place. Sequence is: Knit, pull cord, slide, knit, pull, slide, and so on, until the cord is long enough.

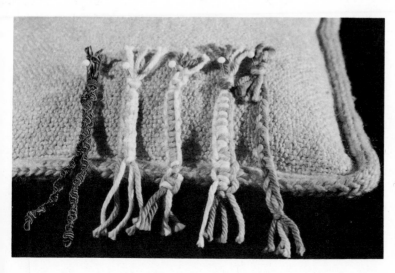

7-26. Knotted cords and braids. The background is a pillow with knitted cord sewn around the edge. Pinned to the pillow, *left to right:* A sturdy round cord in macramé, two sinnets of half knots, twisted together as in 7-22. Gimp cord in two colors. The next three are based on half hitches and square knots. The last, *at right,* is a four-strand plait.

7-27. Both ends of a Tibetan sash. In the end shown at *left* twined rows, each a different color, extend into weft fringe. The fine cotton is twisted into a round cord. The narrow top border is plain weave tapestry, stepped into triangles, with small slits. The wider band is patterned in several colors, woven and wrapped into narrow strips, occasionally caught together. At *right* the same techniques are used in this end of the sash, but with an entirely different pattern and use of slit and plain weave. Both ends are left with a long warp fringe, which twists into round cords.

7-28. Tibetan sash ends. Just one end is woven with a band of slit and plain weave tapestry, and both ends have rows of twining that continues into a long weft fringe, somewhat twisted on itself. Details of the pick-up pattern are shown in figure 7-29.

Macramé cords

The big challenge of macramé is to try and do it all the ways you can think of! Unlimited, when you count color-ways and combinations of the simple knots. More ideas and methods will be found in *Macramé: the Art of Knotting* and *Color and Design in Macramé* by Virginia I. Harvey, who has also written articles for *Handweaver and Craftsman* on the subject of braids, plaits, and cords. Also see *Practical Macramé* by Eugene Andes.

BELTS AND SASHES, GIRDLES AND BANDS (7-27—7-44)

Although the several techniques represented in this group fit into other chapters, we thought it might be more interesting to put belts all together for comparison and study.

Belts and girdles are important in every weaving culture and appear everywhere. They are used as necessary working parts of a costume, as carrying straps, as trimming and enhancement. Sometimes they are worn in layers, or several worn one above the other for a wide girdle effect. They are also worn as badges of office, an indication of ceremony, position, or status. Braids and bands widen into belts and girdles, and are almost interchangeable. A narrow belt may be applied to a border by sewing, or a firm band may be perfect for a narrow tie belt. In most primitive cultures where weaving is done, bands and belts are woven for practical purposes over and above holding pants or skirt in place.

7-29. Details of Tibetan sash shown in figure 7-28. The pick-up patterns on the double weave are rich in symbolism, as most ethnic designs are. These small geometric patterns are particularly pleasing. Very dark blue and off-white alternate in the center patterns. Almost escaping attention, faint orange and tan motifs are woven along the edges, and are equally interesting.

7-30. Two Habitant ski belts from Quebec. Long, to wrap and tie over sweater or parka. The sash at *right* is about five inches wide, the fringe was originally eight inches long. At *left* is an interesting use of open warp weave in a narrow tie belt. Warp is fine white wool, woven areas are in all colors of the rainbow. Courtesy of Mrs. Gordon Hart and Joan Hunter.

FUNCTIONAL, FANCY, OR BOTH

If you look through costume books you will be fascinated by the many forms belts can assume and the many ways to wear them. In figures 7-27, 28, 29 we show details of two Tibetan sashes that combine beauty and utility. These sashes are worn wound firmly about the waist so the shirt can serve as a secure pocket to hold the owner's possessions safely in place. Both sashes are very old and the colors have mellowed to lovely soft shades. Together they comprise a study of half-a-dozen techniques: slit-weave, wrapped warp, and plain-weave tapestry are all in these three-inch bands. Note the intricate woven borders and marvelous fringes. These are from the collection of Mr. Earl Dome, who brought them from Tibet many years ago. The photographs are by William Eng. *Warp and Weft from Tibet,* by William A. King, gives an account of motifs used in Tibetan rugs, banners, and bells.

• Woven ski belts are worn in Canada to keep sweater or parka snug and add a decorative note as well. One shown is a wide, double weave in colorful worsted with long fringe. Another, a tie-belt, has narrow open warp with many-stranded bundles of bright wool woven in, like soft pompons. Plain weave covers the warp in between. At the ends, small bead cylinders are strung on groups of three or four warps. (Figure 7-30.)

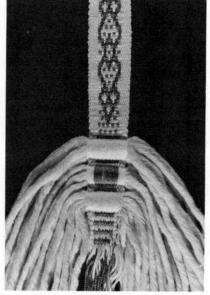

7-31. Cerise and white tasselled tape less than an inch wide, used to fasten a rectangular cloth head-covering for a woman of U.N. Long, New Territories, Hong Kong. Ties under the chin. Pick-up warp pattern, with color reversed on the other side. Weft fringe is made by inserting large bundles of coarse, soft cotton twine into a shed, and leaving long ends. The warp ends hang free in a fringe. Collection of Mrs. E. H. Lund, Eugene, Oregon.

7-32. Detail of tape in figure 7-31. (Photographs by William Eng.)

7-33. End finish on a Sprang-technique white cotton pajama string from Pakistan. Warp ends are wrapped, then divided into two, then four, and tightly wrapped with the same fine cotton, left in small tassels at the ends. Collection of Mrs. E. H. Lund.

Right:

7-34. Tapestry-weave hair band from Guatemala. These long, narrow bands are woven with many colors in fine cotton thread, patterned with tiny figures, leaves, flowers, birds, animals, geometrics. Slits, plain weave tapestry, grid, hatchings, outlining techniques and more are used in small scale. End is a fluffy, layered pompon. Costume and Textile Study Collection, School of Home Economics, University of Washington.

Below:

7-35. In Huichol, Mexico, men wear these very unusual decorative belts, sometimes several of them at once, along with other woven belts of different widths, either embroidered with cross-stitch on cotton, or woven in double weave. This very fine one is double weave, with the pattern in bright blue and yellow-orange. Buttonholed edge and fat tassels are red-orange. The patterns are from clay-stamp designs. Each of the nine pocket units is made from a woven rectangle about five inches long, folded and stitched with paired buttonhole around the edge. Then all are fastened together at the top corners. Two are real pockets, with the top edge left open. Two strands of wool are tightly twisted and knotted for a tie. From the collection of Mr. and Mrs. Fred Hart.

• Tasselled tape is used by women of Hong Kong to fasten their cloth hair-covering. (Figure 7-31, 32.)
• The Sprang-technique pajama strings from Pakistan are both handsome and useful. (Figure 7-33.)
• Woven Mexican and Guatemalan hair bands are long, narrow, and intricately woven. Some are incredibly long, and are wound around and around to fashion distinctive hats and hair-styles. (Figure 7-34.)
• Bands and belts are a means of holding and carrying great loads slung on the back, supported by bands on head and shoulders, like the Indian tumpline in figure 2-16.
• The pocket belts, woven sashes, and head bands of the Huichol Indians in the highlands of Mexico are beautifully patterned, colorful and decorative, but serve a function, also. (Figure 7-35, 36, 37.)
• Color symbolism is represented in our crisp black and white Crios from Ireland, made for Aran Island funeral wear; gaily colored ones are for all other occasions (figure 7-38). This picture also shows a buckled Gaucho belt from Argentina.

Below are notes on more fascinating belts and bands and uses of them that we have observed. Keep an eye out for these and others from around the world, as well as the ones pictured above.
• The narrow tape used to hold a Japanese kimono in place is covered by the wide, beautiful obi.
• In Cuetzalan, Mexico, three-yard-long plain-weave white cotton girdles are

7-36. Detail of one of the pockets shown in 7-35.

7-37. Head band from Huichol, Mexico. Blue and orange double weave, fine wool, about one- and one-quarter-inch wide. The warp ends are divided into four groups, smoothly twisted and knotted. Note that the small design just before the fringe is different on each end. From the Collection of Mr. and Mrs. Fred Hart. (Photograph by William Eng.)

7-38. Belts from Argentina and Ireland. Both belts are black and white wool, but quite different in construction and method. From South America comes the slit-weave tapestry, with alternating black-and-white rectangles, each one containing the same geometric design. The buckle is a double loop of stiff wire, one loop wrapped in black, the other in white. Adjustable and simple. From the collection of Zada Sigman.

The warp-patterned sash, with warp ends braided, comes from the Aran Islands. Men wear these over their heavy sweaters. Usually, they are woven in bright colors. From the collection of the author.

7-39. Igorot festival girdle from the Philippines. Although this is much like strong canvas webbing, thick and heavy, it is flexible. Warp-face pattern. The warp is soft cotton string, about 50 per inch. The weft is many-ply (about 75) cotton, about the size of cotton rug yarn. Ends are left in a straight, long fringe, with two rows of Philippine edge securing the weaving and making a braid-like finish. From the collection of Irma Robinson.

woven to be wound twice around the waist, knotted at the left with ends hanging.

• Hopi Indians make very special plaited or fingerwoven wedding sashes, using as many as one hundred shedding sticks in the process.

• In a Mexican market an occasional find might be woven belts with the warp ends left unfinished so the new owner can knot and embellish the ends as he wishes.

• As a badge of office: Seen emerging from the Cathedral at Cobh, Ireland, the officiating pastor walking ahead of the funeral cortege, wearing a wide sash of soft white fabric slanted from shoulder to opposite hip, ending in a large rosette.

• A Roman girdle held a tunic at the exact length proper for the station in life of the wearer.

• Narrow tape or tasuki cord Japanese women use to tie kimono sleeves up out of the way has its counterpart in Mexico, where an old custom was to tie full *huipil* sleeves out of the way when grinding and cooking. Some tapes were woven of cotton, and some special ones of silk, or a regular narrow belt was used.

• A Laplander belt is worn low on the long blouse, gathering in the fullness.

• Sam Brown belts, and cartridge belts of the military, Roman sword belts, and so on. Girdles for show and fashion, for utility, status, or flash of color.

7-40. Assomption sashes. *Left:* English-woven. *Right:* Canadian-Indian, finger-woven. Named for a parish in Canada, these finger-woven sashes of many colors—mostly red—were made by Indians in the mid-nineteenth century for the Hudson's Bay Trading Company. The typical arrow design is shown in the authentic Indian sash, at *right.* The sash at *left,* machine-woven in England, of coarse yarn, is a fair imitation, but the reverse side is different, while the true finger-woven ones are identical on both sides and are of very fine mercerized cotton yarn. From the David Sellen Collection, Thomas Burke Memorial Washington State Museum, University of Washington.

7-41. Belts made at Camp Nor'wester, Lopez Island, Washington, under the direction of Marty Holm, counselor. *From left:*
a. Finger weaving or braiding. Diagonal stripe.
b. Finger weaving, plaiting. A flame design, with arrow shape in the middle.
c. Card weaving, by Paule Peterson.
d. Finger weaving, by Theresa Rand.
e. Card weaving. (a,b,e by Marty Holm. Photograph by Richard Weatherford.)

CONSTRUCTION

The methods of constructing belts, sashes, and so on run the gamut of simple plain weave, twisted cords, plaiting, and knotting through warp patterns, pick-up and double weaves, tapestry, macramé, finger and card weavings, to the elegant brocades, silks and gold threads of obis, and ceremonial girdles of precious stones and threads. And our list is limited to those done only by a weaving or knotting technique! There are also those made of metals, leather, beadwork, embroideries, and so on and on.

Finger weaving

Finger-woven or plaited sashes are detailed in *Crafts Design* and books by Verla Birrel and Raoul d'Harcourt. Assomption sashes (figure 7-40) and Hopi Indian wedding sashes are woven in narrow or wide strips. The afghan in chapter 8, figure 8-19, was woven in the manner of an Osage Indian sash, then the strips were joined together; each strip is complete, and can be used as an independent sash. Make bands or sashes in your choice of technique, then join them in some appropriate way for blankets, ponchos, or scarves. (Figure 7-41.)

7-42. Part of the top side and reverse (*left*) of a sash from Guatemala, over two yards long, and about five inches wide. Firmly woven of fine cotton. Warp face with outlined patterns made by overlay brocade technique. Note that the design is just indicated on the reverse side by a slight denting where the pattern weft catches the warp. Ground colors are red and white. The different patterns, divided by plain bands, with changes of color in each, are never exactly repeated. Every rich color is used. Fat tassels of green, purple, and blue are attached to the folded point at the end, which is finished with purple zigzag stitch.

CRAFTSMANSHIP

Some of the finest workmanship and most sophisticated patterns are expended on belts. It is interesting to find them turning up in almost every textile collection. In the three books on weaving by this author dozens of belts are shown and discussed—and I wasn't even trying to feature belts. They are always there, and they illustrate a variety of techniques and master craftsmanship. Aside from their interest and beauty, representing regional design, and often superb technique, their portability makes them appealing to tourists and collectors.

7-43. Detail of 7-42. Some of the many patterns. From the collection of Gloria Huntington. Acquired in Huehuetenango, Guatemala. (Photographs by William Eng.)

7-44. Woven warps at the end of a long, patterned sash from Huichol, Mexico. Courtesy of Mr. and Mrs. Fred Hart. (Photograph by Paul Macapia.)

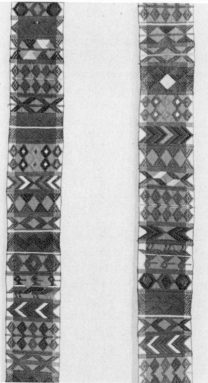

TECHNIQUES

Inventive Peruvian master craftsmen were very fond of passementerie trims—that is, very ornate tapes. Methods included twisting, twining, plaiting, and braiding, plus variations of needle-weaving, needle-knitting, and tapestry weave. *Textiles of Ancient Peru* by Raoul d'Harcourt is filled with excellent photographs and drawings to help you visualize and perhaps reconstruct some of these elegant trims. The most elaborate are composed of miniature figures in a complex tabbed edge on a woven tape.

SAMPLING

When you do sampling and studies for bands and belts, you might make them the size of bookmarks. In six or eight inches of weaving plus warp fringe you can do a great deal of experimenting. Put on about three yards of warp, an inch or so wide, and try lots of belt ideas. Try some tapestry techniques like the Guatemalan hair bands, or new color combinations in woven stripes. Combine different weaves with leather (see chapter 5), then make these into belts.

Our notebook sketches and directions for quick reference follow.

Notebook

Herringbone hem (D7-1)

The stitches can be worked close together or far apart.

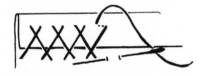

Simple hemstitching (D7-2)

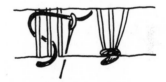

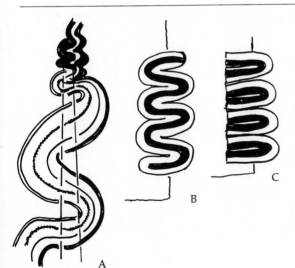

Peruvian undulating-edge tape (D7-3)

A. The system of weaving this scalloped band over two warp ends is shown with just four wefts, but it can be made with more. The order in which they are woven is 1, 2, 3, 4 then 4, 3, 2, 1, repeated until the length is woven. Just like playing musical scales. It is most effective when woven with contrasting wefts, and the use of different colors will help while learning to do it. The loops can be tightened or left quite loose. Be sure that each loop just touches the others.

The edge can be woven along with a plain or patterned fabric by catching in over and under two or more of the fabric selvedge yarns. The two warp ends for the edge band are put in outside of the warp for the width of fabric.
B. The top side.
C. The reverse side.

Peruvian saw-tooth tape (D7-4)

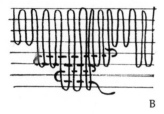

A

B

C

A. First stage of weaving the points.
B. Weaving weft into the warps to shape the points.
C. The point-wefts tightened up, and ends darned in. Skeleton warps removed. The first four warps are permanent ones, and form the heading band. The next four warps are skeleton warps, which are pulled out after the points have been woven.

How to weave Peruvian saw-tooth tape

As a separate banding, in classic Peruvian style, it can be woven on any kind of loom or frame. No shed is required for narrow tape, but for a wide one, a shed will help. Weaving is done in two stages: (1) Weave over all warps to shape the point (D7-4A). (2) Weave across the points, tighten up, and remove skeleton warps (D7-4B).

The warp and weft
The spacing and number of warps determines the width of the heading and depth of the points. Our small example in figure 7-22 was woven on eight warps. Finished band is about an inch wide. Warp is mercerized cotton, but linen or fine wool will do. Weft is fine, soft wool. Other yarns could be used, but wool will pack in the best for smoother points.

NOTE: Spliced weft in a narrow tape is difficult to hide, so carry as much weft as possible. Begin and end a new length at the straight edge.

The weaving
A blunt tapestry needle is a convenient shuttle for a narrow tape, and a necessity when weaving the points so the skeleton warps will not be caught in. This tape will be reversible if care is taken to tuck in ends. We suggest you do your first ones in fairly coarse scale, to help get the "feel" of the right tension in the points. Follow sketches A, B, and C, and this procedure:
• Weave several rows back and forth the width you want the heading throughout.
• Gradually add one or more warps at a time, weaving in steps down to the last warp.
• Reverse the order, and weave stepping up to heading.
• The heading rows between points determine the point spacing.
• The above wefts now become warp, and are woven back and forth to complete the points. This weft replaces the skeleton warp.
• Tighten the point weft, darn yarn ends in. Pull skeleton warps out.
Now you have a firm tape with points along one side, ready to be sewn to clothing, mats, or what you wish. For a real challenge try rick-rack, with points on both sides—the Peruvians did!

Adaptation by the author
Like the undulating tape, the points can be woven along with your cloth. Add enough extra warps at the selvedge for the width of the border. Take the weft around warps needed to shape the points. The weaving and tightening can be done while the weaving is still on the loom, and skeleton warps pulled out later (C). Weave points on both edges if desired. (See figure 7-22.)

Plaited, braided, or basket-edge finish (D7-5)

Especially durable for an edge on a rug. Made with needle and yarn.

Joinings

Joinings and edges are interrelated and it is hard to separate them. They are equally important. An edge usually needs preparation in some way before the joining takes place. In the section on edges, chapter 7, we gave several finishes that can be either left as an edge or used as a base for joining two pieces of fabric. Joinings also slip over into the field of embroidery, because most of the techniques must be done with a needle. There are inconspicuous joinings and there are decorative joinings, each kind having its rightful place. In this chapter weavers will find directions and ideas for the many ways of joining pieces of weaving. When large projects are woven in units on small looms a knowledge of how to go about designing the joinings into the whole is required. (See *Weaving is for Anyone* for more on this subject.)

An early-day direction for joining is found in the *Book of Exodus* where it is told how to make the curtains for the Tabernacle—of fine twined linen with loops of blue on the edge of each, opposite to one another, coupled with gold clasps. Another reference, this to the making of the goat-hair tent, calls for brass clasps and loops to join the pieces.

Weaving narrow lengths or small units, joining them beautifully with stitches, shows finesse and a thorough design effort. For example, a wall of handwoven draperies with each panel joined to the other by hand, in a stitch that adds to the woven pattern, is a real work of craft and design.

A year-long study of finger techniques by the Seattle Weavers' Guild, planned and directed by Virginia Harvey and the author, with the able and enthusiastic help of all the members in their study groups, provided a wealth of ideas. When one study group of about ten members was asked to research and do examples of decorative joinings for handwoven fabrics, they all protested that there was nothing to explore on the subject. Their surprise—and delight—at discovering hidden talent for experimenting with stitches was a joy to behold. With some gentle prodding and suggestions, they began to find ideas and examples. The result of their study was a group of about 80 joining ideas and worked samples, many of them original uses of old stitches. More about these further on.

Sometimes woven pieces are joined so the seam is hardly noticeable. This is

8-1A. Inconspicuous joining. African Kente cloth, made of narrow strips. The strips are woven with areas of pattern and plain weave, then joined in a block pattern, without too much careful matching of lines. (Photographs by William Eng.)

8-1B. Detail of 8-1A.

most successful if the fabric has an uneven texture or a patterned weave. Generally, if you want to join two flat, fine, plain-weave pieces it is better to recognize the seam by using a stitch that does show and is obviously a part of the whole design. It need not always be a bold line. A very delicate joining can be made on fine linen with the same thread as that used in the weaving. On very old weavings, sheets, coverlets, tablecloths, strips made into clothing, pieces were often joined with sewing thread with no attempt to make a design element of the seam.

Some strip weavings are joined quite casually with large stitches just adequate to hold the piece together. Kente cloth strips are sewn with no attempt to disguise or ornament the join (figure 8-1). At the other extreme is the exquisite sheer white shirt from India (figures 8-2A, B, C).

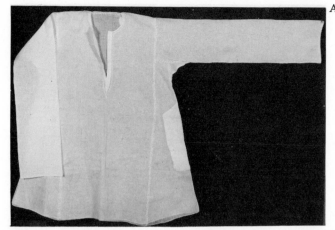

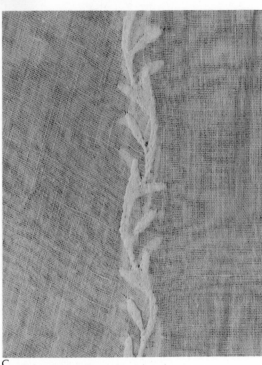

8-2A, B, C. Sheer white shirt from India. Details, many times enlarged, show the fine intricate work done at the neckline and seam joinings. Courtesy of the Costume and Textile Study Collection, School of Home Economics, University of Washington. (Photographs by Audio-Visual Services, University of Washington.)

A SHIRT FROM INDIA

Unbelievably delicate and beautiful seaming and neck finish has been worked on this sheer white linen shirt, above, by some careful and imaginative craftsman in India.

For the binding around the neck and the facing around the front slit several layers of the sheer material are used, with edges hemmed on the top side. On the sheer body of the shirt, a row of openwork and graceful clusters of knobby embroidery in white has been added to ornament the opening. All construction seams are made important by the fine detailing, even to the seams where the underarm gusset is put in. Surely a shirt for a very special occasion, such as a marriage.

TWO KINDS OF JOININGS

Inconspicuous: Ancient and slip-stitch methods. See suggestions for joinings that hardly show given in our notebook pages at the end of this chapter.
Conspicuous or *decorative:* Our illustrations, descriptions, embroidery stitches, sketches, lists, and references will all help you learn some fancy joinings and how to choose them.

REQUIREMENTS FOR A JOINING STITCH

The most important and obvious requirement is that the joining stitch—joins! And *holds* the seam together. Tablecloths, afghans, coverlets, ponchos, anything subject to constant lifting and handling *must* be joined securely. If not properly put together, the sheer weight of the joined pieces will cause the stitches to pull apart. Be sure the stitches are fastened well at the beginning and end of the seams. Try a sampling of carefully chosen stitches. Often a combination of several stitches will do a better job. We show some examples of joinings that work.

CASE HISTORIES

Here are several stitches and joinings that have served well on articles in constant use for a number of years.

Coverlet

This was woven in three strips. The warp is worsted, weft is thick unspun white wool. Warp ends, secured by one row of overhand knots, are trimmed to a one-inch straight fringe. A joining that would give a little and not be too rigid was needed. It had to be strong enough to hold when the coverlet was lifted about. After some experimenting, we worked a row of blanket stitch along the selvedges, except for the two outside ones; they were left as is, because the lumpy edge formed by the fluffy wool looked right. A simple crochet stitch joined the strips, worked through each separate blanket stitch, from side to side. The joining is compatible with the weaving. (Figure 8-3.)

8-3. Coverlet of unspun wool joined by crocheted band on blanket-stitched selvedges.. By the author. (Photograph by Don Normark.)

A poncho

Sturdy garment made of two strips, woven of very fine unspun wool in natural gray alternating with nettle-dyed gray-green. A slit was left for a neck opening. The join, although too subtle to show in a photograph, has held through years of the rugged use the item was made for—to wear for sailing, doubling as a bunk blanket, for campfire and terrace sitting. Along the bottom, a narrow hem was sewn with the warp-wool, then "Y" stitched. A Raised Chain Band stitch makes a firm joining, the full length of the two strips, except for the neck slit. On each side of the joining, a row of "Y" stitch goes up and along the selvedges at the neck slit, and on down the back joining. All stitches are in the same dark-gray handspun yarn, blending with the gray unspun wool. (Not pictured.)

Draperies

We think it is important to join handwoven material by hand, even when the seams are long, for the most careful machine stitching will sometimes pucker or distort, especially on loosely woven or extra heavy textiles. As examples, we describe two sets of draperies with quite different requirements for joining. One, a semi-sheer cotton woven with thick and thin textured yarn, plain weave, with rows just nudging each other, was done in 28-inch strips. The strips were joined to fill two windowed walls. Selvedges were overcast together in the same cotton as the warp, and the seams were lost in the full hang and nubby texture.

The other, a linen and silk material, has two weights woven on the same warp, with the same weft. Half was loosely woven, half beaten closely to be opaque. Lengths were joined and hung together on one track, covering a window and wall and an opening between rooms, above a counter. Where the heavy section is seen from both rooms, the hem and seams were finished on both sides. To echo the line pattern of squares in the heavy raw silk, a buttonhole stitch in the same silk was worked over all seams and along the hem on the "wrong" side. (Not pictured.)

Seams of embroidery stitches on a weskit

An embroidered wool over-vest or weskit, reminiscent of Old World costumes, was made with seams loosely stitched on a sewing machine. The seams were then embroidered with the Chevron stitch as a joining, and the machine stitching was pulled out. The fine black wool yarn holds the seams together with no gaps or pulls. This was a structural experiment that worked well. The rest of the vest was embroidered in a variety of stitches. Side seams were laced through embroidered eyelets. The background material, not handwoven, is a wool coating material in camel tan. Embroidery was done in silk and wool yarns, black, white, and light camel tan. (Pictured in figures 8-4A, B, C on next page.)

MEXICAN AND GUATEMALAN JOININGS

Mexican and Guatemalan weavers and embroiderers create textiles so rich in color and variety of techniques—many on one garment—that it was difficult to select the few we have space for here. Privileged to study and admire the constantly growing collection of Fred and Leslie McCune Hart and the treasures in their shop, La Tienda, Seattle, they also permitted us to photograph representative pieces. We suggest a perusal of the large and lovely book on Mexican

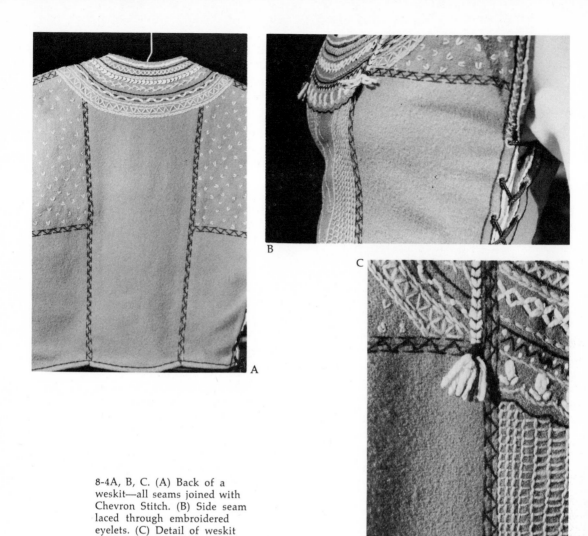

8-4A, B, C. (A) Back of a
weskit—all seams joined with
Chevron Stitch. (B) Side seam
laced through embroidered
eyelets. (C) Detail of weskit
front. By the author.
(Photographs by Kent
Kammerer.)

costumes by Donald and Dorothy Cordry. In common with Peruvian craftsmen, Mexican and Guatemalan textile weavers produce intricate work on simple equipment.

Huipils (blouse or dress)

Huipils are made in blouse or full dress length. Although made and worn in different ways in different villages and states, the construction is basically about the same. Usually they are unshaped strips, three panels wide, front and back; panels are joined with two seams, front and back up to the shoulder. Side seams are usually joined with a small opening left for the arm, but sometimes they are joined only part way—occasionally sides are left open. Necklines are shaped into an oval, square, or V. In some the only decorated panel is the front one, but more often all panels will have embroidery or woven designs, from a narrow shoulder band to an all-over pattern. While in a certain village the general plan is the same, each weaver or embroiderer uses her own fund of design

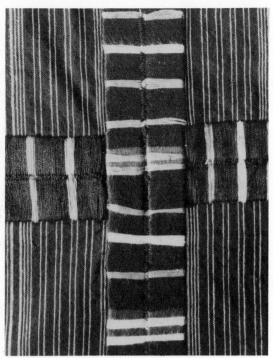

8-5. Detail of a *huipil*, dress length, Chinantec Indian, Mexico.

8-6. Detail of a skirt from Chichicastenengo, Guatemala. Note the wide joining.

knowledge, making each garment different and individual. Each one is a completely fascinating study of color, pattern, and techniques. The illustrations that follow are all from the collection of Fred and Leslie McCune Hart, photographed by William Eng.

Figure 8-5: Detail of a dress-length *huipil*, Chinantec Indian, Mexico. Several techniques and almost every color are found in this dress. The ground weave alternates wide bands of very fine red cotton, with blue and green lines, and bands of white coarser cotton plain weave, with lines of open-weave Leno. Embroidered motifs cover much of the ground in both areas. The front and back panels are joined in wool worsted. The seam was first put together with an overcast stitch, then a one- and one-half-inch stitch was worked, crossing over from side to side. Colors were changed about every inch, ranging through greens, blues, purple, pink, and orange. The same stitch and colors in cotton floss join the side seams. Often in these handcrafted textiles some charming little personal touch is found. In this one about an inch of joining in the all-wool row is worked in cotton floss—and it is a lighter and different yellow than any of the rest.

Figure 8-6 shows a detail of a skirt from Chichicastenengo, Guatemala, done in navy blue and white stripes, very fine cotton plain weave. Woven in two narrow strips, it is joined both horizontally and vertically. The joining of shiny, stranded floss in clear bright red-orange, green, white, dark brown, royal blue, and yellow is a very strong design element. The ground fabric is quite stiff, therefore when an inch hem is turned back on each of the joining edges and the closely worked stitch is crossed from side to side, the wide band is raised slightly from the cloth. It looks and feels padded. The stitch is the same on the reverse side.

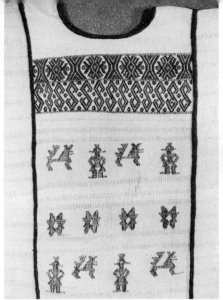

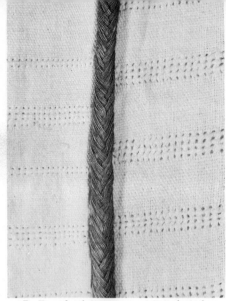

8-7A. Front panel of a white-and-red *huipil*. Mixe Indian, Oaxaca, Mexico.

8-7B. Detail of joining in Mixe *huipil*. Rows of Leno weave.

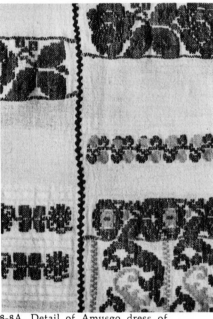

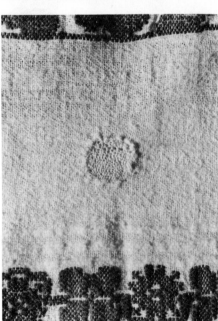

8-8A. Detail of Amusgo dress of crepe-like cotton.

8-8B. Beautifully sewn darn in the center front of the Amusgo dress.

8-9. Part of a richly embroidered dress from Chichicastenengo, Guatemala.

Figures 8-7A, B show details of a white-and-red Mixe *huipil,* dress length. The ground weave is white cotton, with rows of Leno. Center panel has laid-in figures in red and a wide row of pattern. Note the plain weave, without Leno rows, at the neck. A thick plaited edge of the stranded red cotton is worked around the neckline, around the sleeve openings, and down the side, joining the front panels. The joining stitch is very thick and rounded. Stitches cross over each other in such close formation that they look like a braid.

Figure 8-8A shows a detail of an Amusgo dress-length *huipil* made of very fine tightly-spun white cotton weave, with a crepe effect. Occasional bands of heavier stripes in larger size yarn produce a rippled seersucker effect. Pattern bands in different widths are woven and/or embroidered all over, in green, purple, and pink. The seam joining, in purple only, is closely-worked button-hole, from side to side, giving the look of rick-rack.

In figure 8-8B we see a round hole perfectly filled in with a fine looped stitch. It was so well done, delighted us so, that we had it photographed. Later, in the Cordry Mexican costumes book, we found a reference to a group of women who customarily do their mending in this way. Thought you would like to see it, too.

Figure 8-9 displays the yoke and shoulder embroidery on a white cotton dress from Chichicastenango, Guatemala. Six-strand cotton floss in rich colors is used for the pattern and the joining of three panels. The neck finish on this is somewhat unusual, in that it is shaped and turned back in a narrow over-cast hem. The pattern works up around it in a planned manner. The join is multi-color, in the same stitch as used on the skirt and *huipil* shown in figures 8-5, 6. Here, the stitches are short and loosely spaced, so the effect is more open. Note how this stitch is taken down to the bottom of the pattern, then the selvedges put together and pulled up tight with a large black overcast stitch on the top. This is a characteristic type of seaming, with the edges sewn into a ridge. The sleeve edge is plain selvedge, and the side seams are also overcast in black.

Although the joining in figure 8-10 is not a true joining, we are putting it here with the group of Mexican and Guatemalan costumes. The Otomi Indians of Hidalgo weave this unusual *quechquemitl* with an ingenious shaped shoulder woven in, joining the straight woven bands of the front and back. Warp yarns are put in, back and forth, then the weft is woven in with a very long needle used as the shuttle. Our example is an old one, which has been washed, and the wool is tightened and somewhat matted. The word quechquemitl means "neck," and at first glance these shoulder coverings look child-size. They are worn high on the neck and shoulders, and slip on over the head.

8-10. Otomi Indian, Hidalgo. *Quechquemitl* with unique shaped shoulder. (Photograph by Paul Macapia.)

C-12. A sampler of embroidery joining stitches. (Photograph by Jacqueline Enthoven.)

EMBROIDERY STITCHES FOR JOININGS

It is most important to become acquainted with a number of embroidery stitches. The more the better—and we predict you will try lots of them. Suggestions follow on sampling and learning the stitches and we also suggest investigating the wealth of good books on stitches presently available (see bibliography). There are stitches for almost any type of joining—tight, loose, flexible, fancy, discreet, or flamboyant.

NOTES ON DOING JOININGS

• Anchor the work. For the neatest result, find a way to fasten down the two pieces to be joined. This is essential when a stripe or pattern must be matched.
• Pin or baste together when the edges are overlapped, such as in top-seaming or over-sewing, etc.
• Small articles can be pinned or basted to paper or muslin, side by side to keep in alignment.
• Edges that just meet, without overlapping, can be basted together lightly with an overcast stitch that does not draw them too close. Weight or fasten the pieces at the top, so you can work on them with slight tension; use heavy books, covered brick, clamp into a clip-board, pin to your ironing board. You will find a way that fits your project and your own method of working. We find that for smaller pieces, our weighted plastic tape dispenser is perfect.
• Warning from a very old book on needlework: "Never pin the work to your knee"!

SAMPLING

We found it useful to do a sampler planned to be an attractive wall-hanging reference work. It is shown opposite, in color. Another way to learn is by doing a great many small examples on cloth of all weights and weaves, using different yarns and embroidery threads. Figures 8-11, 12, 13 show a group of embroidery-stitch samplers made to discover good joiners. Worked by two able

8-11. Examples of embroidery joining stitches, worked by Lassie Wittman. *Top, left to right:* Blanket stitch, whipped, blanket stitch with cross stitch (both of these can work as an insertion, making an open joining). Chevron stitch in several sizes, worked here as a fairly loose join, but note how it was used as a tight joining in the weskit, page 198. *Bottom, left to right:* Closed and open feather stitches. Crested chain.

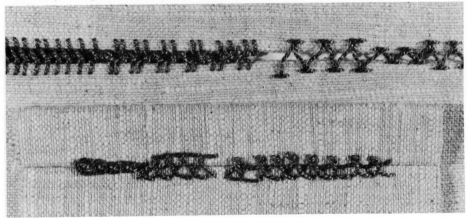

8-12. *Top down:* Blanket or buttonhole, three stitches alternating from side to side. Single buttonhole. Fishbone—a very firm one as worked here, quite small and close together. Single and double feather stitch. These are looser joins, but will work well. All worked by Lassie Wittman. (Photographs by Kent Kammerer.)

Right:

8-13. Three joinings worked by Pat Albiston. (From *The Stitches of Creative Embroidery* by Jacqueline Enthoven.) *Left:* Sorbello stitch. Classically, this stitch is worked to make a small, puffy square. Here, the looped·center is over the joining slit, and the arms reach out and sew into the two edges. *Center:* Loop, Centipede, or Sienese stitch. As a filling stitch it is worked between two parallel lines, making it useful for joining two strips. The legs fasten into the two edges, the bodies make a continuous raised line over the slit. *Right:* Threaded straight and back stitches. A line of stitches down one edge is threaded with loops, which are caught down on the opposite edge, making a joining that is flexible, but holds the two edges together well (Photograph by Kent Kammerer.)

stitchers, Lassie Wittman and Pat Albiston, in the familiar named embroidery stitches, so you can look them up—and find others. Making samples like this, a few inches of several stitches on one cloth, is an excellent way to compare various stitches for usefulness as joinings. Some will be snug, some too loose, some will move enough to be flexible, but still hold well. Such exercises are very much worth your time and will be valuable additions to your reference file. We do all our trials and experiments with edges, joinings, hems, and such on hand-woven pieces—thus our store of experiments is useful for both weaving and finishing ideas. Make samples of non-decorative joins and some inconspicuous ones.

NOTE: One way to try out a stitch, or work out an adaptation, is to punch holes at the edges of two file cards, with either a needle or a small punch. Then do your joining stitches from edge to edge. If you put all necessary information with sketches on the cards, you will have a handy file for reference.

ON ORNAMENTAL JOININGS

• Baste a narrow hem on each edge to be joined. Work over each edge with buttonhole (blanket) stitches—in groups of three, singles, high and low, slanting—whatever grouping suits your design. Join the buttonholed edges together by weaving in and out with needle and thread. Catch the opposite stitch and pull up as tightly or as relaxed as you require.

• A buttonhole edge is a very good beginning for a number of chained, laced, over-cast, crocheted, or knotted joinings. It holds a hem in place when the added firmness is needed, or it helps firm up an unturned selvedge.

• Another join, beginning with a buttonholed edge: A detached running stitch is threaded under the long stitches and carried across to the other edge, back and forth. The ground fabric is not caught. This is most successful when the vertical stitches of the buttonhole are far apart enough to show the threading, especially when two colors are used and the joining thread is larger than the other. It can be pulled up close, or left quite loose.

• Couching is an excellent joining, and can be very showy. Use where you can have a raised band at the join, and where you want the two sides to be close, firmly held, with seam covered. Pin the two edges, or loosely catch with basting. Pin, when they overlap—baste when they must just touch. Lay a bundle of yarn along the seam. Sew on with almost any stitch that will go over from side to side and catch the yarns down onto the fabric. Straight stitches in groups or singly, buttonhole—one row going each way—two rows of "Y" stitch, chain stitches, slanting or straight—you choose.

• Chevron, herringbone. Most varieties of cross stitches are natural joiners.

• Lacings. Get the maximum use and beauty from the novelty spun yarns—slub, bouclé, mohair loop, large size and lofty yarns—by using them to interlace stitches. They do not need to go through the cloth, they lie on the top surface. Your stitches can be made loosely and be of the size needed to accept these yarns.

• Threading, lacing, or overcast stitches combined with an edge stitch have many ways and uses. Overcast, chain band, threaded running stitches, and so on.

• A joining seen on pouch bags or edging on a garment (Peru): Sew a row of small loops—overcast or buttonholed—along an edge. Lace the two edges together. These loops are sometimes made as a bar, sometimes as a picot—like button, hook, or belt loops on a dress. Sew a few strands to the cloth, making the size loop you need. Cover it completely with buttonhole, wrapping, or overcast, forming a little cord. Suitable either for decoration only, or for joining.

INSERTION JOININGS, OPENWORK SEAMS, FAGOTTING

These joinings are usually open, somewhat flexible, can be quite ornate. Part of the stitch fills space between two edges in a lace-like effect. Machine-made lace, bobbin and hairpin lace, tatting, crochet—all can be a part of an insertion joining. Some of the insertions made with stitches follow—and there are more (see figure 8-14):

Ladder insertion. Double or crossed back stitch—this one is also worked on sheer material, so the crosses at the back show through.

Italian hemstitch. Any of the plain or fancy hemstitches can be made along the edges, then interlacement worked from side to side, catching the edges together.

Antique hemstitching, where one thread is taken around the hem, can be adapted as a joining. (See "Hemstitching" page 167.)

Openwork seams based on the buttonhole stitch—buttonhole insertion. (See Mexican and Guatemalan joinings.)

When Jacqueline Enthoven expressed an interest in joinings we asked her to make us some examples of joinings using embroidery stitches. She chose to prepare a series of insertions. She had planned to do a typical, classical French insertion, white on white, but thought it would not photograph clearly, so it is white on deep yellow.

SAMPLER OF JOINING STITCHES (Figure 8-14)

Any one of these lacy or closed joinings—expertly worked by Jacqueline Enthoven—could make your joined seam the most important design element of your textile. Each has its place—from the completely closed Roumanian Stitch worked in points to the exquisite open arches of the interlaced Cretan Stitch. These joinings would be effective on table linens. For instance, two strips joined with the Interlaced Double Herringbone Stitch would let the dark wood of a table top show through. This sampler was worked with white on a rich, golden yellow.

From the top, these are the stitches used:

1. French Lace Insertion. Close overcast of the folded edge, catching the lace edge every four or five stitches.
2. Joining two edges with Roumanian Stitch.
3. Cretan Insertion Stitch knotted on each side.
4. Interlaced Cross Stitch, between two rows of pin stitch.
5. Interlaced Double Herringbone Stitch.
6. Italian Buttonhole Insertion.
7. Raised Chain Band, joining two edges.
8. Cretan Stitch, interlaced.
9. Knotted Buttonhole (Balkan Knotted Buttonhole).
10. Eskimo Laced Edge. (See this worked in large scale, page 173, directions, 172).

Refer to Mrs. Enthoven's two books, *The Stitches of Creative Embroidery* and *Stitchery for Children*, for more on embroidery stitches and the charming little Brittany bonnet shown in figure 8-20.

Mrs. Enthoven saved the exquisite little dress worn by her daughter, and graciously allowed us to photograph it so you can see how a very fine French embroidery shop created it. A delicate peach-color, very fine linen, embroidered in white. Note the beautiful fine joining. (Figures 8-15A, B.)

Opposite:

8-15A. Exquisite French detailing on a little dress fashioned by the shop of Noël, in Paris. Note the delicate lace insertion joining and edge. All seams are joined in this way. The narrow tie at the collar is finished with a dainty little ruff of net, embroidered at the top. Two minute French-knotted buttons link part of the neck slit together.

8-15B. Detail of sleeve and side-seam joining. (Photographs by Kent Kammerer.)

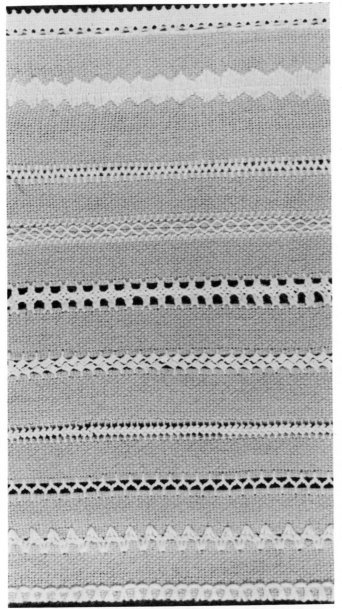

8-15A

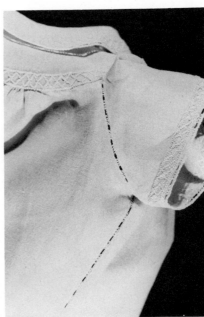

8-15B

FROM THE SEATTLE WEAVERS' GUILD NOTEBOOKS ON WEAVER-CONTROLLED TECHNIQUES

Joinings made with embroidery stitches were worked out by a study group assigned to this subject. Some were invented, some adapted; all work as joinings, and are attractive. Here are a few of those tried:

Cross Stitch variations

Three stitches taken across the seam and a small horizontal stitch at the center, over the seam and caught into the cloth, pulls the three stitches together. This one holds well, if the units are close together.

    Another way: Make the cross and bar with three stitches as above, with the bar longer than the others. Alternate the stitches from edge to edge. Hold down in center with one small vertical stitch, or a cross stitch as above.

• Work Cross Stitches over the seam, vertically or horizontally, with uneven legs (herringbone) close together (looks like plaiting).

• Firmly join with a two-part twisted Cross Stitch. Work a bar across, sewing into each edge. From underneath at the left side of the seam a bit below the end of the first stitch, come up under the bar, over and down through the cloth on the right side; space between, or close-up.

Other stitches that join

• Square chain makes the join. Do some detached Pekinese Stitch along first one side, then the other.

• Interlaced band. Double Chain Stitch, overcast joining.

• Vandyke Stitch. Straight or slanted, open or closed.

• Crossed Buttonhole Stitch. Each side is different, when worked over a seam, so another row can be made facing the other way, and give a nice, complicated cross arrangement, simply made. The top of the crosses can be threaded or overcast to make crosses within boundaries.

• Buttonhole along one edge. As other edge is buttonholed, take the needle through each stitch on the first edge. They will be laced with no further stitches needed.

• Simple overcast, horizontal or straight. Change color as Mexicans do. Close together.

STILL MORE WAYS TO JOIN

• Spanish bedspreads made of three strips of fabric, joined by loops at the sides made with stitching or crochet. Laced with handwoven tape. Fringes all around the edge.

More joining ideas from Guatemala

• Joining with wide (one- to one-and-one-half inch) bands or blocks of cloth in two colors, perhaps red and yellow. (See figure 8-6.)

• Selvedges set so close to each other and stitched with an overcast so tight, it makes a ridge. (See figure 8-9.)

• Shoulder seams joined with a Herringbone Stitch.

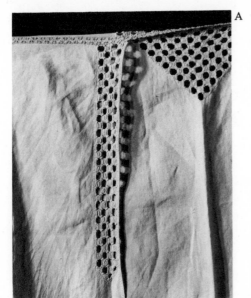 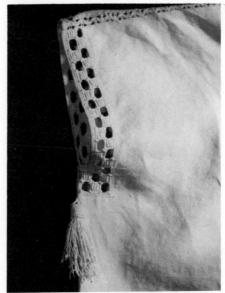

8-16A, B. From Italy, a joining and an edge finish. This fine linen robe has cut-work embroidery and a lace insertion joining at the shoulder seam. Courtesy of the Costume and Textile Study Collection, School of Home Economics, University of Washington. (Photographs by William Eng.)

- Place a cord along the edge. Overcast to stitch it on the fabric (couching). Put two of these edges together with Stem or Overcast Stitches.

Joining with lace

Figures 8-16A, B picture details of a robe from Florence, Italy. The exquisitely crafted finishing touches on this full, very fine white linen robe show great care and planning. The back and front are joined at the shoulder with an insert of delicate lace, which continues on across the back of the neckline to the opposite shoulder. The armhole is shaped, and a band of open cut-work embroidery is worked into the linen ground. To further enhance it, a small tassel, with knotted top (which looks much like the squares in the cutwork) is attached. At the front edges, there is a band of the same cut-work, with the edge, from top to bottom, finished in a fine hemstitching. At the back of the neck, the cutwork is made in a triangle, and you can see the reverse side of it in the photograph, showing the careful workmanship.

JOININGS ON A GREEK DRESS

Figures 8-17A, B, C show details of a Greek dress or shift, from Trikeri. The joining of sleeve, shoulder, and part of the side seam is the same type of buttonhole insertion found on Mexican and Guatemalan garments—even to the changing of color every inch or more. One sleeve seam and most of the side seams are only partly sewn in color, the other sleeve seam all in color. The plain seams are narrow French seams, all done by hand. The sleeves have a row of insertion stitch, then a row of flower clusters in a tiny Cross Stitch, and an edge of picots, all in changing colors. The bottom is encircled with embroidered birds in Cross and Satin Stitches, bordered with picots. Tight, small buttonhole stitch edges the neckline. The slit is bordered with dark-red picot,

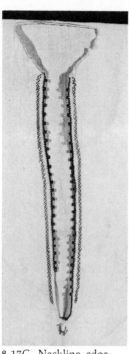

8-17A. Sleeve joinings on Greek dress. Note the whimsical use of color in all details.

8-17B. Bottom edge.

8-17C. Neckline edge.

narrow hem turned back and hand-stitched, then a row of miniature Cross Stitch (note how the design changes). The bottom of the slit is reinforced with a filling of detached buttonhole, and a wee cross-stitched creature is embroidered there. Compare this reinforcement with those in chapter 7, page 171. Logically, some of these details belong in chapter 7, but we want to keep all details on this Greek dress together. Courtesy of Costume and Textile Study Collection, School of Home Economics, University of Washington, Gift of Blanche Payne. (Photographs by William Eng.)

MACRAMÉ SEAM JOINING

A band of macramé almost an inch wide is a handsome way to join two quite heavy fabrics. We can visualize this on panels of drapery, to join strips for a blanket or spread, seams in a coat. Eight cords were used, with a diagonal double half-hitch forming a diamond bar. The knotting and the joining was done at the same time, by taking a small straight stitch with the knot-bearing cords as each cross was completed. The ends are finished off in a simply knotted tassel. If this finish is not suitable for your purpose, the ends can be turned back and darned in. (Figure 8-18.)

Other combinations of macramé knots will work as joinings. Refer to the bibliography for books on macramé.

8-18. Macramé band joins textured fabric. The join is made as the knotting is done. By Pat Albiston (Photograph by Kent Kammerer.)

8-19. A simple crochet chain curves from side to side, joining finger-woven strips to make an afghan. (Photograph by Kent Kammerer.)

8-20. Brittany bonnet. White embroidery on royal blue flannel. The joining is a row of single crochet on each edge of the seam, whipped together. This makes a slightly flexible join. Note the sassy little Stem Stitch circle and the tassel. By Jacqueline Enthoven. (Photograph by Kent Kammerer.)

CROCHETED JOINING

An afghan, woven in strips, is joined by a beautifully done crochet chain stitch. The strips are finger-weaving, over a forked stick, similar to Swedish, Osage Indian, and other Indian plaiting; as weaving directions are lengthy we refer you to *The Textile Arts* by Verla Birrell. For joining, chainstitch in matching wool is taken from side to side and caught into each edge with one stitch. The long fringe hangs free below the points made in the weaving process. (Figure 8-19.) Made by Mrs. Dorothy Bush Albiston.

Also see the crochet joining on the little shaped bonnet pictured in figure 8-20.

JOINING WITH FIVE STRANDS

A useful, firm, and very handsome joining, worth working through the detailed directions that follow. Refer to figure 8-21, worked in large scale. It joins and decorates all in one passage, can be tight or relaxed. Composed of four strands laid on the surface, sewed with just one strand, it allows use of large or nubby yarns; the catch thread can be fine. All five strands can be different colors and yarns, making the design potential abundant. The ends at the beginning and end of the seam can be darned in at the back or extended into tassels, braids, or what you will. Use for joining edges of pillows, sections of handbags, skirts,

211

8-21. Five-strand catch-stitch joining in three versions. *Left:* An over-large one. *Right:* Wool on wool—brown and white, with a fine linen catchdown. *Center:* On multi-warp cotton, joined with soft, nubbed white cotton bouclé, with wool catchdown. Variation in sequence.

clothing, and household textile seams. It is a kind of mixed breed—looks like chain stitch, is something like couching, a little like braiding, and can have an arrow or a chevron-stitch pattern.

Step-by-step directions

Make a social occasion of it if you have long seams to join. With one person to place the yarn, one to catch the yarn down, it goes very quickly. However, the directions are for one pair of hands.
• You will need both hands for the sewing. Edges are pulled somewhat taut during work, so secure the cloth to a clipboard or weight it down on a table.
• Align, and baste the two edges so they just meet, using a loose overcast stitch. Do not pin, or the edges will overlap.
• Measure four lengths of yarn, to cover the seam, allowing a slight take-up. If ends are to be knotted, add length for that.
• To start, catch the four ends, lying side-by-side, with needle and sewing thread.
• Make a straight stitch over the top of the two inside strands, left to right. Lift these strands to the outside.
• Bring the other two strands to the center, side by side, and catch down. Your needle will be at the back, ready to come up for this stitch. Take care not to pucker or draw in the edges.
• Continue, alternating the pairs, and catching down, until seam is covered.
   The ends can be finished as suggested, or turned up with the plain hem of the article. If the hem is a straight fringe, the seam ends might be a large ornate tassel for punctuation. A variation on the chain-stitch appearance: Twist the middle pair of yarns over the outside pair, after each catch stitch. You are always working with the same pair, and the result is an arrow or chevron.

Less Conspicuous Joinings

Antique joining stitches: Start from the under side, bring thread up, over to the other edge, under, then up and over, and so on. There are several variations of this, one with a loop knotted over the crossing. (See figure D8-1.)

One variation is related to the antique joining, but with a stitch brought over at the end of each long stitch, at the inside edge. It is a little stronger, and has a nice row of small stitches in the slit. This was discovered by Virginia Harvey when she was trying out the crossed joining stitch shown in figure D8-2.

Laced joining: Something like the Antique, but each stitch on returning to the other side is laced under the previous stitch.

Invisible Joining: See the bedspread project on page 248. The joining thread matches the weft, is sewn from side to side, horizontally, and locks just like another weft. Particularly "invisible" in a textured or wool fabric. This method is found on Peruvian rugs.

FOUND ARTICLES (RE-CLAIMED, RE-RUNS, RE-JUVENATED)

A planned joining of a newly-woven fabric is an interesting project, but if you *really* want a challenge see what you can do with bits and pieces. In our first book, we dwelt on "scrap weaving" and showed a collage of handwoven left-overs.

Any long-time weaver who has done a lot of sampling and yardage has boxes of odd pieces of woven cloth of every kind—and a mountain of thrums. You can't just toss them out, and you can make only a certain number of collages, needle cases, glasses cases, tiny cocktail napkins, and rag mats out of these oddments. Some practical articles that will use up a lot of small pieces are:
• Wools: Patchwork afghan, quilt, bedspread, long skirt, pillows, tote bags, or baby carriage coverlets (if your weavings are the proper delicate colors).
• If your weaving ran to cottons and linens, the same idea can be used to make patchwork tablecloths and mats, aprons, skirts, pillows, and so on.
• Heavy wool and pile weave samples might be incorporated into a rug or floor pillows, or upholstery for a small chair or stool.

Turn your thoughts in this direction and you will have more possible uses than scraps. Borrow from our pioneer ancestors and fabricate those samplings and cuttings into something new and useful, and gain an added bonus. They will all be there, a patchwork reference when you plan new weavings. The thrums are useful, too, to add pile or stitches. My own plan: to make one smashing quilt or rug, then out go the rest. I will have shelf room and can start over!

Since these pieces are more or less expendable, anyway, use them to try out methods of joining and finishing edges. These trials may be a prelude to a really handsome planned woven article. You will do it with an experienced hand, and then you will have a two-fold reference work—weaving and stitches.

Sort the scraps for color, texture, and type of joining stitch you want to make. Do an elaborate cutting or shaping job if you are so inclined. Perhaps the shape of the scraps make the jig-saw, as is. These can be put on a backing of muslin, if they can be fitted tightly together or if the joining stitches will cover gaps. For backing that will show, use a large piece of handwoven or other suitable background. With lots of bits and pieces, and loads of ideas, you will no doubt assemble more combinations than you can complete.

A curious thing is apparent. When you spill out a box full of your weaving left-overs they seem to blend in with each other, even without sorting. There is a family resemblance. Quite a few have the same or similar yarns in them. Many were color-related when they were samplings for a special use—say a dozen variations of weave, texture, and color, all on one warp, to show a client. These, cut apart, joined with appropriate stitches, will make an elegant floor pillow, not only handwoven, but assembled and joined by hand. Remember the patchwork quilts that covered you at Grandma or Great-Aunt's house? And the fun of waking in the morning light, studying the dozens of joining stitches, shapes and patterns of the cloth—dreaming about who wore them where? Let's continue this lovely idea and do it with our extras from handweaving. It just might be you are making a real family heirloom. Add to your weaving skill, know-how of many techniques, and your designing eye. Since it is almost impossible to wear out a good piece of handwoven fabric, maybe a skirt, place-mats or tie would profit by a new life as part of a quilt.

Another way to use your needle techniques: Put to use the damask banquet cloths and enormous napkins your mother stored away. Join the napkins decoratively into a table cloth or runners the size you can use (and care for). Dye them, or use as is. A damask pattern will suggest a joining or edge stitch. Appliqué or embroider a motif over the worn spots.
Join today.

Our notebook sketches and directions for quick reference follow.

Notebook

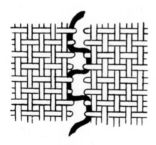

Two inconspicuous joinings (D8-1)

When done with a matching sewing thread the join is minimized.
A. Slip stitch. Joining thread is pulled tight enough so that the edges just come together.

B. Antique or Ancient. This stitch can be decorative if a contrasting or large thread is used. Hardly noticeable with a fine, matching thread. It can be worked with stitches straight across, or with stitches slanting.

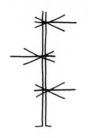
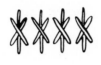

Cross Stitch variations (D8-2)

Cross Stitch is a versatile joining stitch. These stitches join by putting the "legs" of the stitch on opposite sides of the join. They straddle the seam. The two pieces of material can be fastened just touching or overlapped as desired. These five are some of the many different ways of spacing, length of cross, and extra stitches added.

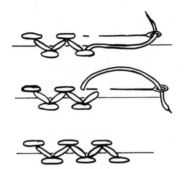

Chevron Stitch (D8-3)

Chevron Stitch is a join that brings, and holds, the two edges together, but has a bit of "give." This is the join used on the weskit shown in figures 8-4A, B, C.

Couching (D8-4)

Couching is a most useful technique for covering the seam, holding the laid on yarns with any kind of stitch you wish. This sketch shows a simple overcast stitch with uneven spacing used for couching. Try Buttonhole, "Y," Ladder, Chain, and Cross Stitches as a beginning.

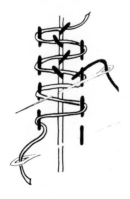

Overcast, or lace join (D8-5)

A joining made in three passes. First, a row of running stitches is worked along each side of the edge, on each of the two pieces to be joined. Next, yarn is laced back and forth, drawing up so the edges just touch. This does not go into the cloth. Last, work a slanting stitch from side to side (slanting Antique), catching down the lacing. This can be done with three sizes and colors of yarn, or all in the same color and size, or whatever mixture your design requires.

Ancient Knotted join (D8-6)

This join is a variation of Ancient join.

Raised Chain Band (D8-7)

A row of chain stitch is worked along the edges of the fabric to be joined. These rows are laced with the yarn on the surface only. This worked efficiently for us on a poncho. A decorative but secure join that withstands wear.

A closing, rather than joining, from Borneo (D8-8)

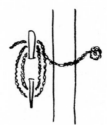

Two ways to hold a front opening, found on jackets made by the Iban or sea Dayak people of Borneo. Good example of using materials at hand. These fastenings are joinings—in a way. As described in the book *Iban or Sea Dayak Fabric and their Patterns*, the jacket (*Kalambi*) that these people weave, twine, and trim has a particular distinction of its own. The side seams are laced in an open back-and-forth stitch, something like the slanting antique stitch, tied at the bottom. An opening is left under the arm, so no shaping is necessary. (This is also done in some Norwegian jackets, made from unshaped straight lengths. It gives the ease needed without having to fashion a shaped armhole.) The sleeve seams are joined with a counter hem. For the simple fastenings, twine is knotted through one side of the opening. A thorn is put through the other side, vertically. The twine is wrapped around a few times—like securing a boat line around a cleat.

Another version: A cord is fastened on each side of the opening. Small squares of felt or fabric are threaded on the ends. Flip the ends over each other to tie. The Iban use little squares of red and yellow flannel strung on. This material was also used to bind some edges of the jacket.

Both these ideas can be easily adapted by using a carved wood pick or a slim metal pin instead of the thorn. The twine can be a fine macramé sinnet or crocheted cord. The little squares threaded on could be felt, thin metal, or wood. Very good for fastening a wool shawl or a coat.

Fringes

Fringes and edges are closely related. Sometimes an edge is especially prepared to hold fringe. However, because edge finishes do not always involve fringe, and because preliminary treatment of an edge before fringing does not always require a separate step, we have separated fringes and edges into two chapters. Some of the fringe-edge treatments may work well without the fringe, and we will note this. When you are planning an end finish, look at the edges and joining chapters, too. Fringes add motion—swingy movement—a feeling of gaiety, which is probably why fringes are so important a feature in primitive dance costumes. Fringe can be modest one-half-inch straight warp-end fringe, or it can be elaborated through all lengths and complexities to a fringe that is the most important part of a weaving. Maori mantles, Samoan grass skirts— these are nothing but fringe, with just a narrow heading of weaving or twining to hold them together.

In figure 9-1, we show a purely decorative object from Peru, thought to have been used by some important person to embellish his costume. The upper section is believed to be much older than the lower two-thirds. It is a study in techniques. Starting at the top: a rolled, ridged hem, oversewn with plaited stitch; plain rep weaving; patterned tapestry weave; sewed on, a plaited piece; sewed onto the plaited part, long, heavy, twisted fringe with stripes of different colors. Each tightly-twisted fringe ends in two short twisted ends. Down each side of the top section, heavy cord is sewn on, ending in elaborate tassels made of plaiting and twisted fringe. It is thick, heavy, and feels padded.

• A small legend about fringe: In Indonesia, baskets festooned with long fringe are hung in huts, in the belief that evil spirits will become entangled in the fringe. These are called Spirit Traps.

Even though this chapter is over-long, we have much left over. There are so many exciting possibilities in contriving fringes that we were able to include only a sampling of the ingenious and elegant methods seen and thought of. They are so much fun to work with—giving an edge with long warp-ends to a weaver is like giving a blank canvas and paints to an artist!

9-1. Early Peruvian weaving with fringe. From the collection of Mrs. Charles Chapman. (Photograph by William Eng.)

C-13. Tapestry: student work. Bottom is fringed with wrapped warps. Hanger at top has row of chaining. C-14, 15 show details of top and bottom. Instructor: Larry Metcalf, Director, Department of Art, Seattle Pacific College. (Photographs by Larry Metcalf.)

THE FIRST FRINGE

Who devised the first fringe? With the interlacing of warp and weft, the ends were there, and something either had to be done with them, or they could be left hanging, so—fringe! The very first weaver of all must have been the first to leave—or create—the first fringe. The Bronze Age skirt we reconstructed, shown in figure 9-59, is fringe. Queen Nefretiri of ancient Egypt was depicted in a fine linen draped costume with fringed edge. American Indians used fringe, cutting leather into fringes for decoration. Northwest Indians had a version of the family roller-towel, a tassel or fringe of shredded cedar bark. Their capes, skirts, and the Chilkat blankets all had fringes. Spanish shawls, Mexican rebozos, Scandinavian rugs, Peruvian woven-tab fringe—everywhere fringes come and go in importance in textile history. As we write this book fringes are having their day once again on clothing. They appear on everything—shoulder bags, shawls, jackets, skirts, jewelry, and even on shoes and boots.

9-2. The innate beauty of plain weave and plaid in Paula Simmons' handspun natural color wools needs nothing more than a long, straight warp fringe, with a single knot. By weaver, spinner, shepherd Paula Simmons, Suquamish, Washington.

9-3. Painted warp continues into the warp ends. Knots, casually spaced, but with care, are an effective edge for this subtle wall hanging. See the entire piece in chapter 5, figure 5-38, and note the knotted top finish. By weaver Hope Munn. (Photograph by Kent Kammerer.)

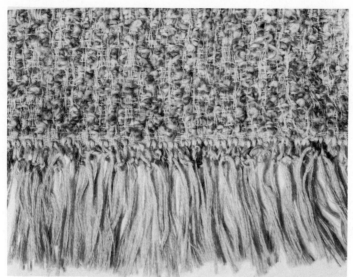

9-4. A soft, fluffy afghan woven with curly mohair yarns is edged
with a full fringe of fine yarns matching the ground weave.
Several strands are attached to the edge by hooking through, then
knotting in a seemingly casual, loose knot echoing the textured
weave. Woven by Sylvia Tacker. (Photograph by Harold Tacker.)

USES

Fringes are not always a desirable finish for a handwoven article, and should
not be an automatic way of completing an edge just because the warp ends
are there. Traditionally, fringe is never used on some weavings—for instance
a Gobelin tapestry. On the other hand, they do offer an excellent way to add
an elegant, special richness to otherwise plain items.

Wherever fringe occurs be sure to plan and design it into the project. This
is especially important if you want an elaborate knotted edge and must allow
plenty of yarn for the knotting. More about this later. It should always be
appropriate for the article, and right in scale for its use, worked as a continua-
tion of a design idea, as an accent, or as the main design element. Often the
best treatment of fringe is just simple knots to protect the weft, with fringe
hanging straight and unadorned. It is tempting to get carried away with ideas,
and sometimes hard to know where to stop.

TYPES OF FRINGE

Fringes are of two basic types: structural and applied. Either can be knotted,
plaited, or otherwise treated for beauty or utility.
Structural fringe, warp: This is an integral part of the woven fabric utilizing
the warp. Structural fringe may have a heading completed on the loom as part
of the weaving, at the beginning and/or end; or extra warp length may be left
at each end to be finished after the weaving is removed from the loom.
Structural fringe, weft: Fringe can be woven at and beyond the selvedge, using
the main weft or additional weft. A skeleton (or extra) warp acts as a guide to
control the length of the weft fringe. Skeleton warp is fastened in tension, but
is not threaded through the heddles. It is pulled out after the weaving is
finished.

9-5

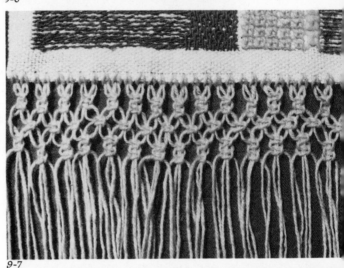

9-6

9-7

9-5. Warps, knotted and manipulated in layers, beads added, for a hanging that is all fringe and macramé. Student work. Teacher, Betsey Bess, Art Department, University of Washington. (Photograph by Audio-Visual Services, University of Washington.

9-6. A wool-needlepoint flat shoulder bag from Greece is bordered across the top with small points, knotted. A few strands of wool are put through the tip of the point and tied into little tassels. A length of round braid in two colors along the seams forms a continuous shoulder strap. Courtesy, Irma Robinson. (Photograph by Kent Kammerer.)

9-7. A macramé fringe in flower-like patterns is attached to the edge of a stitchery composition. Woven by Jill Nordfors. (Photograph by Flo Wilson.)

9-8. Small hanging in all macramé fringe is attached to a piece of driftwood. Done mostly in square knots and half hitches, two colors, separating and jointing in tassel-like forms. By Flo Wilson. (Photograph by Flo Wilson.)

9-8

Applied fringe: This is woven, knotted, crocheted, or prepared in some other way as a separate band and fastened on with stitches, decorative or plain, or yarns added to the edge. Many of the structural fringe methods can be used to make applied fringes by weaving them on narrow headings or bands, with or without a skeleton warp.

FRINGE CHART, OR LIST

In sorting out the ways of fringes, we made a form of chart or list. Perhaps it will help you, too:

Structural fringe (integral part of warp or weft)

Warp fringe
• Ends left plain, twisted, knotted, plaited, braided, wrapped, woven tabs.
• Weft protector edge finishes—may leave a fringe or ends may be turned to the back.
• Finished on the loom—Woven tabs, hemstitched, headings, etc.
• Finished off the loom—Knotting, twisting, braiding, etc.
• Headings or bands woven for spacing of fringe or as part of the preparation or design of the finish.
Weft fringe
Weaving weft is extended out at the selvedge, or beyond the selvedge over a skeleton warp. May be left as loops, or cut and completed like a warp fringe.

Applied fringe (woven separately or fabricated off the loom)

• Woven, crocheted, knotted, and other methods. Made as separate band to be sewn onto the fabric.
• Needlework fringes made on the fabric with added yarns.
• Extra yarn added to warp ends or selvedge, with needle or crochet hook.
• Fastfringe. Made over a gauge and applied with fancy stitches.

PLANNING FOR FRINGE

Fringes must be carefully planned for when you design your weaving. If you want to use the warp as fringe, choose the proper yarn, color, number per inch, extra length, allowing enough for your chosen method. A fringe, to be a well-integrated part of your woven material should not be just a casual after-thought. If you want a weft fringe, you must choose the right weft yarn for that purpose and plan room for a skeleton warp, if needed. Be sure to allow enough total warp to provide fringe of the desired length *after* knotting, braiding, or whatever you plan to do. And allow for some on both ends, if necessary. On a wall hanging, where you want to do an important involved garnishment with braids and knots, be sure to leave a really long length of warp. As much as a yard may be needed for a fancy finish.

A very loose formula is to add about one inch to the length for each row of knots. Example: For a finished fringe five inches long, with two rows of knots, allow about seven inches. The length needed will be variable, depending upon the kind of knot, how tightly tied, and so on. It would be wise to do a sample of the fringe you have in mind, in the yarn you plan to use. Measure the length of yarn before you begin, to see exactly how much take-up there is in your particular material and method. After this, add a little extra, to cut and even the ends.

STRUCTURAL FRINGE—WARP

The simplest form of structural fringe is to leave ends of warp unwoven, secure the end of the weaving with hand stitching, cut the ends even, and leave it plain and unadorned. This is sometimes the best of all treatments for an otherwise rich fabric, or for a textile that is supposed to be unobtrusive—IF the warp is set close enough and the warp is attractive enough to be left that way. From this most unimaginative of all methods you can go into the many ways of knotting rows and groups: tapestry-woven tabs; macramé knotting; adding in extra ends; twining; needlework; and on and on, as far as imagination, time, and the woven article will permit. Some Mexican rebozos, for instance, are more knotted fringe than woven area. This kind of finishing can be the most exciting part of the whole project. If the fringed edge is the most important design element, application of tassels, pompons, bands, and corded headings will add to the enrichment.

Fringe can be on any or all four sides of a fabric, ends or selvedges. Each piece in need of a fringed edge will suggest its own need as to color, length, and intricacy of design.

HEADINGS FOR FRINGE PREPARED ON THE LOOM

NOTE: Remember to prepare the heading at the beginning *and* end of the weaving, if you want the same treatment at both ends.

For straight fringe, no grouping: Along the last row of weft, catching through between the warp ends, overcast, outline, or chainstitch for a simple heading—more than one row and different kinds of stitches for an elaborate heading. Here are some fringe-heading ideas gleaned from studying photographs of Peruvian textiles. These methods are probably not at all the way they were actually done, but they suggested these stitches and would be attractive ways to top off a fringed edge:

Embroider a ridge with several rows of outline stitch, very close together; three or four rows of chainstitch, worked back and forth; buttonhole stitch, with the bottom of the stitch on the fabric, the vertical sitches caught around the last row of weaving, between the warps. This looks like a row of small squares.

Headings to group warps for knotting or plaiting: Make two or more rows of wrapped or outline stitch. Each stitch is wrapped around the number of warps needed in each group. Pull stitches tight to make the division.

Working knots for fringes

Simple knot or overhand tie (see sketch D9-4). This is the simplest knot used in tying a fringe. To make a smooth knot, be careful to put the knot in place against the fabric edge before tightening. Hold the strands at the point where the knot will be placed, at the edge of the fabric. Bring all the strands up and over, making a loop. Put all strands through loop, pull tight.

Slip knot (Windsor knot). Tied just like a man's necktie. A good knot that permits the fringe to lie smooth and flat. Take half the yarns in the group

9-9. This little triangular padded tassel suspended from the corner of a green linen bag from Italy seems to have a vitality of its own. At each corner mercerized white floss, also used in the embroidered pattern, has been attached and knotted. Note the joining on the bag: Horizontal catch stitch wrapped to form a round cord joins the two sides; rows of hemstitching adorn the edges. Courtesy of the Costume and Textile Study Collection, School of Home Economics, University of Washington. (Photograph by William Eng.)

9-10. A small mat from Italy, with ornamental tassels at each corner, hemstitching, and detached embroidery, is related in technique to the bag in figure 9-9. Two warps with inserts wound and knotted in a fascinating lumpy finish are attached to a needle-worked ball. Courtesy of the Costume and Textile Study Collection, School of Home Economics, University of Washington. (Photograph by William Eng.)

9-11. Otomi Indian (Mexico) *quechquemitl* of plain-weave handspun wool, white and dark red. The edge is an applied fringe, alternating red and white. A row of stitches, two rows of counter-chaining make a heading. The handspun yarn twists upon itself in pairs and bunches to make an uneven crinkly fringe. The red yarn, finer and a bit over-spun, curls up and is shorter than the white, although about the same when pulled straight. A good example of material dictating the design. This self-levelling fringe is more effective and different than a weaver might have thought of doing. Notice the meandering, simple row of stitchery within the boundaries of a double stripe in the ground weave. Courtesy Leslie McCune Hart, La Tienda, Seattle. (Photographed by William Eng.)

and carry under, then over the other half. Bring the first bunch of yarns down through the loops and pull up tight. Ease the loop up to the heading. This knot can be made with just one strand—the left one—making the tie over all other ends in the group.

WHAT AND HOW

Ideas for structural warp fringes and how to do them

• Straight fringe is made by simply stopping the weaving and leaving warps unwoven to the length desired for the fringe, or wefts can be pulled out until the warps are the length you want.

NOTE: In a finely woven fabric it helps to use a blunt-end needle to pull the weft yarn down without disturbing the warp ends too much.

One of the considerations is raveling of the fabric. When the yarn is fine and closely sett, and has a tendency to cling, there is not much of a problem. Washing will usually mat or shrink the fabric slightly so the wefts will stay in place above the fringe. An easy way to secure the edge with hand-sewing

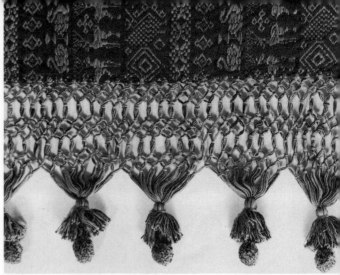

9-12. Detail at the end of a very narrow tapestry belt from Mexico. (See figure 7-34, chapter 7). This layered pompon, made separately of very fine cotton, was tied to the warps of the belt. From La Tienda, Seattle. (Photograph by William Eng.)

9-13. At the edge of a black and teak-brown pick-up weave textile from Guatemala warps separate and come together in a rhythmic, lacy pattern. Simple knots are at each division. Groups of warps come together in a short, thick tassel. Attached at the center, giving a fillip to the very end, is a round, clipped ball of the same yarn. Collection of the author. From La Tienda, Seattle. (Photograph by Kent Kammerer.)

is to overcast with needle and thread. Machine stitching as a finish is out of place on an otherwise carefully handcrafted textile, except when it is a necessity for protecting the woven area and for strength and wearability. In such cases, machine stitch and then cover it with a decorative needle stitch. (See "Edges," chapter 7, and "Joinings," chapter 8.) Needlework, such as a Buttonhole Stitch, Running Stitch, Outline, Chainstitch, or hemstitching, adds a nice touch and also keep the final row of weaving in place. They can all be done on the loom, at either end of the weaving. These stitches are inconspicuous when matching warp or weft yarn is used, or they can be bold and decorative in color.

Cutting the fringe

An important part of making all fringe, but especially a straight fringe, is cutting the ends in an even, straight line. One way to do this: Lay the article on a table so the fringe lies along the table edge. Straighten and smooth the fringe, using a comb, fingers, or brush if necessary. Use the table edge as your straightedge, and cut with sharp scissors. Press your palm down firmly to hold the fabric in place. Heavy books, a cloth-covered brick or flatiron make good weights when you need both hands to smooth and cut. Some fringes are casual and may look better untrimmed. But when a fringe is meant to be precise and even, it should not look hacked off.

KNOTTED FRINGE—GENERAL NOTES

Ways of knotting fringe are as varied as the number of weavers doing them. Here are some of the basic knots and a few ideas. These can be used in combinations and ways suitable to the kind of weaving they adorn.

• At the beginning of the weaving, and again at the end, beat the several first

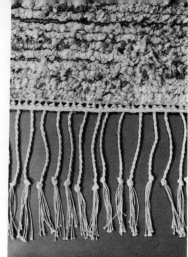

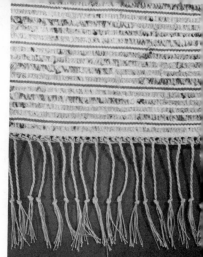

9-14. A funny little hanging made by the author to see what happens to warps treated as fringe, with tension released by cutting. A Soumak or overcast row is put in where the weaving ends. Curly mohair for texture, a small slit to hang it by. (Photograph by Kent Kammerer.)

9-15A, B. Top and back of a short-pile rug with long slender warp fringe. An unusual effect is created by knotting the warps, adding a row of chaining, then twisting bundles of warp held by a simple knot. Single ends hang free in a fringe. Student work, University of Washington. (Photograph by Audio-Visual Services, University of Washington.)

and last weft shots very close, for a firm heading to tie the fringe knots against. When the knotting is finished, this difference in the beat will not be noticed.
• The number of warps tied together depends upon the size of the yarn and the effect desired. When you want a regular rhythmic repetition, a tied fringe should have the same number of threads in each group. If the ends cannot be divided evenly across the warp, space the extras so they will not be noticeable.
• Sometimes the design of the weaving will suggest an unbalanced grouping of fringe. In an uneven warp stripe, group all ends of each stripe together. (Figure 9-14.)

WEFT PROTECTORS

Keeping the last rows of weft from raveling out is of prime importance. Refer to "Edges" in chapter 7 for more on this subject. We include here the ways that secure and protect the wefts, but also can result in a fringe or be a heading for fringe. When the warp ends are worked these ways, a safe and neat edge is made—one that will take a lot of wear; a very good choice for rugs. Note that most of the weft protectors are based on the simple hitch—over, around, and up.

Hidden stitching

This works especially well on wool or a plied yarn. When you wish to have a plain straight fringe with no knots or other ornamentation, sew in a line of invisible stitches. Leave a long end of weft in the first row of weaving. Then thread this end into a needle and sew through the center of each warp immediately below the weaving. This will protect the weft from coming unwoven. If it shows, it will look like another weft.

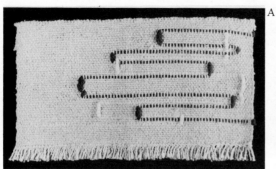
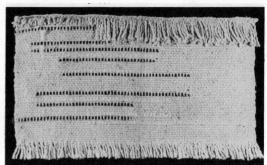
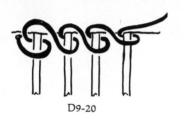

D9-20

9-16A, B. Both sides of a fabric with laid-in pattern, one edge finished with a fringe, the other with fringe turned to the back. (A) Fringed, overcast, or Soumak. Overcast around warp ends with matching yarn. Over one warp, then over two, and over three. A secure edge, easy to work. (B) Plain. Short warp ends, each in turn woven over and under the next three and pulled up at the back. They can be clipped quite close and still be a safe edge. (Photograph by Kent Kammerer.)

Overcast or Soumak edge, with needle and yarn

Although similar to the Soumak heading suggested for grouping warps, this is done off the loom if you have very short warp ends but do want a straight fringe. Weight the cloth on the table so you can pull down on each warp as you work on it. Thread a blunt needle with matching yarn. Start at the selvedge, then sew over and around the first warp end. Pull up. Hold the next warp end taut, sew over, around, and pull up, and so on across. The fringe will slant, but can be pulled down all across to straighten.

Short warp ends (Figures 9-16 A, B and D9-20)

When warp ends are very short, these weft-protectors are useful to know. They can be done on almost any length warp ends, some off the loom—some either on or off. They can be done over groups of ends. Be sure to take the warp ends in order. Be guided by the size of the yarn and firmness of the weaving. Use the same yarn as in the weaving. Matching, for a neat, beaded edge. Contrasting or heavier for a decorative line at the top of the fringe.

SEVEN FAVORITES

The following seven weft-protecting edges are serviceable, fun to do, and lend themselves to all kinds of additions and adaptations—multiple rows, or added rows of stitches above them for a handsome edge, as you will see in the illustrations.

Until I become familiar with the steps of a weft-protecting method, I make a little chant—for Czech Edge, for instance, "under-over-down-up-pull." It helps to get the rhythm and sequence. When working with the warps on a fabric with cut ends, be sure to take the warps in sequence as they are in the weave.

Many of these weft protectors are similar, but each has its best use and works best on a certain size warp. You may want to try several before finding the one right for your material.

Half Damascus

The Half Damascus weft protector edge involves just two warps (or pairs) working at a time. The ends will lie up on the fabric and can be cut quite short, darned into the cloth, or, on a rug, covered with applied tape. When worked from the top side, the edge will be ridged on the back. (Figure 9-17.)

Warp 1 over 2, under and up. Pull snug to the weft. 2 around 3, under and up; 3 around 4, and so on. The rows can be repeated for a band which turns back up on the fabric, and acts as a hem.

Exploring the possibilities of this edge, which can be fringed or plain, we found that if continued row after row, a plait-like band is made. It rolled back up on the fabric, like a turned up hem, after three passes. The ends lie on the back pointing up. So—another version was created! It can be clipped, a short fringe can be left, or the band can be made deep enough so that cut ends can be tucked in and the band hemmed. It looks like an applied border, but is a part of the main fabric. If a hanging fringe is desired, a second stage is worked and it is then Damascus.

Damascus

The Damascus edge brings all warp ends down into a fringe, after the row of Half Damascus has been knotted. A ridge is formed on the top side. The fabric can be turned or worked on the same side as the first pass. The working end, and the one that becomes the fringe, is the one at your right, up on the

9-17. Half Damascus weft protector edge. One row of Half Damascus. An assortment of fringes. The small pile-weave swatch shows this technique as it looks as worked, with the ends pointing back up on the fabric. The corner is turned up to see the edge from the right side, with no fringe down, as in the other example. Author. (Photograph by Kent Kammerer.)

9-18. Damascus edge finish, with corner folded back to show reverse side. (Photograph by Kent Kammerer.)

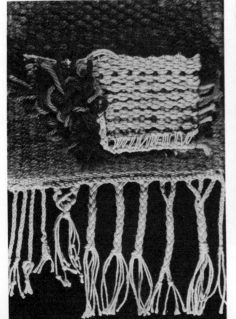

cloth. It is taken over, around through, and down into place as fringe. Both passes are worked on the right side; the fringe covers the first ridge row and the second knotted row is against the cloth. The fringe is flat and hangs in a normal position. The stages can be repeated over and over, to make a wide band. (Figure 9-18.)

Seen on a Greek carry-all bag

Around the top edge of the bag, the cotton warp ends were knotted like the Half Damascus, in two or three rows, to bring it over and flat on the outside. See D9-9 in notebook section for sketch and description.

Philippine Edge

This makes a plaited-looking edge. One row is sufficiently secure, and the fringe is straight and flat. The wrapping motion is the same as the Half Damascus and the Indian Edge, but a different sequence of warp ends. It is wrapped over two ends at a time, then the "up" end is brought down beside the two. The left end is dropped, and the other two are wrapped by the next warp end. Hold warps 1 and 2 firmly with your left hand, while putting 3 over, around, back and up. Pull simultaneously down on 1 and 2, up on 3, to tighten.

This edge finish is fast and rhythmic, as are the others. Very useful to finish rugs, hems on clothing, table textiles. More than one row gives a ridged band. (Figure 9-19.)

9-19. Two examples of the Philippine Edge. *Top:* Bottom edge of a brushed wool coat. One row of Philippine Edge, and a row just above it worked in buttonhole stitch. *Bottom:* Wool flat-weave rug on linen warp. At left is one row of Philippine edge. At right, two rows. By the author. (Photograph by Kent Kammerer.)

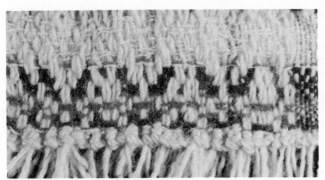

9-20A. Indian Edge. One row, worked right to left on the edge of a heavy, Indian spun wool and silk jacket. By the author. (Photograph by Kent Kammerer.)

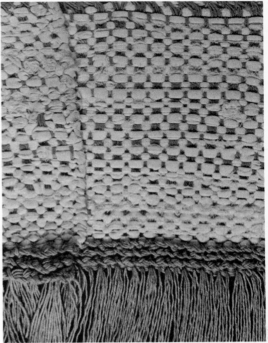

9-20B. Indian Edge on a rag rug. Seven rows, with rug turned over each time, so the ridged band is identical on both sides. Note turned-over edge in the photograph. By the author. (Photograph by Kent Kammerer.)

9-20C. Indian Edge border used to make a shaped textile. Our strange little sample here is a mere hint at the possibilities. When the rows are reversed, the line of the selvedge changes—in or out —so you have the option of shaping or making an undulating edge. This shaping can be used to make a neckline, armhole, or hemline. Worked in single warp, double, and four warps at a time, in both directions, loose and lacelike, or solid. Resembles crochet, very elastic. Finished with a row of collected edge. (Photograph by Kent Kammerer.)

Indian Edge

The Indian edge is a versatile, fast, and easily worked weft-protecting edge. One pass results in a clean row of knots with flat fringe coming from beneath. The ridge makes a nice shadow-line above the fringe. When the fabric is turned over and another row is worked, you begin to make a band. If this is repeated—turning the fabric over each row—you see you are making a textile! It is stretchy, with the look of crochet. Try rows of single ends, then double. The edge tapers in when the knot row is always started at the same edge. Reverse the starting edge, and the shaping occurs in the opposite direction. It starts out exactly like the Half Damascus, but, unlike that method, the working warp end is brought down between the next two warp ends, and dropped. Remember that the discarded warp just brought down is always between the two warps being knotted, and the knotting is always done in front of the middle warp. (Figures 9-20 A, B, C.)

A

B

9-21. Collected-edge samplers. *Top left:* Collected in groups of four, a little braid at the outside edge. *Right:* Collected all the way across, from right, ending in a short brush of warp ends. *Bottom left:* From the middle, collecting both ways. *Right:* Groups collected, separated into colors of the checked weave. (Photograph by Kent Kammerer.)

9-22A, B. Woven Edge. A very secure rug finish that makes a woven band with warp ends on the back. The ends can be cut quite close, or darned in. A plait is made with the remaining ends. This protective edge can be started in the center of the rug with a plaited tail at each side. Note the two small chained mounds in 9-22B. This is a chaining technique for surface interest. Good texture on a flat-weave rug, where several wefts are being woven in each shed. With fingers or crochet hook, lift a loop of the wefts, chain it, then tuck back down in the shed. A large chain should be caught down with an extra weft yarn with a loose end, which is carried along for this purpose.

9-23. A collected edge neatly finishes the end of a wall hanging woven of thick bundles of Scotch broom stems, with warp of heavy yarn and narrow woven tapes. Woven by Hope Munn. (Photograph by Kent Kammerer.)

9-24. Edge seen on a Czechoslovakian towel. Our example shows how it looks with two warps in a group (*left*) and four warps in a group (*right*). (Photograph by Kent Kammerer.)

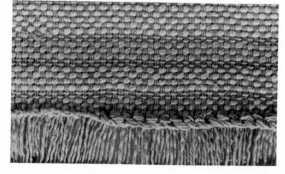

Collected edge

We call this the "Collected Edge," because each warp end is taken along and collected by each warp in turn until its length is used up. Similar to the Accumulated Edge in macramé. A great variety of edges are possible with this. If you start in the middle, the edge slants and thickens toward the edges, ending in a little brush. The whole edge can slant in one direction, ending in a tassel at one side. A straight edge can be made by collecting only a few, then starting a new collection. The illustrations show some of the ways, and there are more than these. (Figures 9-21, 23, D9-15.)

Woven edge (Figures 9-22A, B, D9-17, D9-18)

From a Czechoslovakian towel

A plait-like edge finish with fringe was found on a towel in the Costume and Textile Study Collection, School of Home Economics, University of Washington. To do this edge, work with the cloth toward you, starting at the right side. Work with single or more warp ends, depending on the size of your warp and how coarse and prominent you want the heading. Warp 1 to the left, under 2, up, over to right, down between 1 and 2. To tighten, pull 1 up and 2 down, at the same time, with the ends at an angle to the edge. Pull warp 1 straight, for fringe. 2 is then ready to knot over 3, and so on. Count on about one-half inch of take-up, and allow this amount when leaving ends for a fringe. (Figures 9-24 and D9-16.)

LOOPS INTO LOOPS, OR TWINED LOOPS

On a primitive loom or a frame, warp ends can be lifted off as loops instead of cutting. Twine them, and you have a rounded edge. This would be a natural for the top of a wall hanging, as all you need to do is put a rod through the loops.

Start with the first loop. Slip loop 2 through it, twist loop 1 between 2 and 3, slip loop 3 in, and so on, until loop 1 is full. Then take loop 2 and twine as far as you can, then 3, and so on. Leave some in the center as we did for a

9-25. Loops into loops, or twined loops. *Top:* Long loops in the center of the edge, worked from each end toward the middle. Loop 1 twines with loops 2, 3, 4. Loop 2 twines with 3 and 4. *Bottom:* For a plain, banded edge. Keep twining each loop as far as it will go, until all loops are used. This makes a very firm, reversible hem. By the author. (Photograph by Kent Kammerer.)

looped fringe, or continue until all loops are used up. For a balanced curve, work in from each end. Or work from the middle out, for still another effect. This edge is secure enough for hard wear on a rug edge. (Figure 9-25.) Be sure to . . .

- Always twist the loop in the same direction, for a smooth regularity.
- Make a full twist between loops.
- Keep pushing the twined rows up into place, while pulling down on loops.
- Keep the tension as even as possible.
- After all loops are twined, you can make some adjustments in the tension.

A crochet hook is a help in catching the loops through, especially when the twining loops become very small and difficult to work. If you plan a deep-edge band, leave quite long loops—as much as two inches or more. In our banded example, the loops were about one inch long. The looped example had loops about three inches long.

WARP PROTECTORS

A long fringe, especially on a rug or a household fabric often laundered, will become a bit ragged with wear. You can prevent this in many cases by providing "warp protectors."

The methods in chapter 7 covered warp ends worked into bands or taken up into the weaving to protect the warp. Rows of knots, or ending each warp or group of warps in a knot at the end will also serve as a protection, as will braiding warp ends almost to the end, then wrapping. Wrapped warps are a whole style in themselves (see figures 9-44—54). If the fringe seems to be getting frayed or tangled, you can always do more knotting, weave them into bands, turn them into a hem, darn the ends up into the weaving, wrap them, or add fresh fringes.

BRAIDED FRINGE (Figures 9-26—9-36)

Braiding groups of yarn is familiar and used often, especially on rugs, for very good reasons: It wears well, does not tangle, is neat, tidy, attractive—and fun to do.

The size of the braid groups will depend on the number of warp ends, heaviness of the yarn, design of the whole weaving and its use. Divide warps into groups of three or more ends. Braids are finished with a slip knot or one strand wound round and round several times with the end tucked in. Individual ends below the braid can be left as is, or knotted. One idea: Make a knot like the one you put at the end of a sewing thread. This is a perky finish. The over-all design of the weaving may suggest an unbalanced grouping of ends to be braided. In our example shown in figure 9-26 all the ends of warp in each flat-weave area are grouped into one fat braid. The ends below the pile weave areas are divided into small groups and braided. Thus the design element of a flat band between pile areas is carried on right into the fringed edge, creating the pleasing effect pictured.

- Instead of letting the braided groups hang straight, you can cross and knot them into pairs. This is such a simple process, but it looks like quite a sophisticated fringe. Two ways are shown in figure 9-28. You will think of others. Try groups of four, crossed and knotted, alternating with three hanging straight.

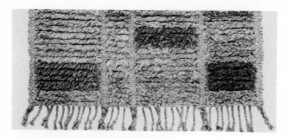

9-26. Fringe divided into groups relating to the woven pattern. The flat-weave warps are grouped in a large braid, the warps below the pile-weave areas are divided into smaller braids. By the author. (Photograph by William Eng.)

9-27B. Detail of RAVEN.

9-27A. Coarse, shiny black binder-twine, plaited and woven into submission by Hope Munn, who calls it "RAVEN" and says "never-more!" She disciplined a difficult material, and made an elegant hanging of it. The graceful curved end finish with tassels would be suitable for a sash or stole. (Photograph by Kent Kammerer.)

9-28. A rug-like small hanging in all white yarns, wool and linen. Nearly half of it is braided fringe, delicately accented with small beads. Woven by Beverly Ernst. (Photograph by Kent Kammerer.)

9-29. Detail of a shoulder band on a bag from Colombia. The two ends are sewn together with warp ends on top, all braided into one fat little finial. Courtesy of Sonia Ann Beasley. (Photograph by William Eng.)

KNOTTED FRINGE

On very long warp ends do a knobby fringe by knotting it on itself as many times as you can or want to. The cut end can be darned into the edge of the fabric. Or do half-hitches, two warps on to themselves.

ADDED FRINGE ENDS

When the warp is set apart and too sparse, or the yarn is too fine for an adequate fringe, additional ends can be put in. This method is also used to add fringe to selvedge edges or an edge that has already been hemmed. Sometimes a matching fringe is wanted on all four sides, disregarding the warp ends. It is much easier to do when the fabric is on the loom under tension, but can be done after the material is off the loom. Yarns can match the warp or be different in size, color, and texture.

9-30. Braided warp ends with handspun wool added for a full tassel border on a flat-weave rug of handspun and dyed wools. Woven by Nell Scott, Toppenish, Washington. Courtesy of Henry Gallery, University of Washington. (Photograph by Audio-Visual Services, University of Washington.)

9-31. Sometimes simplicity is the best. Heavy two-ply white wool warp in a wall hanging done in Greek Soumak technique is braided and wrapped. Woven by Sonia Ann Beasley. (Photograph by Kent Kammerer.)

9-33. Wall hanging of narrow strips, with warps divided and plaited. Very much a part of the total design. See the whole hanging, in chapter 5, "Tapestry." Woven by Hope Munn (Photograph by Kent Kammerer.)

9-32. On a rug from Greece, six pairs of warp are drawn together for a widely-spaced small braided fringe. From the collection of Irma Robinson. (Photograph by Kent Kammerer.)

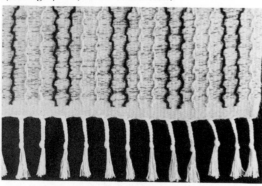

A

B

9-34A,B. Beautifully conceived and worked edge for a double-weave hanging. Plain lead washers from the hardware store hold and shape the fringe. Figure 9-34A shows a hanger at the top, with the dark and light warp layers woven through and tied into a perky brush as a finial. Along the bottom (9-34B) is a single row of the washers, with dark warps, then light warps brought through the center hole. Wrapped and tied, with fringe left hanging. This whole long hanging has so much happening on it that we have used it in three different chapters. Look for the different treatments between the separate pattern areas and views of the whole piece. Weaver, Bernice O'Neil. (Photograph by Kent Kammerer.)

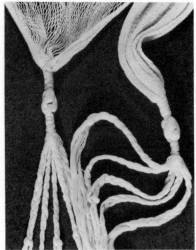

9-35. Very fine white cotton Sprang-technique pajama sash from India. This elastic, expandable technique narrows down to a point, then the warps are wrapped, plaited, wrapped again, then subdivided into groups and made into several small three-strand braids. Courtesy of Jeanette Lund. (Photograph by Kent Kammerer.)

9-36. Deep fringe on a fine linen towel, in the Scandinavian manner. The open pattern is made by braiding the very fine warp, dividing and bringing the warps together, ending with a row of small knots and straight warp ends. Because it has been pressed so often, and treasured for years, the delicate little braids hardly show in the photograph, but you can follow the pattern. Woven by Gertrude Mortensen. (Photograph by Kent Kammerer.)

Method for adding fringe

Cut yarn twice the length you want for the finished fringe. Double the yarn over, put crochet hook through the fabric and catch the looped yarn. Pull through. Pull ends through loops to tighten (see "Working knots"). After these extra yarns have been added, you can knot, braid, or treat them any way you wish, or just let them hang free. They are securely fastened, and will lie quite flat and smooth.

STRUCTURAL FRINGE—WEFT

Weft fringe is usually made while weaving the main fabric. The weft rows are extended out from the selvedge in short loops, long loops to be cut, or a twisted or straight loop made around a skeleton warp. References on Peruvian weaving call the extra warp a "skeleton warp," and it is sometimes referred to as a "loom string." It is not threaded into the heddles, it is merely a gauge put alongside the selvedge to regulate the length of the weft fringe and is removed after the fringe and the weaving are finished. As the weft is taken around this extra warp, it can be twisted around itself on the pass back into the shed. Even when the twisting is not done, this kind of fringe will twist a bit when released. *Warning:* Always be sure that a selvedge is woven between the rows of weft that go out into the fringe. At least every row or two of weft should be returned at the selvedge before the next fringe weft is woven.

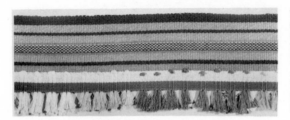

9-37. Here is the idea source for the two weft fringes showin in figures 9-38 and 9-39: a band of tightly-woven cotton on an Igorot skirt from the Philippines. Along one edge, the weaver inserted little bundles of fine cotton in color groups. Apparently no attempt had been made to even up this small fringe, or to put the inserts in evenly. See this in color on page 52. Courtesy of Zada Sigman. (Photograph by Kent Kammerer.)

9-38. Front of fringe inspired by the edge shown in figure 9-37. We thought of this as the front, and made a little loop at the turn of each extra weft as it went back out to the edge. We liked the straight, firm selvedge that occurred.

9-39. The reverse side is also attractive, and if you do not want the selvedge line or the loops, use it this way. The colors are a rich, warm brown, with yellow and yellow-orange fringe. By the author. (Photographs by Kent Kammerer.)

9-40. Twisted weft fringe, made over a skeleton warp. Twill weave. Between weft stripes we ran extra fringe wefts out to an extra warp, twisted before being woven into the ground weave. At the turn, a slight loop. Design possibilities are many. The extra weft can be woven as a stripe, uneven rows, blocks, and more. Each insert can be a different color, independent of the others. Be sure to weave a good selvedge in between. (Photograph by Kent Kammerer.)

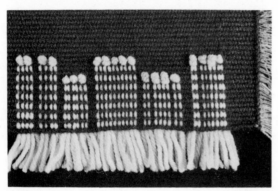

9-38

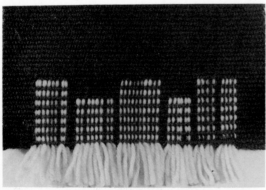

9-39

9-40

Other ways to use a loom string

For fringe added to the selvedge as weaving progresses, put this extra warp along-side the selvedge, spaced for the correct length of fringe. Below are some suggested methods:
• Fringe whipstitched to the edge, using the loom string as a gauge. Use a needleful of fringe weft.
• A single strand knotted around the selvedge, moved out and around the extra warp. This can be done as a continuous strand, or cut pieces knotted at the edge without the gauge.
• Woven tapestry tabs can be made along the selvedge edge. This involves two sets of operations. First, a number of wefts are continued out around the skeleton warp. These become the warps of the woven tab. The weft for the tab is woven in, parallel to the selvedge. (See figures 9-55, A, B.)

9-41. More weft fringe samplings. *Left:* Blue and brown, alternating plain weave and twill. The plain-weave wefts are taken out into a loop at each selvedge. The twill weave is carried up the selvedge on top to look like an overcast stitch. *Right:* Pairs of weft, plain weave, are woven as separate lengths, with cut ends beyond each selvedge. The ground weave completes the selvedge and helps to hold the pattern wefts in place. We knotted and braided the weft fringe in several ways, just for starters! The bottom edge of this sample is made by looping the warp-end loops into each other. (Photograph by Kent Kammerer.)

9-43. Double-fringe hem. A method similar to this is used on heavy Spanish bedspreads. The outer band of weaving is turned back and hemmed to the weaving, leaving a thick looped fringe. To make this fringe the outer band is woven over several extra warps, but the fringe wefts extending to the outer band are not woven. Ground weave between fringe wefts builds the secure selvedge. If the pattern of the two bands match, the material is reversible when hemmed. Adapt this for other uses, too, where you want a good full fringe, uncut. Woven by author. (Photograph by Kent Kammerer.)

9-42. Fringe woven on all four sides. The dark fringe is the warp; the light loop fringe on each side was made with a skeleton warp outside of each selvedge. One weft shot between each loop makes a selvedge. (Photograph by Kent Kammerer.)

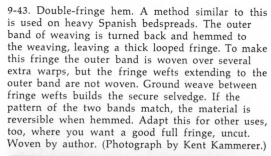

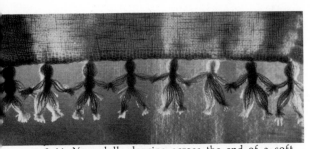

9-44. Yarn dolls dancing across the end of a soft white wool shawl. They are right at home, because they are made from the same yarn as the shawl. They owe their crinkly contours to the fact that they were fashioned from woven wefts, pulled from the cloth. Made like a tassel, wrapped and tied at neck, waist, wrist, and ankle. Hands held together by a stitch, and another stitch or two fastens the heads to the selvedge. By Mary Hanson, for a grandchild. (Photograph by Kent Kammerer.)

9-45. Warp ends. The top edge of a bag from Yugoslavia has a wrapped warp fringe. One group of warps is wrapped with wool about half-way. Another wrapped group is brought to it, and they are wrapped together, leaving the warp ends free for a short fringe. Fashioned in pairs all around the top, of the bright wools woven into the tapestry of the bag. The handle is two wrapped strands, loosely twisted together. Full tassels are sewn at the edges. Courtesy of Ann Johansen. (Photograph by William Eng.)

9-46, 9-47. The ends of two free-form wall hangings. Figure 9-46 shows warps held by willow twigs. wrapped, woven and twisted, then released into thick fringe. Figure 9-47 shows groups of three warps covered with plain weave, twisted, then a few rows of plain weave. Small bundles of warp are wrapped and twisted, left in a fringe. Adult student work. Teacher, Larry Metcalf, Chairman Art Department, Seattle Pacific College. (Photograph by Larry Metcalf.)

9-48A, B. Wrapped warps. A height in glamour is reached in this elaborate hair decoration from India, which women braid in with their hair. Very fine black silk yarn is wrapped with shiny gold thread in an intricate pattern. *A* shows the fringed end, *B* shows the over-all pattern. Peshawor, West Pakistan.

9-49. Wrapped and tied tassels at the end of a green-and-white Sprang pajama sash from India.

9-50. A Sprang sash with warp ends plaited into a knob, then wrapped and tied. All three, courtesy of Jeanette Lund. (Photographs by Kent Kammerer.)

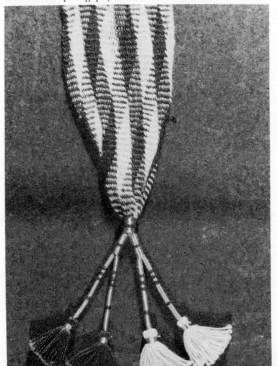

9-51. Rows of Soumak, wrapped warps, and half knots over warps make up this large ornamental warp-end finish. By the author. (Photograph by Kent Kammerer.)

9-52. A short jacket, woven and shaped, has this deep fringe across the back. The warps have been wrapped in different-size bundles with several kinds of the yarn used in the weaving, twisted and connected into loops. Woven by Bonnie Meltzer. (Photograph by William Eng.)

9-53 A, B. Feathered fringe. Warps-ends wrapped, finished with feathers. By Larry Metcalf, Director Art Department, Seattle Pacific College. (Photograph by Larry Metcalf.)

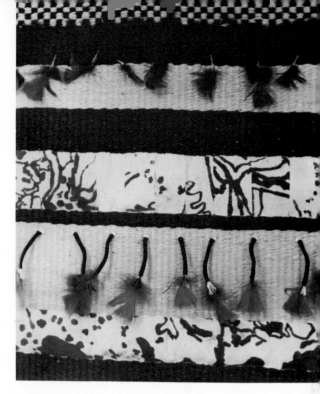

9-54. BLUE FEATHER. Detail of a large wall hanging. Bands of painted fabric alternate with wrapped and feathered fringes sprouting from bands of plain-weave tapestry. Woven by Lin Lipetz Longpre, Director of The Factory of Visual Arts, Seattle.

Woven tab fringe

9-55A. An ancient Peruvian technique tried by two modern-day weavers. The plain weave of a small tapestry is continued into a woven tab fringe. Weave it as you do a Kelim or slit weave, but do not join at the ends. The warp ends are used to sew a bead on each tab. Woven by Gladys McIlveen. (Photographed by Kent Kammerer.)

9-55C. Detail of Peruvian wrapped oval tab. Warp ends are wound in a figure 8.

9-55B. A sampling assortment of woven tabs and fringes. *Top:* At left are two weft-fringe tabs. One is plain weave with a small pattern laid in; the little Peruvian oval below was made by taking wool in a figure 8 over the warp ends. The fringe is plain weave over two and three groups of warp ends, then separated and a half knot put over some warps.
Bottom right: A row of warp tabs, woven on the loom. Some plain, some with inlaid pattern. Warp ends were darned back in. *Left top:* More ways to wrap, knot, and group warp ends. *Left bottom:* Three woven tabs with warp ends left as fringe. All woven by the author. (Photograph by Kent Kammerer.)

APPLIED FRINGES

The uses of applied fringes really is unlimited. Enhance all of these, and more: Cuffs, collars, sleeves, fronts of coats and jackets. Around bottom hems. On scarves, four sides or just ends. Handbags, pockets, hat bands, pillows, bedspreads, coverlets, mats, and rugs. The methods of making fringed bands and tapes are many, too. The big advantage of making your own is that because you have woven the fabric from the same yarns, your color blends and textures will be exactly right.

Fringe woven separately and sewn on

Here is a way to weave two strips of fringe at once. This can be done on any kind of loom—two or four harnesses, back-strap, inkle, or frame. A shed is convenient for weaving a number of yards. With more than two harnesses, you can weave a more elaborate pattern in the heading. (Figure 9-56, right.)

How it is done

Put two warps on your loom, side by side, with space between. You weave two headings at once, taking the weft across from one to the other, so the weft between headings is the fringe, to be cut down the center. Be sure to weave a selvedge between fringe wefts on each band. The bands can be different colors, or identical. Woven bands with weft loops: These bands can be woven for belts, or to apply as a trimming. Use many colors, or different yarns and weights. (See samples shown in fiigure 9-56.)

Weave a band, running weft out as you wish along the sides, looping evenly, in groups, or at random. In our illustration note at far left spaced bunches of loops that look like little bows along the band. Twill weave meandering up the center branches out into loops along each selvedge. Taking the weft out along just one side, gives you a looped fringe with band. Do some sampling on this idea, and you will find many ways to make a pattern using only two colors, or more. We made our samples in wool worsted, but for crisp, tight, stiffer bands we suggest linen, mercerized cotton, gimp, narrow braids, or cords.

Using the weft for a fringe

To really match your cloth, ravel some of the weft and use the raveling to make an edge finish. The yarn, crinkled from being woven, has a different look that is attractive and unusual. Make tassels, little yarn dolls (figure 9-44), Fastfringe, or hook it into the warp fringe or a hem.

Strip fringe

The strip fringe made on an Oriental two-warp loom (see *Weaving is for Anyone*) is good for rugs, but can also be made with finer yarns for a light fringe touch. You can make miles of this fringe—a Ghiordes knot on two warps, made with cut ends of yarn (figure 9-57). The two warps make the heading, the strips of fringe can be sewn anywhere on your fabric. Use an embroidery stitch or sew it on invisibly. A Seattle weaver made fringe from the very fine wool used to weave a light-weight coat fabric. It was sewn along the front edge with a "Y" stitch and made a perfect finish.

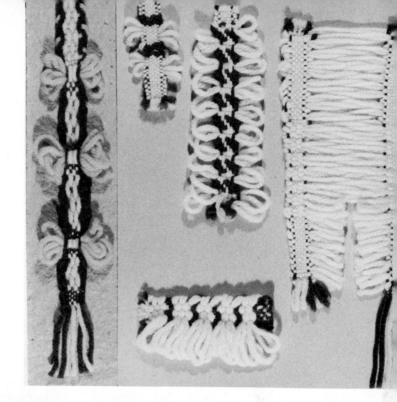

9-56. Woven applied fringes and bands. Weaving two fringes at once is shown at right.

9-57. Two-warp pile fringe or strip fringe. Examples shown in figure 9-56, 57, by the author. (Photographs by Kent Kammerer.)

9-58. Fastfringe. We dubbed this fastfringe because it does work up rapidly. See directions in the text. These are but a few of the ways you can apply it. The row of chainstitch that holds it together in the making can be at the center, top, or wherever you want it. The other stitches that hold it to the edge or area make an important accent. Outline, buttonhole, more chain stitches, and "Y" stitch are some that we used for these effects.

Fastfringe

We devised and named this, although no doubt others have figured out how to do it. It is so simple, so fast, and can be used in so many ways, all depending upon how you apply it to fabric. (Figure 9-58.) Another way is to crochet the chain holding the loops.

How to do it

Working from the skein of yarn, make loops around a gauge. With fingers, needle, or crochet hook, work a row of chainstitching across, around the warps. Yards can be made in one piece. Fasten the chain stitch by pulling the end through and tightening. Then comes the creative part! Flatten the chained loops so the row of stitching is at the top, center, or wherever you choose. Gauge: Cardboard or a length of wood. We tried a piece of wood one-by-two inches and found the one-inch thickness a good base for the chainstitch. Cardboard works, too, stitching down the center.

Winding: Tape the yarn end to the gauge. Wind loosely enough so you can slip the loops off with ease. Place the yarns side by side, with tension as even as possible.

Chainstitch: When the gauge is full, do a row of chainstitch over two yarns at a time. Leave a tag end of yarn at each end, to sew through the fabric when you attach the fringe. When the full gauge has been chainstitched, slip most of it off, wind and sew another group until you have the length you need in the fringe strip.

Attaching the fringe: Have the cloth hemmed and ready. The fringe can be fastened to the selvedge, but the result is better on a firm thickness such as a hem.

Lay cloth on a table and pin a length of fringe along the edge. The simplest attachment is a running stitch in matching yarn, through each chain. After the fringe is attached, the loops can be cut for a straight fringe, a combination of cut and uncut, uneven lengths, or left all loops. Add colors and stitches to widen and ornament the edge. You can sew an elaborate band of stitchery on and around the chainstitch, or along the top. Our examples are only a beginning. This fringe is a good one to use for a spot of embellishment, tassel-like, a bow or butterfly. Buttonhole, backstitch, "Y" and cross stitches are fast, simple, and most effective. The fringe can be placed on the hem either to cover the hem and cloth or at the very edge so the fringe hangs free (a lengthening idea!). You can make it very full, or wind your loops so they barely touch. Color changes can be made as you are winding the loops, or narrow pieces can be made separately in different colors and attached in patches, layers, rows, or spots. A really free-wheeling readily-adaptable technique.

EGVEDT SKIRT (TWISTED CORD FRINGE)

A swingy, fringed skirt, looking a bit like the familiar grass skirt, is a part of the Costume Collection from Jutland, in the Danish National Museum, Copenhagen. It intrigued me enough to try a simulation of it. We think the technique is a useful one to add to your fringe list. Try it as a window screen or room divider, or made of soft wool, quite dense, as a small cape or shawl: or simply as an interesting wall hanging. Where you want a fringed edge—long or short— not too fly-away—this method would work well. Try it on the ends of a sash. (Figure 9-59.)

The original skirt of two-ply wool yarn, worn by a young woman of Egvedt hundreds of years ago, was wide enough to wrap twice around, with the waist-band extended into ties. The ends of the ties were twisted and wrapped like the skirt edge—another belt idea. It was interesting to find that a similar warp fringe finish was found in Peru on a Nazca tunic.

9-59. Our miniature reconstruction of the Egvedt skirt—nothing but twisted fringe with a wrapped-circle end finish. (Photograph by Kent Kammerer.)

Experiments in reconstructing the Egvedt skirt fringe

Our first try at this was made from a photograph and description. Later, a sketch seen in *Costumes of the Bronze Age in Denmark* (bibliography) confirmed the end-finish method as in figure 9-59 and described below as Method 1. Another way, which seems easier, with fewer steps, is weaving a twisted weft fringe with waist band, Method 2 below.

Method 1. On a warp long enough to allow for twisting pairs of warp and for a woven waist band at the top, weave a band of plain weave. The wefts in each row are taken out to the selvedge and long cut ends left. These will be the warps to weave on the extension of waist band into ties, so allow for this and the twisted and wrapped warp ends. Cut off the loom, tie the long warps together in pairs at the bottom, twist, separate into a loop, wrap, making a small oval loop about an inch long. This will help to keep the warps twisted up to the waist band. A length of yarn, knotted or twisted cord, can be threaded through the loops and fastened to the outside fringe at each side.

Method 2. Weave a waist band and twisted fringe as a weft fringe over a skeleton warp. No tying of warp pairs is necessary, and the extended heading for the waist tie is woven before and after the section of weft fringe. For directions see figures 9-40, and D9-21 in the notebook section. Our frontispiece, "A Banner of Techniques," shows fringe done both ways.

WRAPPED OVAL FRINGE FROM PERU

One of the matchless edge finishes devised by the Nazca weavers is a plump oval tab. The basis of it is a loop of warp. Provide this by weaving a weft fringe, tie cut warp ends as in method 1, Egvedt skirt, or use warp loops at beginning and end of fabric woven on a backstrap loom. A thick, padded look results when a large bundle of warp ends is used. After the warps twist a turn or so, wrap back and forth in a figure 8 until the tab is full and covered. Tabs like this can be made as a separate tape and applied, or made from warp ends as an integral edge. (See 9-55 C and D9-22.)

A BEDSPREAD PROJECT INCORPORATING
EDGE FINISHES, JOINING, AND FRINGES

Planning to weave a bedspread in two strips, we were provided with an opportunity to summarize and bring into one article a number of the techniques from chapters 7, 8, and 9. Before embarking on such a large weaving, we followed our own advice and did some sampling (figure 9-60).

To be considered

• All four edges—selvedges, top, warp ends at top and bottom.
• Method of joining the two strips of fabric, which included any special selvedge treatment on the joining edges.
• Reversible? Yes, therefore, the woven pattern should have minimum overshots on either side. Neat craftsmanship must be practiced on both sides. Joining and edge finishes must also reverse well.
• Warp set at suitable spacing for a full structural fringe and firm fabric.
• Weft spaced for an adequate weft fringe and balanced weave.
• The loom pattern must produce a good selvedge.

Design decisions and the sampling

Because of the beauty of our soft, grayed yellow-green, vegetable-dyed hand-spun Swedish yarn, we found that our final sample was much more understated and simple than we had been prepared to do—and almost too subtle to show well in our photograph.

Warp and weft: The same heavy wool.

Sett: Pairs of warp, in the same reed and heddle, 6 per inch.
Threading: M's and O's, with blocks of plain weave and pattern. Chosen for simplicity, variation in rectangles and squares, and suitable overshots. Woven at random, so careful pattern matching would not be necessary at the joining.
Loom: A four-harness floor loom.

The weaving

A skeleton warp was put on the loom to gauge the weft fringe along the side. Beating was firm and close. With careful attention to the selvedge edge to be joined, a length twice as long as the finished sample was woven and cut from the loom. This piece was cut in two, a few rows of weft removed, and it was ready for . . .

The finishing

Joining: We had planned a double blanket stitch to relate to the ground pattern, but found that an invisible joining was best. A horizontal stitch, from edge to edge, blended in and looked like the weft. Later, with needle and yarn, we continued any strong overshot across the edge, adding to the no-join illusion.

Top edge: No fringe, Half-Damascus weft protector method. One pass put the warp ends flat, at the back, and made a firm ridge. Later, for more security

9-60. Sample for a bedspread.

and firmness, we put in a row of outline stitch with the same yarn. Ends were cut close, for neat reversibility.

The long sides: These edges were complete and needed nothing further, having been properly woven with a selvedge in between the weft fringes, and the skeleton warp removed.

The bottom edge: This is where we planned to do something quite elaborate and gorgeous, and left warp ends about 25 inches long. After many tries with braiding, knotting, and so on, we realized that all it needed was a long, very full looped fringe to repeat that of the sides. The double warps were threaded back into the last row of weaving and darned in. The loops were left at about five inches. As a final touch, we stitched a small border, emphasizing the woven pattern.

From the exercise in planning and trial, we can now confidently go ahead with the pleasant task of fabricating a bedspread.

A FINAL WORD ON FRINGES

By now you will have learned that fringes are fun, fast, and a real challenge. There is a fringe for about any project you can dream up—and I just can't resist saying that every fabric, with its four edges to be enhanced, is a fringe benefit!

Notebook sketches and directions for quick reference follow.

Notebook

Planning for fringe (D9-1)

Separate warps into bundles while still on the loom, making a heading for fringe.

Adding fringe to an edge of fabric (D9-2)

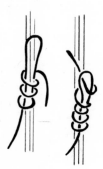

Lashing fringe, or lashing a wrapped warp (D9-3)

Here is a tip from the Boy Scouts and sailors. One of the ways to make a very secure wrapping with ends that do not show:

Make a loop in the lashing yarn, place along the group of warps to be wrapped. Cut end at the bottom, loop at the top. Begin wrapping at the bottom. Wrap the warp bundle evenly and snugly. After enough wrapping has been done, complete by pulling the cut end of loop, drawing it through until the loop is under the wrap. Pull down on bottom end and up at top end, to tighten. Cut ends close.

Overhand knot (D9-4)

A simple overhand knot that puts the ends of the fringe hanging straight. Tie one strand or a bundle this way.

Fringe variations (D9-5)

A few ways to separate, cross, add beads, pompons, or tassels to fringe, straight or plaited.

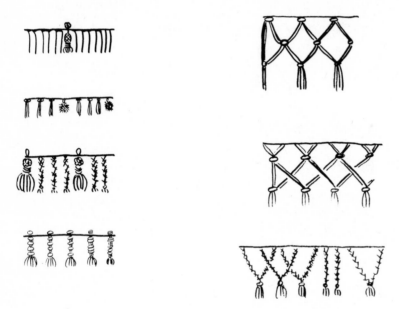

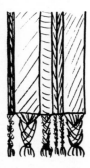

Fringe related to fabric (D9-6)

When your woven pattern is in stripes or definite divisions of color or pattern, plait the fringe in groups of warp ends from each pattern.

Fringe on a double-woven rug (D9-7)

All the white warp ends were plaited into wide fringe. The black warp ends are shorter, and are plaited so they alternate on top of the longer white fringe. Woven by Lila Winn.

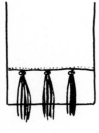

Fringe over a hem (D9-8)

Take a tuck or false hem above the bottom of the hem and attach fringe or tassels. Or turn up a deep hem, stitch decoratively or plain, then add fringe so it hangs over the hem.

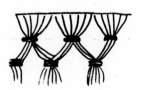

Fringe from a Greek bag (D9-9)

Six warps are caught to the cloth with one stitch—a running stitch the width of the bag. In the second row, the warps are divided and caught down with a double stitch over three warps from each group. Ends are cut in a short fringe. This whole edge was only about one and one-half inch deep. It could also be done on a larger scale.

Fringed trim on *huipils* (D9-10)

On white rib-weave *huipils* from Yalalag, Oaxaca, Mexico, a row of twined silk (or rayon) threads (twined during the weaving, in the old ones). Both ends of the pattern weft are left in a long full fringe. This same idea was seen on a fine cotton, with the band in zigzag pattern woven of fine cotton thread, ends in a fringe.

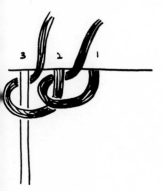

Half Damascus (D9-11)

First stage of Damascus, and a very good edge in itself.

Damascus (D9-12)

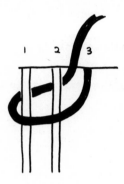

A. first pass.

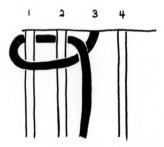

B. Ready for second pass, working with warp ends 4, 3, and 2, dropping 1.

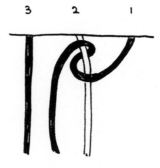

A. First pass, warp one over two, and down.

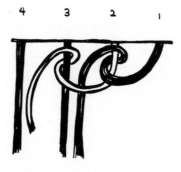

B. Second pass, warp two over three, and down.

Collected Edge (D9-15)

A. The system of wrapping. No warp ends are dropped, but each one in
succession is added and wrapped.
B. Progression along edge of fabric.

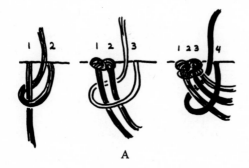

A

B

Edge from a Czechoslovakian towel (D9-16)

This procedure creates a plait-like edge finish with fringe.

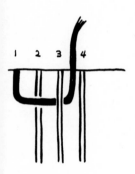

Woven Edge (D9-17)

Each warp is woven, in succession, over and under two or three warp ends, then the end is darned into the fabric.

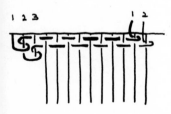

Wrapped and woven (D9-18)

Each warp is wrapped around the next warp, then the ends are woven in over the next several warp ends. The end is again wrapped over the last warp end, and either clipped close or darned in. The ends are brought out over warp ends in succession.

Twined edge (D9-19)

Warp ends are twined, in succession, and pushed up close to the body of the fabric. No fringe ends.

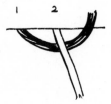

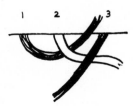

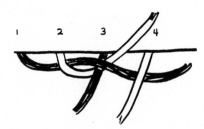

Very short warp ends (D9-20)

Ends too short to wrap or knot. Sew with needle and thread, preferably matching the warp, or the same. Pull the stitch up close to the cloth edge.

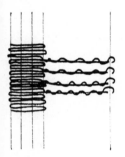

Egvedt skirt woven as a weft fringe (D9-21) Method 2.

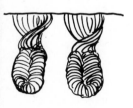

Peruvian wrapped oval fringe (D9-22)

From Nazca. Warp ends are wound in a figure 8.

An author's reflections

I am haunted by the shades of all of the other techniques and variations—those I missed or didn't have time for. I am startled awake in the middle of the night with the thought: did I include that one, or didn't I? Or, why didn't I weave that adaptation, or suggest this way to proceed? This text has been like trying to cram an encyclopedia full of information into a tiny box. We have skimmed—but in some depth. Where something is missing—or lightly touched—we regret . . . just no more room or time.

We hope we have helped in a small way to place techniques in proper and accurate slots. We hope we have opened a few doors to new or different methods.

We may well have put "our neck in a noose," but feel confident that it will be a properly knotted, named, and trimmed one!

Jean Wilson
March, 1972

Glossary

Arc (Bubbling): Curving or slanting the weft in the shed so it will be relaxed and not pull in at the sides when beaten.

Beater: Device to move the weft down into place against the weaving. Can be a comb, fork, fingers, or warp stick. On a loom with heddles, it is the movable frame which holds the reed.

Basket weave: Two wefts over and under two warps, or equal numbers of warp and weft.

Bobbin: Length of weft wound and inserted into shuttle. Also butterfly, hand-bobbin, hand-hank, or tapestry needle.

Cartoon: Drawing for tapestry design. Elaborate and colored, or a simple sketch.

Changepoint or color change: Where weft of one color is dropped and another begun—particularly in tapestry weaving.

Doup: A string "half-heddle" with no eye. Added around a dowel to lift warp into a repeated pattern.

Ends: Single warp threads. Warp ends.

Fiber: Filaments, natural or synthetic. Wool, silk, etc., as taken from the source, before it is processed.

Floating warp: Extra warp at selvedge, twisted into the selvedge as a filler, as weaving proceeds. Loosely tied to the loom frame, for adjustment. (Navaho rug selvedge.)

Gauge: Used in pile weaving. A stick, rod, ruler, etc., to regulate the size of loops.

Harness: Frame that holds the heddles.

Heading: Beginning- and ending-rows of weaving. The first few rows are strips of cardboard or heavy yarn to help even up warp spacing. The end rows protect weaving when it is cut off the loom; can be used for a hem, as a special treatment for fringe, etc.

Ground weave: The foundation or background. The main body of the weaving when pile or pattern is added.

Heddles: String or metal devices with an eye, through which the warp ends are threaded. Suspended in the heddle frame.

Imbrication: Pattern weave on surface—usually describes twined basket weaving. Pattern is on outside only.

Loom: A frame to hold warp ends in tension. A device on which to weave.

Loom-controlled patterns: Those that are threaded through the heddles in a certain order, raised and lowered by treadles. Cloth is woven in a pattern. Ex.: twill, diamond, honeycomb, etc.

Pile weave: Added weft, raised above the ground fabric. Looped or cut.

Plain weave (Tabby): The simplest of weaves—over one warp and under one warp, with a single weft.

Reed: Like a comb, set into the beater frame. Originally made of reeds, now of metal.

Row, pick, throw, shot: A line of weft woven in.

Selvedge (selvage): Edge at each side of weaving. Where weft returns around the outside warp.

Sett: Number of warp ends per inch, on the loom.

Shed: The wedge-shaped opening created when alternate warps are raised and lowered. The space where weft yarn travels across the warp.

Shuttle: Holder for a quantity of weft yarn, which slides across the warp, in the shed. There are many sizes and types for different yarns and uses from large wooden rug-shuttles to blunt tapestry needles to weave tiny spaces.

Skeleton warp: Extra warp tied to front and back beams, with a space between it and the main warp. The weft is carried around this warp to make a weft fringe. The space determines the length of the fringe. The skeleton warp is pulled out when weaving is finished.

Supplementary weft: Pattern weft. Extra wefts to add pattern, texture, pile.

Tapestry: Patterned textile. Weft is not thrown the full width of the warp but is manipulated by hand into patterns with many color changes in any row.

Tags: Bits of wool, slightly twisted or unspun, put into the weaving for small spots of pile.

Take-up: Amount of warp used up in weaving of a given length. Heavy yarns "take up" more of the warp length than fine ones.

Tension: Condition of warp, tied down at each end so threads are taut, allowing the weft to be inserted and beaten down.

THRUMS: Ends of warp left when weaving is finished and cut off the loom.

TREADLES: Pedals that are tied to the harnesses for foot control of the raising and lowering of heddles, which make the weaving shed.

TWILL WEAVE: Weft woven over two warps at a time, in a loom-controlled progression, on a diagonal.

WARP: The lengthwise threads fastened to the loom. The foundation of weaving.

WARP FRINGE: Ends of warp left unwoven

when the fabric is completed, retained as a trim or finish.

WARP PROTECTORS: Braiding, knotting, wrapping, or other treatment of the warp fringe to keep it from tangling.

WEFT: The yarn woven through the warp.

WEFT FRINGE: Weft carried out beyond the selvedge, sometimes around skeleton warp (see Skeleton warp).

WEFT PROTECTORS: Extra rows of weaving and hems, stitching, knotting, and so on to keep weaving from ravelling out.

Bibliography

Here are the books and other publications I turn to most often, and have found to be the most helpful and interesting.

Beutlich, Tadek. The Technique of Woven Tapestry. New York: Watson-Guptill, 1967.

Bird, Junius. Paracas Fabrics and Nazca Needlework. The Textile Museum, Washington, D.C.: National Publishing Co., 1954.

Birell, Verla. The Textile Arts. New York: Harper, 1959.

Black, Mary E. New Key to Weaving. Milwaukee: Bruce, 1957.

Brohalm, H. C. and Hald, Margrethe. Costumes of the Bronze Age. Copenhagen, Denmark: Nyt Nordisk Forlag. Arnold Busck, Oxford University Press.

Collingwood, Peter. The Techniques of Rug Weaving. New York: Watson-Guptil, 1968.

Cordry, Donald and Dorothy. Mexican Indian Costumes. Austin, Texas: University of Texas Press, 1968.

D'Harcourt, Raoul. Edited by Grace G. Denny and Carolyn M. Osborne. Textiles of Ancient Peru and Their Techniques. Translated by Sadie Brown. Seattle: The University of Washington Press, 1962.

Dillmont, Theresa de. Encyclopedia of Needlework DMC Library.

Emery, Irene. The Primary Structures of Fabrics. Washington, D.C.: The Textile Museum, 1966.

Enthoven, Jacqueline. The Stitches of Creative Embroidery. New York: Van Nostrand Reinhold, 1968.

Gunther, Erna. Art in the Life of the Northwest Coast Indian. Portland, Oregon: Portland Art Museum, 1966.

Groff, Russel E. Card Weaving. Robin and Russ Handweavers, 533 North Adams Street, McMinnville, Oregon 97128.

Harvey, Virginia I. Color and Design in Macramé. New York: Van Nostrand Reinhold, 1971.

———. Macramé: The Art of Creative Knotting. New York: Van Nostrand Reinhold, 1967.

Holm, Bill. Northwest Coast Indian Art. Seattle: The University of Washington Press, First printing, 1965. Paperback, 1970.

House, Florence E. Notes on Weaving Techniques. (Out of print. Check libraries and museums.)

Jobe, Joseph, ed. Great Tapestries: The Web of History from the 12th to the 20th Century. Translated by Peggy Rovell and Edita Lausanne Oberson. New York: Time-Life Books, 1965.

Jones, Jeanetta L. Embroidery Weaves for Linens. Westfield, Massachusetts: Jeanetta L. Jones, 1964. Revised edition, 1966. A folder of mimeographed directions, good working drawings, plus woven examples.

Karasz, Mariska. *Adventures in Stitches.* Funk and Wagnalls, 1959.

King, William A. *Warp and Weft from Tibet.* Reprint by Robin and Russ, McMinnville, Oregon.

Kybalova, Ludmila. *Coptic Textiles.* London: Paul Hamlyn, 1967.

Mead, Sidney M. *The Art of Taaniko Weaving.* A. H. and A. W. Reed, Sydney, Australia: Wellington-Aukland.

O'Neale, Lila M. *Textiles of the Early Nazca Period.* Chicago: Field Museum of Natural History. (Several books on Peruvian and Highland Guatemalan textiles. Most quite old, and out of print, but worth looking for in libraries.)

Payne, Blanche, *History of Costume,* Harper and Row, 1965.

Roth, Ling. *The Maori Mantle.* Halifax, England: Bankfield Museum. (Another work by Ling Roth is out of print, but may be found in museum libraries.)

Wilson, Jean. *Weaving is for Anyone.* New York: Van Nostrand Reinhold, 1967, 1972.

————. *Weaving is Fun.* New York: Van Nostrand Reinhold, 1971.

Periodicals

C. I. B. A. (libraries only)

Shuttle Craft Guild Monographs, The, published over the years by the late Harriet Tidball, distributed by the Craft and Hobby Book Service, P. O. Box 626 Pacific Grove, California 93950. Especially recommended:

No. 12. Contemporary Tapestry, 1964.

No. 15. Guatemala Visited, Atwater, Mary M., 1946, reprint 1965.

No. 21. Two-Harness Textiles, The Openwork Weaves, 1967.

No. 28. Weft Twining, Harriet Tidball and Virginia Harvey.

An abundance of valuable research material is available for the looking. Watch for new books, for reprints, magazines, archaeological journals, and museum publications.

Index (Page numbers in Italics indicate illustrations)